PSYCHOLOGICAL
TESTING OF
HISPANICS

PSYCHOLOGICAL
TESTING OF
HISPANICS

Edited By

KURT F. GEISINGER

American Psychological Association
Washington, DC

Published by the
American Psychological Association
750 First Street, NE
Washington, DC 20002

Copies may be ordered from
APA Order Department
P.O. Box 2710
Hyattsville, MD 20784

This book was typeset in Century Condensed by Techna Type, Inc., York, PA

Jacket illustrator: David Diaz
Jacket designer: Grafik Communications Ltd.
Printer: Braun-Brumfield, Inc., Ann Arbor, MI
Technical editor and production coordinator: Deborah Segal

Library of Congress Cataloging-in-Publication Data

Psychological testing of Hispanics/edited by Kurt F. Geisinger.
      p. cm.
    Based on a conference held at the Lincoln Center campus of
Fordham University.
    Includes bibliographical references and index.
    ISBN 1-55798-169-8 (acid-free paper)
    1. Hispanic Americans—Psychological testing—Congresses.
I. Geisinger, Kurt F., 1951–.
E184.S75P79   1992
155.8'468073'0287—dc20   92-8394
                                        CIP

Printed in the United States of America
First Edition

APA Science Volumes

A PA expects to publish volumes on the following conference topics:

Cardiovascular Reactivity to Psychological Stress and Cardiovascular Disease
The Contributions of Psychology to Mathematics and Science Education
Developmental Psychoacoustics
Emotion and Culture
Lives Through Time: Assessment and Theory in Personality Psychology From
    a Longitudinal Perspective
Maintaining and Promoting Integrity in Behavioral Science Research
Stereotypic Behavior
Temperament: Individual Differences in Biology and Behavior

As part of its continuing and expanding commitment to enhance the dissemination of scientific psychological knowledge, the Science Directorate of the APA established a Scientific Conferences Program. A series of volumes resulting from these conferences is jointly produced by the Science Directorate and the Office of Communications. A call for proposals is issued several times annually by the Science Directorate, which, collaboratively with the APA Board of Scientific Affairs, evaluates the proposals and selects several conferences for funding. This important effort has resulted in an exceptional series of meetings and scholarly volumes, each of which individually has contributed to the dissemination of research and dialogue in these topical areas.

The APA Science Directorate's conferences funding program has supported 22 conferences since its inception in 1988. To date, 14 volumes resulting from conferences have been published.

Wayne J. Camara, PhD
Acting Executive Director

Virginia E. Holt
Scientific Conferences Manager

Essays in honor of Anne Anastasi

Contents

Part Three: The Testing of Hispanics in Industry and Research

Part Four: Cultural and Clinical Issues in the Testing of Hispanics

Conclusion

Contributors

Anne Anastasi, Department of Psychology, Fordham University

Nancy A. Busch-Rossnagel, Department of Psychology, Fordham University

Wayne J. Camara, Science Directorate, American Psychological Association, Washington, DC

Wendel J. Callahan, Poway Unified School District, San Diego, CA

Giuseppe Costantino, Sunset Park Mental Health Center of Lutheran Medical Center and Hispanic Research Center, Fordham University

Thomas F. Donlon, Thomas Edison State College

Richard P. Durán, Graduate School of Education, University of California, Santa Barbara

Lorraine D. Eyde, U.S. Office of Personnel Management

Giselle B. Esquivel, Graduate School of Education, Fordham University

Kurt F. Geisinger, Department of Psychology, Fordham University[1]

Gerardo Marín, Department of Psychology, University of San Francisco

Michael L. O'Brien, California Institute of Integral Studies, San Francisco

Amado M. Padilla, Graduate School of Education, Stanford University

María Pennock-Román, Educational Testing Service and Princeton University

Barbara S. Plake, Buros Institute of Mental Measurements and Department of Educational Psychology and Social Foundations, Teachers College, University of Nebraska

Robert A. Ramos, NYNEX Corporation, White Plains, NY

Orlando Rodriguez, Hispanic Research Center and Department of Sociology, Fordham University

Cynthia Board Schmeiser, American College Testing, Iowa City, IA

Roberto J. Velásquez, Department of Counselor Education, School of Education, San Diego State University

[1] *Now at the State University of New York at Oswego.*

Preface

M uch of the science and practice of psychological testing has emerged in conjunction with the discipline of differential psychology—the study of how people differ from one another. Psychometrics, sometimes described as the science of mental testing, emphasizes the mathematical, statistical, and methodological perspectives on psychology and forms the quantitative foundation for differential psychology. To be useful to psychologists, psychometrics must be integrated with knowledge of the content of psychological science in general and differential psychology in specific to solve the major social, ethical, and interpretative problems facing those who use psychological tests. This volume focuses on the proper use of tests with an important minority group in our society—Hispanics. Hispanics differ from many of the other underrepresented groups in our society, both because they use Spanish in whole or in part rather than English and because they represent different cultures. The intent of this book is not to provide pragmatic prescriptions for using tests with Hispanics. The focus, rather, is jointly on science and broad issues of practice. Although solutions to important questions are always desirable, the study of important issues in the psychological testing of Hispanics remains in its infancy, and in many cases, this volume raises more questions than it solves. In this book, research questions requiring further study are identified and, in some cases, solutions are proposed. If this book is successful, it will have laid a foundation for future study and practice in the testing of Hispanics.

The conference on which this book was based was organized into five sequential sessions and held at the Lincoln Center campus of Fordham University. The first session, chaired by Anthony Cancelli, featured Anne Anastasi's introductory remarks. The second session concerned technical and social issues in testing. It was chaired by Orlando Rodriguez and consisted of presentations by Kurt Geisinger, Michael O'Brien, and Thomas Donlon, which were followed by comments from Cynthia Schmeiser. The third session focused on educational issues in testing Hispanics and was chaired by Giuseppe Costantino. Presentations were made by María Pennock-Román and Richard Durán, but Barbara Plake's scheduled discussant comments were not able to be heard as she had a death in the family prior to the conference. The fourth session related to the testing of Hispanics in industry and research. Chaired by Lorraine Eyde, it featured presentations by Robert Ramos and Nancy Busch-Rossnagel, as well as comments by Wayne Camara. The final session looked at the testing of Hispanics in clinical settings and included a wrap-up and was chaired by Gerardo Marín. A single presentation made by Roberto J. Velásquez was discussed by Giselle Esquivel. Amado Padilla then provided a recapitulation on the entire conference. The papers presented at the conference were generally summarizations of the chapters in this book due to time limitations. Following the conference, Gerardo Marín agreed to draft a chapter on acculturation to complete the book.

The essays provided in this volume are in honor of Anne Anastasi, whose publications in the fields of differential psychology and psychological testing have provided a foundation for these disciplines. Although the planning, organizing, and writing that went into the February 9, 1991, conference "Psychological Testing of Hispanics" occurred without the intent to use the conference to honor this pioneer of psychology, shortly before the conference, many of those involved realized the appropriateness of making this text in honor of Anastasi. A poll was taken, and the participants at the conference, other than Anastasi herself, unanimously decided to dedicate the book in this way. Anastasi has been the recipient of virtually all of the scientific awards there are, her most recent being the 1987 National Medal of Science Award. The inscription of that award stated the following:

> As a scientist, scholar and teacher whose career has spanned more than a half century, Anne Anastasi has stood unwaveringly for excellence. A prolific writer and an exacting researcher, her publications have made major conceptual contributions to our understanding of psychological traits, environmental and experiential influences upon psychological development, and the construction and interpretation of tests. Her classic texts, *Psychological Testing, Differential Psychology,* and *Fields of Applied Psychology,* translated into many foreign languages, are models of clarity, comprehensiveness and synthesis. They frame the very questions that scientists in these disciplines ask and the manner in which research is conducted. In tackling critical controversies that confront the psychology of individual differences and

their measurement, she has furthered the development of psychology as a quantitative behavioral science. A truly staggering schedule of consultantships, committee memberships, invited addresses, and publications continue to provide an ongoing forum for her probing and incisive examination of salient issues in differential psychology and psychological testing.

In addition to the direct contributors, there are many people without whose help this text and the conference that preceded it would not have been completed. Of course, much of the funding for this conference came from the scientific conference program at the American Psychological Association's Science Directorate. They not only funded much of the project; they also helped to shape it in ways that greatly improved its final form. Fordham University provided much of the remainder of the funds supporting the conference through its sesquicentennial celebration program, of which this conference was a small part. Too many individuals to name from the offices of the Sesquicentennial Celebration, Research Services, Academic Affairs, the Graduate Schools of Arts and Sciences, and Education all provided enormous assistance and support at the proper moments. Anthony Cancelli, associate dean of the Fordham University Graduate School of Education, introduced the entire conference and its first speaker Anne Anastasi. The staff in the Department of Psychology, Jonathan Galente, Peggy Mackiewicz, Patricia Greany, and, especially, the project secretary, Peggy Tarnowsky, provided considerable service for which they were not suitably recompensed. Kevin L. Moreland read the entire manuscript furnishing many helpful comments, as did Jeffrey P. Baerwald, S.J., and others read one or more chapters. Finally, my wife, psychologist Janet F. Carlson, provided support and assistance at every step of the process. To all of these people, I provide my heartfelt thanks.

Kurt F. Geisinger

CHAPTER 1

Introductory Remarks

Anne Anastasi

The chapters in this volume approach the psychological testing of Hispanics from diverse angles, thereby providing a comprehensive view of the topic. Beginning with an analysis of methodological issues regarding test bias and cross-cultural testing, they proceed with ethical and legal questions in test use, with specific problems of testing in educational, industrial, and clinical settings, and with the testing of Hispanics in basic psychological research. The individual chapters demonstrate various ways of improving the use of tests with Hispanics, who constitute an important and growing segment of the population of the United States. Nevertheless, I see the function of this volume and the symposium on which it was based as extending beyond that immediate goal; I see it as contributing to the better use of tests with all persons and as adding to our understanding of the psychology of human behavior as a whole. To this end, let me propose two questions—one practical and one theoretical—that you might bear in mind as you read all the chapters, whatever their specific content.

The Role of the Test User

The first question concerns the qualifications and responsibilities of the test user. A conspicuous trend since the 1980s has been the increasing recognition of the part played by the test user. As contrasted with the test constructor, the test user is anyone responsible for choosing tests, supervising their administration and scoring, interpreting test scores, and using test results as one source of information in reaching practical decisions; an individual test user may perform one or more of these functions. Examples of test users include teachers, counselors, educational administrators, testing coordinators, personnel workers in industry or government, clinicians who use tests as aids in their practice, and many others in an increasing number of real-life contexts. In all of these roles, the test user needs knowledge about both the statistical properties of test scores and the psychological characteristics of the behavior assessed by the test.

For example, test users should be able to think in terms of the standard error of measurement and score bands, rather than in terms of single numbers. They should be able to evaluate differences between scores, not only among persons, but also within the person in the interpretation of multiple-trait scores and score profiles. They should be aware of both random and progressive changes in individual scores over time, and they should base their conclusions on multiple sources of information about each person. Most important, test users should recognize that any test score, whether in the cognitive or affective behavior domains, has both a past and a future. Test scores tell us how individuals perform at the time of testing, not *why* they perform as they do. To find out why, we have to evaluate current performance within the individual's *antecedent context.* In what environmental setting did this person develop? What conditions and events were encountered and how did this person respond to them? From another angle, test users need to consider the individual's *anticipated context.* What is the setting— educational, occupational, societal—in which this person is expected to function and for which he or she is being evaluated? What can be found out about the intellectual, emotional, and physical demands of that anticipated context?

Most current criticisms of tests refer not to the tests themselves, but to improper test use and incorrect interpretations of results (Anastasi, 1985, 1990a; Daves, 1984; Eyde, Moreland, Robertson, Primoff, & Most, 1988; Lambert, 1989; Matarazzo, 1990; Tyler & Miller, 1986). One of the most deplorable of such misinterpretations is provided by popular assertions about the IQ, with its many excess meanings. Even when the obsolete term *IQ* is not itself used, some of its excess meanings are attached to other kinds of test scores. For instance, we still find implications that a score on an ability test is predetermined by heredity and provides a permanent fixed label for the individual. We still find these misconceptions about tests, despite the clear and vigorous statements disseminated repeatedly by the College Board to both users and takers of the Scholastic Aptitude Test (SAT), as well as by the more responsible test publishers in their own test manuals. The urgent need for more enlightened test users has been recognized by committees representing several national organizations, working jointly with major test publishers (e.g., Anastasi, in press; Eyde, 1990; Eyde et al., 1988, in press). Many steps are being taken to improve the training of test users through various channels and at different levels. This is an important movement, which needs general support.

Theoretical Implications of Cross-Cultural Research

The second question that I suggest you bear in mind pertains to the broad implications of cross-cultural research for general psychological theory. As far back as 1937, in the first edition of my book on differential psychology (Anastasi, 1937), I argued that the basic goal of differential psychology is similar to that of all psychology, namely, the understanding of behavior. Differential psychology approaches this problem through a comparative analysis of behavior under varying biological and environmental conditions. By relating the observed behavioral differences to other known concomitant phenomena, we may be able to tease out the relative contribution of different variables to behavioral development. If we can discover why one person—or group of persons—reacts differently from another, we have made some progress toward a knowledge of what makes people react as they do (Anastasi, 1937; Foley, 1935, 1936, 1938).

More specifically, John Dollard—also writing in the 1930s—suggested that "to the social psychologist, the three most indispensable letters in the alphabet are I.O.C. (in our culture)"; he observed that these qualifying letters should be regarded as implicit in all behavioral data whose source is restricted to the investigator's own cultural setting (Dollard, 1935, p. 17). That was in the 1930s, a time when psychology students often remarked facetiously that psychology was the study of behavior in white rats and American college sophomores. Since then, we have made noticeable progress in expanding the populations sampled in psychological research. This progress is particularly conspicuous in the subsequently emerging areas of life span developmental psychology and cross-cultural psychology. Nevertheless, we still have a long way to go, especially in our efforts to integrate the diverse research findings into a comprehensive psychological system.

Obviously, one answer to the familiar emic versus etic question—what is culture specific and what is cross-culturally generalizable?—is in terms of psychological facts versus psychological principles. What is learned may be specific to the culture, whereas the laws of learning apply across cultures. We are more likely to get common results in different cultures when we ask the question "How?" How did individuals get that way? What was the modus operandi that led to a particular way of acting or feeling? A considerable amount of research with Hispanics has already contributed significantly to this approach, which looks to cultural differences in the individual's learning history for an explanation of observed behavioral differences (e.g., Diaz-Guerrero & Diaz-Loving, 1990; Laosa, 1990a, 1990b; Rogler, 1989; Stigler, Shweder, & Herdt, 1989). And in this volume, you will find more about such continuing contributions. (See especially Busch-Rossnagel's chapter.)

But the distinction between culture-specific behavioral facts and generalizable behavioral principles does not tell the whole story. There is also much that can be found in the purely descriptive behavioral facts that is generalizable across cultures. It may be helpful in this connection to consider the hierarchical model of human traits, which has already proved useful in integrating other discrepant findings (see, e.g., Anastasi, 1986a, 1986b, 1988, 1990b). It is now widely recognized that behavior can be described at different levels of this hierarchy, from highly specific skills or affective responses at the base to increasingly broader behavior clusters at successive levels. A familiar example in the cognitive area is provided by the old controversy regarding the composition of intelligence, between the exponents of a single general (or g) factor and the exponents of multiple-factor theories. It has become increasingly clear that no one level of the trait hierarchy represents the one true description of intelligence. The same empirical data can be fitted to categories at any level, and the appropriate level varies with the goals of particular testing or assessment programs. These conclusions apply to affective as well as to cognitive traits.

There is some evidence that the hierarchical trait model may serve equally well in integrating cross-cultural findings. Whereas specific trait manifestations may be highly culture bound, the broader trait constructs at higher levels of the hierarchy may be common across cultures. Supporting data for this hypothesis are provided by a recent investigation of attitudes and personal orientations with regard to work and family. This investigation was itself embedded in a continuing research program, spanning more than 20 years, conducted with Mexican populations (Diaz-Guerrero & Diaz-Loving, 1990). The present investigation comprised two studies. In the first study (Diaz-Loving & Andrade Palos, 1985), three personality constructs that had been identified through factor-analytic research within the Anglo-American culture were measured with a three-scale inventory developed within the same culture. This inventory was translated and backtranslated from English to Spanish for use with Mexican samples. When the responses of the Mexicans were factor analyzed, however, the result was a mishmash of 20 narrow and virtually uninterpretable factors. Following these essentially negative findings, a second study was initiated (Diaz-Loving, Andrade Palos, & LaRosa, (1989). A new instrument was developed with items that reflected culturally relevant representations of the three original constructs within the Mexican culture. With this instrument, factor analysis of the responses yielded three factors, readily interpretable in terms of the original definitions.

What this finding suggests is that some universal psychological constructs may emerge, provided we begin with specific behavior identified as significant within each culture and then work from the bottom up in the trait hierarchy. By beginning with different instruments, each independently developed to comparable specifications within each culture, we may be able to identify broad constructs that are themselves generalizable across cultures. This seems to be a promising approach, whether we are dealing with intellectual traits, emotional responses, attitudes, motives, personal value systems, or any other significant aspect of human behavior.

These then are my two questions—one dealing with the responsibilities of the test user and the other with the contributions of cross-cultural research to the basic science of psychology. I hope you find them helpful as you read this volume—and possibly later, as you reflect on what you have read and integrate it into your own thinking.

References

Anastasi, A. (1937). *Differential psychology* (1st ed.). New York: Macmillan.

Anastasi, A. (1985). Mental measurement: Some emerging trends. In J. V. Mitchell, Jr. (Ed.), *Ninth Mental Measurements Yearbook* (Vol. 1, pp. xxiii–xxix). Lincoln, NE: Buros Institute of Mental Measurements of the University of Nebraska.

Anastasi, A. (1986a). Experiential structuring of psychological traits. *Developmental Review, 6,* 181–202.

Anastasi, A. (1986b). Intelligence as a quality of behavior. In R. J. Sternberg & D. K. Detterman (Eds.), *What is intelligence? Contemporary viewpoints on its nature and definition* (pp. 19–21). Norwood, NJ: Ablex.

Anastasi, A. (1988). Explorations in human intelligence: Some uncharted routes. *Applied Measurement in Education, 1,* 207–213.

Anastasi, A. (1990a). What is test misuse? Perspectives of a measurement expert. *Proceedings of the 1989 ETS Invitational Conference* (pp. 15–25). Princeton, NJ: Educational Testing Service.

Anastasi, A. (1990b, August). *Are there unifying trends in the psychologies of 1990?* Paper presented at the annual convention of the American Psychological Association, Boston, MA.

Anastasi, A. (in press). The test user qualifications project: Commentary. *American Psychologist.*

Daves, C. W. (Ed.). (1984). *The uses and misuses of tests. Examining current issues in educational and psychological testing.* San Francisco: Jossey-Bass.

Diaz-Guerrero, R., & Diaz-Loving, R. (1990). Interpretation in cross-cultural personality assessment. In C. R. Reynolds & R. W. Kamphaus (Eds), *Handbook of psychological and educational assessment of children: Personality, behavior, and context* (pp. 491–523). New York: Guilford Press.

Diaz-Loving, R., & Andrade Palos, P. (1985, July). *Motivación de logro y orientación hacia la familia y el trabajo.* Paper presented at the Primer Congreso Interamericano de Psicología Laboral, Oaxaca, Mexico.

Diaz-Loving, R., Andrade Palos, P., & LaRosa, J. (1989). Orientación de logro. Desarrollo de una escala multidimensional (EOL) y su relación con aspectos sociales y de personalidad. *Revista Mexicana de Psicología, 6,* 21–26.

Dollard, J. (1935). *Criteria for the life history—With analysis of six notable documents.* New Haven, CT: Yale University Press.

Eyde, L. D. (1990, August). *Training and test user qualifications.* Paper presented at the annual convention of the American Psychological Association, Boston, MA.

Eyde, L. D. , Moreland, K. L., Robertson, G. J., Primoff, E. S., & Most, R. B . (1988). Test user qualifications: A data-based approach to promoting good test use. *Issues in Scientific Psychology.* Report of the Test User Qualifications Working Group of the Joint Committee on Testing Practices. Washington, DC: American Psychological Association.

Eyde, L. D., Moreland, K. L., Robertson, G. J., Primoff, E. S., & Most, R. B. (in press). The test user qualifications project. An overview. *American Psychologist.*

Foley, J. P., Jr. (1935). The comparative approach to psychological phenomena. *Psychological Review, 42,* 480–490.

Foley, J. P., Jr. (1936). Psychological "ultimates": A note on psychological "fact" versus psychological "law". *Journal of General Psychology, 15,* 455–458.

Foley, J. P., Jr. (1938). The scientific psychology of individual and group differences. *Journal of Social Psychology, 9,* 375–377.

Lambert, N. M. (1989, August). *The crisis in measurement literacy in psychology and education.* Paper presented at the annual convention of the American Psychological Association, New Orleans, LA.

Laosa, L. M. (1990a). Population generalizability, cultural sensitivity, and ethical dilemmas. In C. B. Fisher & W. W. Tryon (Eds.), *Ethics in applied developmental psychology: Emerging issues in an emerging field* (pp. 227–251). Norwood, NJ: Ablex.

Laosa, L. M. (1990b). Psychological stress, coping, and development of Hispanic immigrant children. In F. C. Serafica, A. I. Schwebel, R. K. Russel, P. D. Isaac, & L. Myers (Eds.), *Mental health of ethnic minorities* (pp. 38–65). New York: Praeger.

Matarazzo, J. D. (1990). Psychological assessment versus psychological testing: Validation from Binet to the school, clinic, and courtroom. *American Psychologist, 45,* 999–1017.

Rogler, L. H. (1989). The meaning of culturally sensitive research in mental health *American Journal of Psychiatry, 146,* 296–303.

Stigler, J. W., Shweder, R. A., & Herdt, G. S. (Eds.). (1989). *Essays on comparative human development.* New York: Cambridge University Press.

Tyler, B., & Miller, K. (1986). The use of tests by psychologists: Report on a summary of BPS members. *Bulletin of the British Psychological Society, 39,* 405–410.

PART ONE

Technical and Societal Issues in the Testing of Hispanics

Introduction to Technical and Societal Issues in the Psychological Testing of Hispanics

Orlando Rodriguez

This introduction provides an overview of selected technical and societal is-sues involved in the psychological testing of Hispanics. In order to gain a perspective for the succeeding chapters, it is useful to begin by thinking of the different kinds of people, each representing different societal roles, who are involved in the psychological testing enterprise. First, there are the test developers or *psychometricians*, who determine test content and engage in the arduous technical process of validation and standardization. Second, there are the commercial agents who publish the tests and make them available to clients. Third, there are the clients—the administrators of schools, industry, and health service systems who use the results of these tests to make decisions. The work of all these professionals, then, impacts—rightly or wrongly—on the lives of the test takers, the people about whom decisions are being made. When the viewpoints and agendas of the people placed in these roles differ, conflict very often emerges. When it does, new networks of people come into play. The judiciary system, the political issue organizations, and government agencies try to resolve the conflict of interests and ideologies represented by these different roles. As Donlon's contribution in this volume makes clear, Hispanics have been prominent in legal and political challenges to the standards that the testing profession and its clients apply to Hispanic students, job-seekers, and users of public services.

Testing is ubiquitous in our society as the method by which standards are applied to its members. Testing may even be thought of as a cultural trait of advanced, industrial societies and could be studied as a subcultural phenomenon in its own right. Psychological testing has become an important arena, because issues of equity in the testing of Hispanics and other ethnic groups have proliferated. We need to question whether the dominant or mainstream standards of society limit the life chances of Hispanics, that is, equal access to the goods and services that are offered by society.

What can happen when the test taker is Hispanic? A response to this question rests on the fact that many Hispanics differ from non-Hispanic White and other ethnic groups with respect to language, culture, and socioeconomic status. Let us briefly review data highlighting the sociodemographic situation of Hispanics and then consider how such characteristics may affect Hispanics as they come into contact with test-taking situations in schools, corporations, and health services.

Population estimates indicate that in 1989 20.1 million people in the United States, approximately 8% of the population, were of Hispanic origin. This represents an increase of 39% from the Hispanic representation in the 1980 census and suggests that by the year 2000, Hispanics will be the most populous minority group in the United States (U.S. Bureau of the Census, 1990). Although Mexican Americans, Puerto Ricans, and Cubans, respectively, are the major national origin groups, Dominicans and Central and South Americans constitute a large proportion of the population. Hispanics are an immigrant population, with half of the population's increase in the last decade due to new migrants. Because of the high proportion of immigrants, many Hispanics can communicate only in Spanish. Compilations from the 1980 Census Public Use Sample show that ¼ of Puerto Rican and Mexican Americans and over ⅖ of Cubans speak English "not well" or "not at all."

Because many Hispanics differ in their language from the majority of Americans, it is not surprising that the issue of language has found its way into psychological testing methodology and conceptualization. Clearly, a test written in

English is inadequate to measure the performance of a person who does not understand English well or not at all. But simply translating a test from English to Spanish does not remove all the problems attending the quest for valid psychological measurement. For Hispanics as well as for other migrants, language ability is not simply described as knowing or not knowing English. Hispanics' linguistic ability runs a gamut from Spanish monolingual to Spanish-dominant bilingual, English-dominant bilingual, equally balanced bilingual, to English monolingual. Thus, it would not be far-fetched to assert that the language in which a test is administered is itself a testing issue. (Marín also addresses this issue in a later chapter in this volume.)

Another issue of potential bias involved in the testing of Hispanics is how to assess Hispanics' performance on tests that were developed, validated, and standardized on a nonminority, White, middle-class population. Although this problem has been most salient in the controversy surrounding intelligence testing of Blacks, similar questions about possible bias have been raised with respect to Hispanics' performance on intelligence tests as well as in mental-health-oriented and industrial testing (Olmedo, 1981). Two contributions in this volume delineate the various issues involved in how bias may creep into the assessment of the test performance of Hispanics. Geisinger surveys selected testing issues related to educational and psychological testing and reviews the separate psychometric techniques used to assess bias in decisions concerning Hispanics' performance on tests. O'Brien, using the specific example of Anglo and Hispanic results in the New York City language assessment battery, focuses on the psychometric problems and solutions that are inherent in comparing test results for Hispanics with those for other groups and provides step-by-step procedures for equating group differences in test scores.

For Hispanics, discussions of equity in access to societal opportunities tend to focus on the the the issue of language barriers. However, Hispanics also differ culturally and socioeconomically from the American mainstream. Are sociocultural differences relevant to assessing Hispanics' performance on tests? Having suggested earlier that testing could be viewed as a cultural trait of advanced industrial societies, I would like now to suggest another hypothesis, namely, that test-taking behaviors are culturally learned behaviors. Thus, at a basic level, the argument may be advanced that most Hispanics are not "test wise." Steeped as immigrants in a traditional culture where test taking is not customary, Hispanics come to the testing situation with a cultural disadvantage. Hispanics do not have a cultural knowledge of the mechanics of testing (e.g., there are several choices, but only one correct choice; the correct answer must be recorded in a given slot and within a given allotment of time), nor do they necessarily adhere to the advanced industrial norms and values encapsulated by the general belief in the legitimacy of the testing enterprise as the standard by which to assess performance. This is not to say that a Hispanic from a traditional Hispanic culture comes to the testing situation conscious of the fact that he or she may hold values that are antithetical to testing. To the contrary, adherence to traditional culture precludes having any such crystallized or defined beliefs with respect to such notions. Therefore, a traditionally minded Hispanic is at a disadvantage in not understanding the implications of tests for future life chances. As in all culturally related arguments, however, the issue is rendered more complex by the fact that, just as Hispanics differ in linguistic ability, they also possess varying degrees of acculturation to American society, ranging from full adherence to traditional Hispanic culture to bicultural involvement to complete immersion into American culture (Rogler, Cortes, & Malgady, 1991). In becoming acculturated, a Hispanic most likely learns and accepts the values and norms sanctioning test results as the standards by which rewards are meted out and opportunities are provided.

Finally, the socioeconomic level of Hispanics is a factor to be considered in assessing how Hispanics fare in testing. Partly because of their position as migrants, Hispanics in the United States have relatively low socioeconomic status. In 1989, 27% of Hispanics were under the poverty level, in contrast with 12% of non-Hispanics. The proportion of Hispanics under the age of 18 who were under the poverty level was even higher—38%, in contrast with 17% among non-Hispanics of the same age group (U.S. Bureau of the Census, 1990). Social class intermingles with culture, because most Hispanics in the United States are poor and it is difficult to distinguish where the impact of class on a particular problem ends and the impact of culture begins. Thus, Hispanics' disadvantage in testing may be due as much to low socioeconomic status as to low acculturation.

These considerations suggest that there are complex theoretical issues underlying the question of how the testing enterprise affects Hispanics' life chances. There are, however, adequate methodologies for addressing these issues. The contributions in succeeding chapters provide the reader with thorough reviews of the techniques and scientific standards necessary to sensitize current psychological testing instruments to language and socioeconomic bias.

References

Olmedo, E. L. (1981). Testing linguistic minorities. *American Psychologist, 36,* 1078–1085.

Rogler L. H., Cortes D., & Malgady R. G. (1991). Acculturation and mental health status among Hispanics. *American Psychologist, 46,* 585–597.

U.S. Bureau of the Census. (1990). *The Hispanic population in the United States: March 1989.* (Series P-20, No. 444). Washington, DC: U.S. Government Printing Office.

CHAPTER 3

Fairness and Selected Psychometric Issues in the Psychological Testing of Hispanics

Kurt F. Geisinger

There are very few things about which most individuals within an academic discipline would agree; psychologists and other testing professionals are certainly no exception. However, most testing professionals would agree that validity is the most important facet in the evaluation of a test and its use. Therefore, consideration of the psychometric approach to test fairness or, alternatively, test bias for Hispanics requires first the development of the concept of validation and its interrelationship with the concept of test bias. Thus, this chapter provides a review of the concept of validity, followed by a definition of test bias and a brief description of some of the models and methods that have been used to study it. Test bias is integrated conceptually with the principles of test validation. Finally, some special issues related to the study of test bias against Hispanics are described.

Defining Validity and Validation

Two conditions confound the simple explanation of test validity. First, test validity refers to a collection of concepts rather than to a singular one. That is, validity as traditionally defined involves several meanings and each of these entails its own empirical methodology. The specific use to which a test may be put determines in part the validation principles and procedures that are applied to the test in that context. Second, test validity has not been a static concept; rather, it has evolved considerably in recent years. Each of these ideas is developed in this chapter.

The Validation Complex

In recent decades, three forms of test validation have been generally recognized: criterion-related validation, content-related validation, and construct-related validation. Each of these methods, for example, appears in the *Standards for Educational and Psychological Testing* (1985), as well as the *Uniform Guidelines on Employee Selection* (1978). These three approaches to test validation are briefly described next.

Criterion-related validation

Criterion-related validity is determined by the degree of the empirical relationship between scores generated by two measures. The degree of the relationship is usually estimated in terms of correlation coefficients between test scores and criterion values. Criterion-related validation focuses on "selected relationships with measures that are critical for a particular purpose in a specific applied setting" (Messick, 1989, p. 17). Thus, as presently conceived, this form of validation seems to be relegated to specific applied uses in specific settings.

Messick in fact suggested the use of the term *utility* to describe this type of applied decision making instead of validity or validation per se. Messick preferred the term utility to validation in such studies because utility leads to an interpretation of the correlations in the context of the particular decision: "predictive efficiency relative to base rates, mean gains in criterion performance due to selection, the dollar value of such gains relative to costs, and so forth" (Messick, 1980, p. 1017).

The importance of criteria in criterion-related validation studies cannot be overstated. The *Standards* (1985) stated, "The choice of criterion and the measurement procedures used to obtain criterion scores are of central importance.

Logically, the value of a criterion-related study depends on the relevance of the criterion measure that is used" (p. 11). In some cases, criteria against which tests are validated are questionably related to success in the domain being predicted. Judgments in court cases in the employment testing arena have sometimes rejected the use of a test because the criterion used to justify the use of the test in the validation study was seen as either inappropriate or trivial. As Cronbach (1988, p. 9) succinctly stated, "Traditional validation puts overwhelming weight on the criteria; and great vulnerability lies therein." Any discussion of criterion-related validity vis-à-vis test bias must also mention that the potential Achilles heel in all criterion-related validation is the requirement that the criterion be free from bias. Should it be tainted, such as in the case of ratings made by prejudiced judges, it will almost necessarily be a similarly biased test that best predicts that criterion. Furthermore, a criterion-related validation that uses a biased criterion and standard procedures to identify test bias will make the test appear fair! Convincing demonstrations that criteria are free from inappropriate bias should be a component of all validation and fairness studies. Linn (1982, 1984) and Linn and Dunbar (1986) thoroughly explained the various aspects of predictive bias.

Content validation

The basis for content validation is "professional judgments about the relevance of the test content to the content of a particular behavioral domain of interest and about the representativeness with which item or task content covers that domain" (Messick, 1989, p. 17). Both Cronbach (1971) and Messick (1980) argued that the content validation strategy must cling to behavioral, domain-specific task language. Measures developed and validated using content validation are frequently used in education and industry and involve carefully developed domain specifications and job analyses, respectively, to delineate the areas to be covered on a given test.

An assessment of content validation comprises both evaluating the relevance of the content called for by the test domain (or plan) and judging how well the test ultimately represents the test plan or domain. Neither test-taking behavior nor test scores are generally considered. Hence, some test theorists (e.g., Guion, 1977; Tenopyr, 1977) have suggested that what has traditionally been called content validity is not truly validity at all. Messick (1989) labeled these two aspects of content-related validation as *content relevance* and *content representativeness.* An assessment of content relevance should include a review of the stimulus and response elements called for by the measurement device. These elements should be contrasted with the stimulus and response characteristics of the domain in question. Ultimately, expert judgment must assess whether the test plan matches the domain in this manner. Content representativeness relates to whether the test specifications, and ultimately the test, provide an appropriate and relevant sample of the domain. Such a determination must be made by mapping the domain, comparing this charting of the domain with the test blueprint, and then assessing how effectively the test approximates the domain and test specification blueprints.

Construct validation

Anastasi (1988) defined construct-related validation as follows:

> [T]he construct-related validity of a test is the extent to which the test may be said to measure a theoretical construct or trait...It derives from established interrelationships among behavioral measures. Construct-related validation requires the gradual accumulation of information from a variety of sources. Any data throwing light on the nature of the trait under consideration and the conditions affecting its development and manifestations represent appropriate evidence for this validation (p. 153).

Thus, as the *Standards* (1974) stated

> Evidence of construct validity is not found in a single study; rather judgments of construct validity are based upon an accumulation of research results. In obtaining the information needed to establish construct validity, the investigator begins by formulating hypotheses about the characteristics of those who have high scores on the test in contrast to those who have low scores. Taken together, such hypotheses form at least a tentative theory about the nature of the construct that the test is believed to be measuring (p. 30).

Such theorizing is never completed. "As psychological science generates new concepts, test interpretations will have to be reconsidered...so validation is never finished" (Cronbach, 1988, p. 5).

Because construct-related test validation includes a definition of what a test measures and how well interpretations based on test scores are borne out, almost all empirical analyses using test scores provide some evidence bearing on construct validation, including those normally performed as content-related and criterion-related validation studies.

Two useful terms describing different aspects of construct validation are convergent and discriminant validation (Campbell & Fiske, 1959). *Convergent validation* refers to substantial correlations between a test and other measures to which it should theoretically relate. Traditionally, convergent validity is subdivided into trait validity and nomological validity. The former is based on correlations of two measures of the same construct and the latter based on correlations among different constructs hypothesized to be related. *Discriminant validation* relates to the freedom from alternative interpretations of a test score; that is, freedom from the threat of method variance and from the suggestion that the test scores emerging from the instrument reflect characteristics other than what is intended. Determining whether a test is free from bias is one form of discriminant validation.

One additional term is useful to the present discussion. *Population validity* is used to describe the evidence supporting the ability to generalize validation results across subgroups. Hence, it is a term used to describe a situation where no unintended systematic variance due to group membership is found.

The Evolution of Test Validation[1]

Toward a unified view of test validation

Messick (1975, p. 956), although admitting that criterion-related validation is appropriate for applied decision making in specific settings, cautioned that "even for purposes of applied decision making, reliance upon criterion validity or content coverage is not enough." Both "Cronbach (1980) and Messick (1975, 1980) have also argued, in essence, that no criterion or universe of content is *ever* entirely adequate to define the quality being measured, that a variety of types of logical and empirical evidence is necessary to support a given interpretation, and that all test score interpretations should be construct referenced" (Cole & Moss, 1989, p. 203). Furthermore, neither content- nor criterion-related validation is sufficient to rule out plausible score contaminations. What is needed is evidence not only that test scores reflect the intended constructs, but also that scores do *not* reflect other influences.

Guion (1977, p. 410) considered criterion-related and content-related validation, concluding that "all validity is at its base some form of construct validity."

---

[1] *For a more complete description of the changes in the concept of validation see Angoff (1988), Geisinger (1992), and Messick (1989).*

It is not clear when so many of the leaders in measurement began thinking that all validation is, at some level, construct validation, a point perhaps first made by Loevinger (1957). The documents that guide the use of tests by testing professionals [e.g., the *Standards* (1985) and the *Uniform Guidelines* (1978)], however, continue to cite the three forms of validation (i.e., criterion-related, content-related, and construct-related); this status quo may have survived because many of the applications to which tests are put in society have traditionally been considered by consumers to be adequately justified on the basis of criterion-related or content-related validation.

The role of values

Messick (1980, 1989) presented a new perspective on test validation. In this perspective, he stated that we not only need to look at our evidence supporting the interpretations and uses of tests, we also need to look at the consequences of test interpretation and use. With regard to test interpretation, he stated that we must appraise the following:

> the value implications of the construct label, of the theory underlying test interpretation, and of the ideologies in which the theory is embedded. A central issue is whether or not the theoretical implications and the value implications of the test interpretation are not ancillary but, rather, integral to score meaning...[T]he consequential basis of test use is the appraisal of both potential and actual social consequences of the applied setting (Messick, 1989, p. 20).

It is not always clear whether Messick perceived the consequences of testing to be part of a general validation paradigm or whether it is information that should be used in addition to validation data in the evaluation of a test. Cole and Moss (1989), however, perceived the consequences of testing as part of an extravalidity analysis of a test. Perhaps one may best think of validation as the evaluation of a test much the same way that a program evaluation is the evaluation of a delivery system.

Test validation as traditionally conceived used only what Messick referred to as the test's evidential basis. However, in reviewing or evaluating a program, one must consider both the intended and the unintended effects of that program. Similarly, Messick argued that the evidential basis for testing relates only to the intended effects; we must also evaluate the unintended impacts of testing. Such effects might be changes in school curricula as educational institutions adapt instruction to a given test, adverse impact on groups underrepresented in employment and educational settings, or labels applied to certain groups of students. Values should guide both test use and test evaluation, hence, such factors need to be considered in evaluating the use of tests and other measurement procedures.

The use of tests with groups underrepresented in many settings within society, such as Hispanics, invokes the consequential side of the evaluation of psychological measures. This aspect of test evaluation is present in the ⅘ rule found in the *Uniform Guidelines.* In litigation regarding testing, judges have frequently chosen to consider such social factors along with empirical evidence in making determinations. In *Diana v. California State Board of Education* (1970), for example, it was ruled that students must be tested in their native language. This case involved the classification of nine Mexican Americans as mentally retarded and their subsequent assignment to special education classes in California, based on ability test scores from both the Stanford-Binet and the WISC ranging from 52 to 68. The tests had been administered in English, and when these students were later given the tests by a bilingual test administrator with the opportunity to respond in either English or Spanish, they showed improvements averaging 15 points—one standard deviation. The court not only ruled that ability tests had to be administered in the student's primary language, but also stated that the tests could not include vocabulary, general information, and other unfair verbal questions (Hills, 1981). (In fact, all Mexican-American and Chinese students in educable mentally retarded (EMR) classes were ordered to be retested using only nonverbal procedures. The interested reader is referred to Elliott [1987] for a reaction to many of the legal and psychological factors involved in this case.) The California legislature followed the lead of Diana and passed changes in the legal code governing education so that these problems would not occur again. A similar case was subsequently tried in Arizona with a similar ruling (*Guadalupe Ord. Inc. v. Tempe School District No. 3*, 1972).

Some may differ with Messick's contention that the consequences of testing should be regarded as validation information per se. However, almost all would agree that such factors deserve attention. Indeed, some of the recommendations that emerged from the National Research Council's recent review of the use of the General Aptitude Test Battery (Hartigan & Wigdor, 1989) indicated that the panel of experts reviewing the use of this test considered the negative, unintended consequences of the test's use almost on a par with the benefits accrued from its use.

Perspectives on Test Bias

Definition

Test bias is intrinsically and closely tied to the concept of test validity because, like validity, it rests primarily on inferences based on test scores. Threats to test validation threaten proper test score interpretation. Just as validation was dominated by the criterion-related approach until the last decade or two (see Geisinger, 1992), so has the study of bias (see Flaugher, 1978). Many of the definitions of bias that have been traditionally provided are difficult to extract from the criterion-related validation paradigm. This point can be seen by considering the dominant models of test bias that have been advanced in the literature. (See, e.g., Hunter, Schmidt, & Rauschenberger, 1984; Jensen, 1980.)

Models of test bias in selection situations have been advanced in the professional literature and generally represent attempts to integrate values and validation. That is, these models reconcile the results of selection studies with the outcomes of those studies from a social policy perspective. In the regression model (e.g., Cleary, 1968), a selection procedure is considered biased when a single regression equation is used for all candidates and one or more groups are systematically over- or underpredicted. Darlington (1971) suggested that members of underrepresented groups should be given a bonus in their criterion scores; essentially, this approach would build favoritism into a selection situation (Cole, 1981). Thorndike's (1971) constant ratio model suggested that a measure is fair only if it selects the same proportion of minority group candidates that would have been selected based solely on the criterion (or using a perfectly valid predictive measure). Cole (1973) proposed a conditional probability model in which the proportion of each group that is selected equals the proportion of that group that achieved a satisfactory criterion score. Peterson and Novick (1976) suggested that decision theory be used in making fair selection decisions and that the social philosophy that values increasing the representation of minority groups be made quantitatively explicit. (Decision-theoretic models can incorporate such quantitative information directly.) Although other models have also been advanced, Cronbach (1976) suggested that the approaches already mentioned were only mathematical models and that finding a satisfactory model required debate and resolution of society's values and social policies. Note that all of these models relate to selection situations, but that selection represents only one use to which tests are put.

Bias, on the other hand, needs to be conceptualized with respect to whatever use to which a given test is put. "The purpose and context of an intended use clearly influence the kind of test we construct or choose, the kind of interpretative meaning we look for in a score, the kind of information we collect to evaluate the test, as well as what is considered bias" (Cole & Moss, 1989, p. 203). Because, as argued earlier, all validation is, at least at some level, construct validation, a definition of bias grounded in the logic of construct validation is needed.

A definition of bias has been provided in the literature that moves beyond the criterion-related models reviewed earlier. This definition, provided by Cole and Moss (1989) states the following:

> An inference from a test score is considered sufficiently valid when a variety of types of evidence support its plausibility and eliminate primary counterinferences. An inference is biased when it is not equally valid for different groups. Bias is present when a test score has meanings or implications for a relevant, definable subgroup of test takers that are different from the meanings or implications for the remainder of the test takers. Thus, *bias is differential validity of a given interpretation of a test score for any definable, relevant subgroup of test takers.* (p. 205)

Threats to validation about which test users are not aware may lead to biased judgments about the test and limit proper test inferences. Just as validation evidence may be criterion-related, content-related, or construct-related, so may documentation of bias be ascribed to these sources. With respect to the content validation approach, problems in making valid inferences may be based on differences across groups with regard to the appropriateness for all groups of a given domain of content or testing format, or for how well specific questions cover the content domain. For example, when Spanish-speaking 10th-grade students write responses on an essay final examination in history, the quality of their responses may be limited by their ability to write the answer in English. English writing ability becomes a source of test score variance, and inferences that assume that the scores are due solely to knowledge of history are incorrect.

Criterion-related evidence may consist of differences in the meaning of criterion values across groups; included in such situations would be cases of intentional discrimination in the assignment of criterion values as well as those devoid of intentional discrimination. Imagine a test for selecting insurance salespeople that is validated against a frequently used criterion of sales volume in dollars of insurance sold. Representatives of minority groups who are hired for such positions are often placed in poorer communities, communities often populated by others of their ethnic group. In poorer communities, less insurance is sold because the residents have less disposable income. Based on this (biased) criterion measure, it appears that the minority salesperson is not performing as well as others situated in more affluent settings. Thus, although the insurance company is not intentionally discriminating, the criterion is nevertheless indirectly biased.

Construct-related bias can be imagined when we take traits and behaviors seen as abnormal in one culture but not in another and apply measures of these constructs indiscriminately in the second culture for purposes, for example, of psychiatric diagnosis. Individuals able to thrive in their own culture could be hospitalized as a result of such bias.

Bias Detection Techniques

Test bias has been scientifically studied for several decades. Typically, reviews of test bias research subdivide bias detection procedures into external and internal methods. External methods are those that evaluate whether the relationship between test scores and an extratest criterion is comparable across groups. There are two types of internal methods. The first attempts to identify those test questions that are differentially more difficult for a given group than other questions composing the test. The second involves factor analyses of test items to identify dimensions of test performance for each of the groups under study; the goal is to demonstrate whether the test measures the same, similar, or different characteristics across the groups. If similar factors are found across groups, the test measures comparable constructs in each group.

This analysis of test bias, however, presents bias as a threat to valid inferences in the same way that validation is presented by Campbell and Stanley (1963) and the *Standards* (1985). Test validation implies documentation of one of several different kinds of inferences. As explained earlier in this chapter, these types of inferences have been historically distinguished and documented as criterion-related, content-related, and construct-related validation. It seems relevant, therefore, to consider the techniques used to study bias as they threaten each of these types of inferences.

Criterion-related validation

Criterion-related validation is documented by relationships between tests and relevant criteria, such as grade point average or indices of job success. These relationships are quantified by correlations and modeled by regression lines. Bias in criterion-related testing is evinced either by different correlations or, more typically, regression lines across groups. Regression lines of different groups are compared for their similarity with respect to Y-intercept, slope, and standard error of estimate—the degree to which the line provides accurate estimations of actual criterion values. (These comparisons are well explained conceptually by Anastasi [1988]. The two lines may be compared statistically using procedures developed by Gulliksen and Wilks, [1950]. Durán [1983], for example, summarized the results of predictive validation research using Hispanics' college admissions tests, and Schmidt, Pearlman, and Hunter [1980], did so for industrial selection.) Evidence that a test is biased would be provided by a regression line for the minority group that is parallel to but above the regression line for the majority group.[2] In this instance, using test scores in an equivalent manner (i.e., using a single regression line) for majority and minority groups would lead to systematic underpredictions of the minority group members' performance. This underestimation is the reason the test is considered biased, but it is the differential accuracy of prediction that compromises the validity of using the test in the same way for both groups. That is, because the precision of predictions would be reduced by using the test in an equivalent manner for both groups, the test's overall criterion-related validity is reduced. Therefore, the reason that this type of bias is a threat to validity is because it systematically reduces the accuracy of predictions.

Content-related validation

No techniques for the identification of test bias have been developed explicitly for content validity, although sometimes individuals, including psychological and

---

[2]*Studies comparing regression lines across groups have not commonly uncovered bias. Rather, they have found that tests (e.g., employment tests) are fair for all groups and may even include some bias in favor of minority groups (e.g., Hunter, Schmidt, & Hunter, 1979). Pennock-Román (1990) reported that her analyses of relationships between the SAT and measures of college performance indicate bias in favor of Hispanic students. Reilly (1973) suggested that such findings are a psychometric certainty; groups below average on the predictive test will be overpredicted by these tests.*

measurement professionals, have informally inspected tests or items from tests and labeled them as biased. However, perhaps the most frequently studied family of techniques in the test bias literature consists of what have been called *item bias detection methods*. Item bias techniques are also known as methods to determine differential item functioning (DIF), across groups and have been used in the pretesting phase in test development to identify and remove those questions from a test that are differentially more difficult for one or more groups. The manner in which most of the available techniques work may be explained as follows: The two factors considered by these techniques are the group-specific difficulty level of each of the questions composing the test and the overall level of ability or knowledge of each test taker. The test taker's level of ability or knowledge is generally indexed by the individual's overall score on the examination or some mathematical derivation of that value. The underlying logic is that the content and thought processes called for by a question determine the difficulty level of that question and should be comparable across groups. Because groups may differ in terms of overall ability for one reason or another, these techniques adjust difficulty levels of individual test questions for these overall group differences. If the difference between difficulty levels for an item for two groups is disproportionately large, even controlling for the groups' overall test differences, the particular test question is considered biased. In the pretesting of an examination, such questions would likely be removed from the instrument under development.

DIF techniques, as stated previously, have generally not been considered to be related to a particular form of test validation. However, because they consider the difficulty level of test items only and do not reflect estimates of ability independent of the test itself, it is hard to conceptualize them as related to any form of validation other than content-related validation. There is typically neither a criterion nor an independent measure of the construct used as indicative of overall ability level in the DIF techniques, although such measures could be used instead of overall test score. If independent measures were used, these techniques could then be considered as indicative of criterion-related or construct-related validation, respectively. In fact, in one study (Schultz, 1992), a great number of test questions on a nationally standardized test used for admission to higher education were identified as biased when the criterion of grade point average was used in place of the test score to represent overall ability.

DIF techniques lead to at least two inferential problems. If an item is surprisingly difficult for one of the groups under study, "one must still judge whether the basis of the differences on items is irrelevant to the construct and, therefore, not an issue of bias (Shepard, 1982)" (Cole & Moss, 1989, p. 211). The second problem relates to using total test score as a measure of the construct in question. Cook and Campbell (1979, p. 61) stated that construct validation requires "*convergence* across *different* measures or manipulations of the same 'thing'." The relationship between a test item and the test for which it is a part is probably not sufficiently different to justify the attribution of construct validity. In fact, Cook and Campbell referred to this problem as *mono-method bias,* and it is a threat to construct interpretability.

Construct-related validation

Reynolds (1982a, p. 194) offered the following definition of test bias from the perspective of construct-related validation: Bias exists in regard to construct validity when a test is shown to measure different hypothetical traits (psychological constructs) for one group than another or to measure the same trait but with differing degrees of accuracy. Reynolds (1982b) suggested a number of different empirical techniques that might identify construct-related test bias. These include differences across reliability coefficients; rank ordering of item difficulties; correlations with other variables, such as age; multitrait-multimethod matrices; and factor-analytic results. Each of these is noted later with primary consideration given to the factor-analytic approach.

Adhering to the foregoing definition of construct-related test bias implies that in order for test scores of two groups to be unbiased, they must be equally accurate. Because reliability coefficients are often used to characterize certain types of test score accuracy, inspection of reliability coefficients across groups provides a method for assessing test equivalence in a preliminary manner. Test-retest and alternate-forms reliability coefficients calculated for different groups can be compared statistically as are any two Pearson product–moment correlation coefficients. Internal consistency coefficients can be contrasted, for example, using a procedure developed by Feldt (1969) to test the equivalence of coefficient alpha (or Kuder-Richardson 20) internal-consistency reliability coefficients. Proof that tests produce scores of comparable reliability across two groups serves as basic information regarding the comparability of test scores. (It should be noted that if one group has more restricted test score variance than the other group—often due to ceiling or floor effects—certain statistical adjustments should be made.)

In any test of cognitive skill or ability, a logical and elementary check on test comparability across groups is a determination that the relative difficulty of test questions is similar. That is, those questions that are difficult for one group should also be challenging for others. Should such a comparable rank ordering not be discovered, one must question population validity of the underlying construct. If test items are rank ordered from easy to difficult within each group, rank order correlations, such as Spearman's rho, may be calculated to demonstrate parity. Reynolds (1982b) suggested that rhos of .90 be taken as indicative of consistency and, thus, of construct-related validity.

The nomological validity of a construct, as previously defined, refers to correlations among psychological constructs hypothesized to be related. Psychological researchers develop and test models of the relationships among constructs of interest. These interrelationships may be conceptualized as single correlations, as in the case of correlations between age and mental ability in children, or as sets of correlations describing networks of variables, which may be studied in either a multitrait-multimethod matrix or a structural equation modeling analysis. In the case of a single correlation compared across groups, a simple test contrasting the correlation coefficients may be performed. In a more complex example, a linear structural equation analysis may be performed with ethnic or minority group status studied for its systemic impact as a variable. (An example of this analysis may be found in Muthen [1988].)

The most common technique used to evaluate test bias from the construct-related perspective is factor analysis. Factor analyses of test results are performed for each of the groups under study, and the results are compared. Reynolds (1982b, p. 201), a proponent of this technique, justified the procedure saying, "consistent factor analytic results across populations do provide strong evidence that whatever is being measured by the instrument is being measured in the same manner and is in fact the same construct within each group". Katzenmeyer and Steener (1977) provided a technique for determining the invariance of two factor solutions, permitting strong statements about the similarity of two factor-analytic solutions.

Gutkin and Reynolds (1980, 1981) compared the Wechsler Intelligence

Scale for Children-Revised factor structures for White, non-Hispanic, White Hispanic, and Black children and found them largely comparable. Rousey (1990)
compared the factor structures of a Spanish-language version of the Wechsler Intelligence Scale for Children-Revised administered to Mexican children to that of
the original English version when administered to both Anglo and Chicano children from the United States. All three samples generated similar factor structures with three factors identified as Verbal Comprehension, Perceptual Organization, and Freedom From Distractibility. Such results provide some initial evidence
that the instruments measure comparable constructs.

In the context of personality assessment, Diaz-Guerrero and Diaz-Loving
(1990) performed a most elaborate factor-analytic comparison. They translated a
personality inventory from English to Spanish. Their initial research, however, indicated that the reasonably literal translations did not appear to invoke the same
construct meanings across cultures. "For example, being dominant and dictato-
rial, which is perceived as an undesirable instrumental characteristic for U.S.
subjects—bad for both sexes, but worse for females were perceived in Mexico
as positive instrumental traits" (pp. 519–520). A better model for the measurement of affective constructs in a cross-cultural, cross-linguistic manner is probably to base measures for each cultural group on definitions of the construct to be
assessed. Scales are then independently developed using culture-specific items
for each of the inventories. Diaz-Guerrero and Diaz-Loving reported that several
English-language measures have been adapted for Mexican populations using
these procedures with great success. One reason these efforts have been seen as
successful is that comparable factor-analytic solutions have been found across the
two cultural groups. These investigators summarized their approach as follows:
"The fact that the same construct and definition can lead to different linguistic
operationalizations, depending on the culture, alerts us to the importance of the
universality of some psychological constructs and at the same time to the culture-specific representation of such characteristics. Although having parallel instruments does not permit a quantitative comparison between two cultures, it
does permit intracultural comparisons and qualitative intercultural comparisons"
(p. 520).

Cole and Moss (1989) expressed concerns about our lack of knowledge regarding the sensitivity of these comparative factor analyses. Perhaps more problematic, except for giant testing agencies such as Educational Testing Service, the

American College Testing Program, and the U.S. military's testing program, are the sample sizes needed to perform these analyses accurately and appropriately.

The Relationship Between Test Validity and Test Bias

When test differences across ethnic, cultural, or gender groups occur, it becomes necessary to ask *why* such differences have occurred. Answers to this question become evidence for or against convergent or discriminant validation. If groups do not differ with respect to test scores and no difference due to group membership was expected theoretically (i.e., no relationship between group membership and the construct is expected), one has evidence of discriminant validation. When groups are expected to differ on the construct and they do so, this is evidence of convergent validation. When there is no adequate explanation for why the groups differ with regard to test scores or with regard to the relationships between test scores and external variables, convergent or discriminant validation may be compromised. From the perspective of construct validation, such unexplainable group differences become a source of test score variance that cannot be interpreted as stemming from the construct assessed. Thus, the test would be seen as biased and less valid than would be preferred.

Test Bias Against Hispanics

It needs to be remembered that in most instances, the study of test bias against Hispanics differs from and is more difficult than that against many other groups, such as Blacks, women, or the elderly. There are at least two ways in which test bias differs when we consider bias against Hispanics. The first of these relates purely to language differences, both in test administration and in the interpretation of test results. The second situation considers differences between Hispanics and the other groups in our society due to cultural factors, with these cultural differences including those related to language.

In some cases, of course, a single test, almost invariably administered in English, is used to test Hispanics as well as all other groups, and interpretations from the test are comparably determined for all groups. In such an instance, traditional test bias approaches may be used. In other cases, however, test forms are prepared in English- and Spanish-language versions.[3] In these cases, it is more difficult to judge the existence of bias, because the test forms differ. The use to which the examination is put determines whether a single English-language test may be used or if two different-language forms need be developed.

Two primary factors confound the interpretations of some tests across Hispanic and non-Hispanic populations: language and culture. Neither of these problems is easily resolved, but language has received more recent attention from the psychometric literature (e.g., Durán, 1988, 1989), even though it is potentially less complex.

Language Differences

The first issue related to language concerns the question, "In which language should the test be administered?" For some testing situations, such as for employment tests where the job is performed solely in English, the answer is clear; in others, such as for psychiatric diagnosis, the answer becomes quite difficult. In educational testing situations, where a child's ability to succeed in future educational endeavors is in question, the decision is also difficult and depends on the specific situation. Sometimes, administering tests in both languages may yield useful information. Nonverbal tests of ability or skill may also be used in some cases. The choice of the language in which to test should be determined by the use to which the examination scores are to be put. Scores from tests of cognitive ability, for example, may need to be interpreted within the context of scores on measures of language ability or acculturation, as described later.

In many employment settings where English-language tests are used with Hispanic applicants, the level of language applied on the test needs to parallel that used on the job (as it does with English-speaking test takers). With written tests, various readability formulas may be used to estimate both the reading levels of the examination and of materials used on the job to ensure that the test does not require an artificially high reading level. Plake (1988) provided a conceptual grounding for such efforts. In the scoring of certain free-response mea-

---

[3] *It should be noted that the translation of existing tests into new languages "presents additional methodological problems that often are not treated properly. For example, direct translations do not ordinarily yield technically equivalent forms because the domains sampled by the different language versions may have little overlap, and the translated items may exhibit psychometric properties substantially different from those of the original English items. Additionally, the interpretation of scores remains difficult, even after translation, because the test content remains culture-bound" (Olmeda, 1981, p. 1083).*

sures, such as the essay questions typically found in graduate school comprehensive examinations, the level of English-language skill necessary for achieving passing scores on the examination should be considered when constructing the questions, scoring the responses, and interpreting the results. (Other techniques for reducing bias in the construction of tests may be found in either Allan, Nassif, & Elliot [1988] or Berk [1984].)

Padilla (1979) noted that there are situations in which it is appropriate for job candidates to be given extra credit for being bilingual. In job settings where such bilingualism is functionally related to job success, such credit is indeed appropriate, although it is rarely given (e.g., civil service settings). Such bonuses, appropriately awarded because the language skills enhance job performance, should be seen as additional to any other advantages provided to members of language minorities in the attempt to increase their representation in the workforce, on campuses, and in advanced instruction. Credit for being bilingual (French/English) is appropriately provided to managers in the public service of Canada, for example.

For the first time in the history of professional standards relating to the development and use of tests, the *Standards* (1985) provide a section on the testing of linguistic minorities. Seven standards were enumerated to provide some guidance toward good testing practice. In general, these standards emphasize attempts to achieve valid inferences from test scores coming from members of linguistic minorities. They accent the notion that tests that presumably measure psychological characteristics when administered to English-speaking test takers, may assess language skills (irrelevant to the construct purportedly being measured) to a greater or lesser extent when given to linguistic minorities. Thus, they attempt to assure valid test use and interpretation. Furthermore, they state that test publishers developing assessment instruments recommended for use with linguistic minorities need to inform test administrators and test users of proper procedures and interpretations with those groups. Those standards follow.

13.1 For nonnative English speakers or for speakers of some dialects of English, tests should be designed to minimize threats to test reliability and validity that may arise from language differences.

13.2 Linguistic modifications recommended by test publishers should be described in detail in the test manual.

13.3 When a test is recommended for use with linguistically diverse test takers, test developers and publishers should provide the information necessary for appropriate test use and interpretation.

13.4 When a test is translated from one language or dialect to another, its reliability and validity for the uses intended in the linguistic groups to be tested should be established.

13.5 In employment, licensing, and certification testing, the English language proficiency level of the test should not exceed that appropriate to the relevant occupation or profession.

13.6 When it is intended that the two versions of dual-language tests be comparable, evidence of test comparability should be reported.

13.7 English language proficiency should not be determined solely with tests that demand only a single linguistic skill. (pp. 74–75).

Adherence to these standards would certainly improve the use of tests with Hispanics across a wide range of applications and, in turn, would reduce threats to valid inferences based on these scores. Unfortunately, it is easy to reverse each of the standards and find examples of test misuse, all of which seem to be frequently committed in actual testing practice.

Cultural Differences

Before beginning a discussion on the influence of culture on test scores, we need to remember that those people referred to as Hispanics include those from Puerto Rico, Mexico, Cuba, and many other countries primarily in Central and South America. Just as significant information about their cultures is lost when all the distinct Indian peoples or nations present in our society are grouped as Native Americans, the grouping of all Hispanic populations together as a single group makes some cultural differences between Hispanics and Anglos less apparent.

All individuals are linked to "the multiplicity of overlapping groups" (Anastasi, 1958, p. 628) to which they belong. Of these, cultural groups are one of the most fundamental. Membership in various cultural groups has been shown to impact many basic psychological functions, such as memory, perception, concept formation, social behavior, and cognitive and emotional development (Anastasi, 1958). Furthermore, cultural group membership is so rudimentary that we sometimes forget to consider cultural limitations in research and theory. For this reason, Dollard (1935, cited in Anastasi, 1958, p. 605) argued that the most important limitation of social-psychological research was the culture in which it was performed.

Scores emerging from psychological tests are indeed subject to cultural influences. Not to reflect culture, of course, would likely mean that the scores would not validly reflect the construct or behavior they were intended to assess. Consider two quotes from Anne Anastasi, and we may glean when such influences represent valid influences on test scores and when they do not. First, let us consider this valid perspective. "Every psychological test measures a sample of behavior. Insofar as culture affects behavior, its influence will and should be reflected in the test. Moreover, if we were to rule out cultural differentials from a test, we might thereby lower its validity against the criterion we are trying to predict. The same cultural differentials that impair an individual's test performance are likely to handicap him [sic] in school work, job performance, or whatever other subsequent achievement we are trying to predict" (Anastasi, 1967, p. 299). Nevertheless, a "test may be invalidated by the presence of uncontrollable cultural factors. But this would occur only when the given cultural factor affects the test without affecting the criterion" (Anastasi, 1950, p. 15).

Cognitive abilities, for example, differ in both quantity and pattern across ethnic groups. The oft-cited study by Lesser, Fifer, and Clark (1965), for instance, demonstrated that four different ethnic groups in New York City (Blacks, Chinese, Jews, and Puerto Ricans) produced different profiles on a battery of ability tests.[4] The four tests in the battery assessed verbal ability, reasoning ability, number ability and spatial ability. Although groups differed in their overall levels on all four scales, their patterns of performance as represented by their group profiles also differed significantly. For instance, the Black sample did most poorly on number and spatial abilities, whereas these scales were the Puerto Rican sample's two best. Minton and Schneider (1980) considered a primary reason for such disparities to be differing value systems within cultures. That different cultural groups adopt different value systems, engage in different activities based on their values, and that these varying activities differentially affect the development of specific skills and abilities appears to be a most plausible explanation for

---

[4]*These findings have been replicated, at least in part, by Stodolsky and Lesser (1967) and Hennessy and Merrifield (1978).*

the different ability profiles across groups. In effect, distinct cultural groups experience differential reinforcement schedules. Within varying cultural groups, different skill patterns are shaped. An associated feature of cultural or ethnic group status is environmental deprivation. Varying levels of environmental stimulation may account for at least some of the overall differences in ability levels. However, environmental deprivation cannot account for the differences between Black and Puerto Rican profiles indicating differing patterns of performance, as found in the Lesser et al. (1965) study, for example.

Proper test score interpretation for some minority groups, such as Hispanics, involves consideration of acculturation. "Acculturation refers to complex processes that take place when diverse cultural groups come into contact with one another. It is an extremely important aspect of the experience of linguistic minorities in the United States. Acculturation is also related to testing issues because it involves the acquisition of language, values, customs, and cognitive styles of the majority culture—all factors that may substantially affect performance on tests" (Olmeda, 1981, p. 1082). Because acculturation can presently be assessed with reliability and validity (Olmeda, 1979, 1981), school and clinical psychologists should include formal measures of acculturation when assessing individuals from other cultures. Marín's chapter in this text provides an initial grounding in the measurement and use of acculturation in assessing Hispanics.

Summary

To understand current concepts of test bias against cultural and ethnic minorities demands appreciation of test validation. The contemporary approach to test validation, including those which have been present in psychology for many years (i.e., content- and criterion-related validation), concentrates on construct validation. Such an approach asks test developers and users to interpret scores in a psychologically meaningful way and to provide theoretical rationales for test use. Proper test use requires both construct-related validation research and trained, well-informed test users.

The goal of construct-related validation research is to determine both the degree to which the test measures the construct to be assessed and the degree to which it is free from inappropriate influences—perhaps the most important of which in our society are those influences based on ethnic and cultural group membership. Culture may influence the psychological characteristic in question and, hence, need to be reflected in the test score if the test is to be valid. On the other hand, such influences may also represent instances of test bias. Careful explanations and theories of the nature of the psychological or educational constructs assessed should determine the extent to which a test is culture- or ethnic-group bound. These explorations are needed as part of construct validation itself.

The techniques used to study and evaluate the presence of test bias have largely been developed in accordance with earlier testing practices and dwell on the criterion-related validation model. Procedures also exist for identifying potentially biased test items on tests that have no criterion. These item bias detection procedures are based on the assumption that the test as a whole is not biased and have generally been used with content-valid, educational tests. Few techniques have been used that approach bias from a construct-related validation perspective, and the field of testing needs such procedures, especially in view of the increased importance given to construct validation in testing today. Comparisons of exploratory factor analyses of test items across different groups have been used as an initial approach, and the use of structural equation modeling or other newer techniques is even more likely to be successful, because the latter allows researchers to use other variables to explore why differences are present. At this time, such approaches have not been frequently applied, and the study of test bias from the perspective of construct-related validation research is in its infancy.

Interpretation of individual test scores demands integration of various findings from general psychological research, as well as validation research, and as such, is far more demanding even than performing ongoing construct-validation research. Complex interactions of psychological, linguistic, cultural, and other background factors affect the test performance of linguistic minorities. Examiners need to be specially trained to test such individuals and to consider language skills, acculturation, socioeconomic factors, and other variables in any assessment of an individual's level of functioning. Improving methodological procedures for the study of test validation and bias is the necessary first step. The second step will be the conduct of research studies demonstrating both the nature of and explanations for differences across groups. Only when such research has advanced substantially can the training of practitioners to interpret the complex interactions be brought to where it needs to be.

References

Allan, R. G., Nassif, P. M., & Elliot, S. M. (Eds.). (1988). *Bias issues in teacher certification testing*. Hillsdale, NJ: Erlbaum.

Anastasi, A. (1950). Some implications of cultural factors for test construction. In *Proceedings of the 1949 ETS Invitational Conference* (pp. 13–17). Princeton, NJ: Educational Testing Service.

Anastasi, A. (1958). *Differential psychology* (3rd ed.). New York: Macmillan.

Anastasi, A. (1967). Psychology, psychologists, and psychological testing. *American Psychologist, 22*, 297–306.

Anastasi, A. (1988). *Psychological testing* (6th ed.). New York: Macmillan.

Angoff, W. H. (1988). Validity: An evolving concept. In H. Wainer & H. Braun (Eds.), *Test validity* (pp. 19–32). Hillsdale, NJ: Erlbaum.

Berk, R. A. (1984). Conducting the item analysis. In R. A. Berk (Ed.), *A guide to criterion-referenced test construction* (pp. 97–143). Baltimore: Johns Hopkins University Press.

Campbell, D. T., & Fiske, D. W. (1959). Convergent and discriminant validation by the multitrait-multimethod matrix. *Psychological Bulletin, 56*, 81–105.

Campbell, D. T., & Stanley, J. C. (1963). Experimental and quasi-experimental designs for research on teaching. In N. L. Gage (Ed.), *Handbook of research on teaching* (pp. 471–535). Chicago: Rand McNally.

Cleary, T. A. (1968). Test bias: Prediction of grades of Negro and White students in an integrated college. *Journal of Educational Measurement, 5*, 115–124.

Cole, N. S. (1973). Bias in selection. *Journal of Educational Measurement, 10*, 237–255.

Cole, N. S. (1981). Bias in testing. *American Psychologist, 36*, 1067–1077.

Cole, N. S., & Moss, P. A. (1989). Bias in test use. In R. L. Linn (Ed.), *Educational measurement* (3rd ed., pp. 201–220). New York: American Council on Education & Macmillan.

Cook, T. D., & Campbell, D. T. (1979). *Quasi-experimentation: Design and analysis issues for field settings*. Chicago: Rand McNally.

Cronbach, L. J. (1971). Test validation. In R. L. Thorndike (Ed.), *Educational measurement* (2nd ed., pp. 443–507). Washington, DC: American Council on Education.

Cronbach, L. J. (1976). Equity in selection: Where psychometrics and political philosophy meet. *Journal of Educational Measurement, 13*, 31–41.

Cronbach, L. J. (1980). Validity on parole: How can we go straight? In W. B. Schrader (Ed.), *New directions for testing and measurement: Measuring achievement progress over a decade* (No. 5, pp. 99–108). San Francisco: Jossey Bass.

Cronbach, L. J. (1988). Five perspectives on the validity argument. In H. Wainer & H. Braun (Eds.), *Test validity* (pp. 3–18). Hillsdale, NJ: Erlbaum.

Darlington, R. B. (1971). Another look at "culture fairness". *Journal of Educational Measurement, 8*, 71–82.

Diana v. California State Board of Education, Civ. No. C–7037 RFR (N.D. Cal., 1970).

Diaz-Guerrero, R., & Diaz-Loving, R. (1990). Interpretation in cross-cultural personality assessment. In C. R. Reynolds & R. W. Kamphouse (Eds.), *Handbook of psychological and educational assessment of children: Personality, behavior, and context* (491–523). New York: Guilford Press.

Dollard, J. (1935). *Criteria for the life history—With analysis of six notable documents.* New Haven, CT: Yale University Press.

Durán, R. P. (1983). *Hispanic's education and background: Predictors of college achievement.* New York: College Entrance Examination Board.

Durán, R. P. (1988). Validity and language skills assessment: Non-English background students. In H. Wainer & H. I. Braun (Eds.), *Test validity* (pp. 105–128). Hillsdale, NJ: Erlbaum.

Durán, R. P. (1989). Testing of linguistic minorities. In R. L. Linn (Ed.), *Educational measurement* (3rd ed., pp. 573–588). New York: American Council on Education & Macmillan.

Elliott, R. (1987). *Litigating intelligence: IQ tests, special education, and social science in the courtroom.* Dover, MA: Auburn House.

Feldt, L. S. (1969). A test that the hypothesis that Cronbach's alpha or Kuder-Richardson coefficient twenty is the same for two tests. *Psychometrika, 34,* 363–373.

Flaugher, R. L. (1978). The many definitions of test bias. *American Psychologist, 33,* 671–679.

Geisinger, K. F. (1992). The metamorphosis in test validation. *Educational Psychologist, 27,* 197–222.

Guadalupe Ord. Inc. v. Tempe School District No. 3, Civ. No. 71–435 (D. Ariz., 1972).

Guion, R. M. (1977). Content validity: The source of my discontent. *Applied Psychological Measurement, 1,* 1–10.

Gulliksen, H., & Wilks, S. S. (1950). Regression tests for several samples. *Psychometrika, 15,* 91–114.

Gutkin, T. B., & Reynolds, C. R. (1981). Factorial similarity of the WISC-R for white and black children from the standardization sample. *Journal of Educational Psychology, 73,* 227–231.

Gutkin, T. B., & Reynolds, C. R. (1980). Factorial similarity of the WISC-R for Anglos and Chicanos referred for psychological services. *Journal of School Psychology, 18,* 34–39.

Hartigan, J. A., & Wigdor, A. K. (Eds.). (1989). *Fairness in employment testing: Validity generalization, minority issues, and the General Aptitude Test Battery.* Washington, DC: National Academy Press.

Hennessy, J. J., & Merrifield, P. R. (1978). Ethnicity and sex distinctions in patterns of aptitude factor scores in a sample of urban high school seniors. *American Educational Research Journal, 15,* 385–389.

Hills, J. (1981). *Measurement and evaluation in the classroom* (2nd ed.). Columbus, OH: Charles E. Merrill Publishing Company.

Hunter, J. E., Schmidt, F. L., & Hunter, R. (1979). Differential validity of employment tests by race: A comprehensive review and analysis. *Psychological Bulletin, 86,* 721–735.

Hunter, J. E., Schmidt, F. L., & Rauschenberger, J. (1984). Methodological, statistical, and ethical issues in the study of bias in psychological tests. In C. R. Reynolds & R. T. Brown (Eds.), *Perspectives on bias in mental testing* (pp. 41–100). New York: Plenum.

Jensen, A. R. (1980). *Bias in mental testing.* New York: Free Press.

Katzenmeyer, W. G., & Steener, A. J. (1977). Estimation of the invariance of factor structures across race and sex with implications for hypothesis testing. *Educational and Psychological Measurement, 37,* 111–119.

Lesser, G. S., Fifer, G., & Clark, D. H. (1965). Mental abilities of children from different social-class and cultural groups. *Monographs of the Society for Research in Child Development, 30* (Whole No. 102).

Linn, R. L. (1982). Ability testing: Individual differences, prediction, and differential prediction. In A. K. Wigdor & W. R. Garner (Eds.), *Ability testing: Uses, consequences, and controversies* (pp. 335–388). Washington, DC: National Academy Press.

Linn, R. L. (1984). Selection bias: Multiple meanings. *Journal of Educational Measurement, 21,* 33–47.

Linn, R. L., & Dunbar, S. B. (1986). Validity generalization and predictive bias. In R. A. Berk (Ed.), *Performance assessment* (p. 203–236). Baltimore, MD: Johns Hopkins University Press.

Loevinger, J. (1957). Objective tests as instruments of psychological theory. *Psychological Reports, 3,* 635–694.

Messick, S. (1975). The standard problem: Meaning and values in measurement and evaluation. *American Psychologist, 30,* 955–966.

Messick, S. (1980). Test validity and the ethics of assessment. *American Psychologist, 35,* 1012–1017.

Messick, S. (1989). Validity. In R. L. Linn, (Ed.) *Educational measurement* (3rd ed., pp. 13–103). New York: American Council on Education & Macmillan.

Minton, H. L, & Schneider, F. W. (1980). *Differential psychology.* Prospect Heights, IL: Waveland Press, Inc.

Muthen, B. (1988). Some uses of structural equation modeling in validity studies: Extending IRT to external variables. In H. Wainer & H. Braun (Eds.), *Test validity* (pp. 213–238). Hillsdale, NJ: Erlbaum.

Olmeda, E. L. (1979). Acculturation: A psychometric perspective. *American Psychologist, 34,* 1061–1070.

Olmeda, E. L. (1981). Testing linguistic minorities. *American Psychologist, 36,* 1078–1085.

Padilla, A. M. (1979). Critical factors in the testing of Hispanic Americans: A review and some suggestions for the future. In R. W. Tyler & S. H. White (Eds.), *Testing, teaching and learning: Report of a conference on research on testing* (pp. 219–233). Washington, DC: National Institute of Education.

Pennock-Román, M. (1990). *Test validity and language background: A study of Hispanic American students at six universities.* New York: College Entrance Examination Board.

Peterson, N. S., & Novick, M. R. (1976). An evaluation of some models of culture-fair selection. *Journal of Educational Measurement, 13,* 3–29.

Plake, B. S. (1988). Application of readability indices to multiple-choice items on certification/licensure examinations. *Educational and Psychological Measurement, 48,* 543–551.

Reilly, R. R. (1973). A note on minority group test bias studies. *Psychological Bulletin, 80,* 130–132.

Reynolds, C. R. (1982a). The problem of bias in psychological assessment. In C. R. Reynolds & T. B. Gutkin (Eds.), *The handbook of school psychology.* New York: Wiley.

Reynolds, C. R. (1982b). Methods for detecting construct and predictive bias. In R. A. Berk (Ed.), *Handbook of methods for detecting bias* (pp. 199–227). Baltimore, MD: Johns Hopkins University Press.

Rousey, A. (1990). Factor structure of the WISC-R Mexicano. *Educational and Psychological Measurement, 50,* 351–357.

Schmidt, F. L., Pearlman, K., & Hunter, J. E. (1980). The validity and fairness of employment and educational tests for Hispanic Americans: A review and analysis. *Personnel Psychology, 32,* 257–281.

Schultz, M. (1992). *A comparison of some recently proposed procedures for detecting the presence of biased test items.* Unpublished dissertation, Fordham University, Bronx, NY.

Shepard, L. A. (1982). Definitions of bias. In R. A. Berk (Ed.), *Handbook of methods for detecting bias* (pp. 9–30). Baltimore, MD: Johns Hopkins University Press.

Standards for educational and psychological testing. (1985). Washington, DC: American Psychological Association.

Standards for educational and psychological tests and manuals. (1974). Washington, DC: American Psychological Association.

Stodolsky, S. S., & Lesser, G. S. (1967). Learning patterns in the disadvantaged. *Harvard Educational Review, 37,* 546–593.

Tenopyr, M. L. (1977). Content–construct confusion. *Personnel Psychology, 30,* 47–54.

Thorndike, R. L. (1971) Concepts of culture fairness. *Journal of Educational Measurement, 8,* 63–70.

Uniform guidelines on employee selection. (1978). *Federal Register, 43*(166), 38296–38309.

CHAPTER 4

A Rasch Approach to Scaling Issues in Testing Hispanics

Michael L. O'Brien

The notion of sample-free scaling abounds in the item-response theory literature, but language-free scaling poses special challenges. The two-fold purpose of this chapter is to (a) consider issues in developing comparable tests for Anglos and Hispanics and (b) devise an equating system for language proficiency tests that expresses scores on an invariant scale to measure growth in one language or to compare skills between languages. In the first section of this chapter, a five-step procedure is proposed for developing comparable tests for Anglos and Hispanics. The second section contains scaling methods for growth-sensitive, language-free measurement with language proficiency tests.

Procedural Steps

Step 1—Scale Development

Within the theoretical framework of Rasch-based measurement, an item response is characterized by the confrontation of a person to a test item. The person's response to the test item depends only on the proficiency of the person in relation to the difficulty of the test item. In the case of language-categorized populations, the response further depends on the extent to which the test-item content has a stable referent between Anglos and Hispanics. That is, would the test item have the same scale value regardless of whether it was calibrated using response data obtained from either population?

Theory defines the scope and interconnections of a psychological variable with other tests and variables. One begins to operationalize a theory by specifying a domain of items measuring skills thought to reflect the variable or construct being measured (Anastasi, 1988). In this process, it is often useful to delineate objectives or diagnostic criteria for item writers. For example, one might devise a measure of language proficiency from reading the relevant linguistic literature and then devising objectives reflecting specific language skills.

Item writers are then summoned to produce a pool of items meeting the specifications of the test objectives. Each item writer needs to be thoroughly familiar with the literature underlying the objectives and, ideally, should have instructional experiences with the variable being observed.

When the item pool has been developed according to the foregoing procedures, it is ready for another review—this time for likely item difficulty. This integral part of scale development requires an expert panel to make predictions regarding the expected difficulty of each item when calibrated. The panel members should read each item and from their expertise assign an a priori rating that reflects their expectation of the item's difficulty (see, e.g., O'Brien & Hampilos, 1988). The rating is based on predictions implied from the relevant literature and from the experience of the panel members who worked instructionally with the variable or construct being measured.

Finally, investigations of concurrent, predictive, or construct validity require the test developer to select existing tests to administer along with the pilot items. It is important to comb the literature for relevant interconnections among related tests and other variables, in which a lawful relationship may be predicted between the newly developed test, on the one hand, and existing tests and other variables, on the other. Predictions are to be made prior to observing empirical data from the new test.

Once satisfactory progress is made with scale development, the test items are ready for tryout with a sample of examinees who are representative of the larger population for whom the test is ideally targeted.

Step 2—Item Calibration

Once the items are administered to a group of examinees, known as the calibration sample, the response matrix is prepared for analysis. At this juncture, the real work of psychophysical scaling methods is set into motion. Whereas Thurstone's (1927) scaling methods were based on normal deviates, modern psychophysical methods use logarithm-based, sample-free item calibrations and test-free person measurements (Rasch, 1980; Wright, 1968). These methods, known as *Rasch models*, predict the probable response of a person to an item, given the person's position on the underlying variable and the item's difficulty in relation to the underlying dimension being measured (Wright & Masters, 1982). Choice of which Rasch model to use depends on the observation format—dichotomous, rating scale, or partial credit (see, e.g., Masters & Wilson, 1988; O'Brien, 1986, 1989).

Scaling the item calibrations from the calibration sample requires use of a Rasch analysis computer program, such as binary calibration (BICAL) (Wright & Mead, 1976). For this discussion, it is assumed that one is developing a test to be used to measure a variable on which Anglos and Hispanics are to be compared. A Rasch analysis is used to estimate the probability of a person's response to a test item. The response probability is derived from the estimated difference between a person's level of language proficiency and the level of difficulty of the language proficiency item. The general form of the Rasch model when item responses are dichotomous is the following:

$$P\left(X_{ni} = 0,1 \mid b_n, d_i\right) = \exp\left(X_{ni}\left(b_n - d_i\right)/1 + \exp\left(b_n - d_i\right)\right) \qquad (1)$$

Wherein X_{ni} is response X (0 or 1) given by person n to item i, b_n is person n's level of language proficiency, and d_i is item i's level of difficulty on the language proficiency test.

The b_n term is estimated from the unweighted sum of correct responses given by each person and d_i is estimated from one minus the proportion of correct responses given (by the calibration sample) to each item.

Applying the Rasch model to test data results in an estimate of b for each person or score (i.e., sum of correct responses). An estimate of d for each item is calibrated independently from the person measure. However, b and d are expressed on a common, logistic scale, centered at $\bar{d} = 0$. Convenient linear transformations of this logistic scale are given by Wright and Stone (1979). For example, norm-referenced scaling for expressing person measures and item calibrations on the same scale is facilitated from the following Rasch Normative Scaling Unit (NIT) transformation of b and d, respectively:

$$\text{NIT}_b = 500 + \frac{(b - \bar{b})}{S_b} \times 100 \tag{2}$$

$$\text{NIT}_d = 500 - \frac{\bar{b}}{S_b} \times 100 + \frac{\bar{d}}{S_d} \times 100 \tag{3}$$

Wherein S_b is the standard deviation of raw language test scores, and S_d is the standard deviation of item difficulty indices.

These NIT transformations create a norm-based scale with $\bar{b} = 500$ and $S_b = 100$ for the elected norming (i.e., calibration) sample. Item difficulty is calibrated on the same NIT scale, with $\bar{d} = 500 - \bar{b} / S_b \times 100$ and $S_d = 100$. The NIT scale is convenient for exposing the confrontation of the norming sample to the test items, as well as for comparing Anglo versus Hispanic samples on the same underlying variable. An illustrative example of these procedures follows later in this chapter.

Items of poor quality are identified through inspection of item-fit statistics. These indices are used to flag items for which the predicted responses were errant. Frequently, items that misfit are miss keyed or tapped into a dimension not intended to be measured by the test. Such items often provide the opportunity for further item editing and even for reconsideration of the initial test development specifications. For example, one might opt to create a battery of tests rather than a single test to measure a variable with orthogonal subdimensions. Large numbers of misfitting items may indicate various problems with the psychological theory on which the items are based or problems with the item development procedures.

After completion of item calibration, the test developer is left with a set of calibrated items and a measure of each person's level of language proficiency. In addition, the concurrent measures selected for validity studies are scored and recorded for each examinee.

Step 3—Item Validation

Finding a "best set" of items does not stop with item calibration. Validity addresses the usefulness of a test for its intended purpose and specification. Hence, one must evaluate whether the predictions made by the expert raters regarding expected item difficulties are reflected in the item calibrations. A formal procedure for this step is presented and illustrated in O'Brien and Hampilos (1988). In any case, the test developer uses item validation to determine which items may be safely retained for use in the test. Often, insights regarding subtle aspects of certain items and the variable in general are uncovered from item validation.

Step 4—Person–Measure Validation

The observed pattern of responses given by each person is compared against the predicted pattern from the Rasch model. This useful feature of Rasch models, known as the *person–fit statistic*, separates a meaningful total score from one that contains surprising individual responses (Wright & Stone, 1979). A diagnosis from the analysis of individual response patterns given to the items composing a test is the essence of person–measure validation from a Rasch perspective. When the test items pass the stringent requirements of scale development, item calibration, and item validation, a misfitting response pattern should be taken seriously because it indicates that the misfitting person experiences the variable differently than implied by its usual manifestations. Often, gaps exist between levels of the person's experience with the variable—such as an individual who functions well on reading activities, but who experiences difficulty writing. For a misfitting person, the total test score is misleading—the real story lurks amidst the analysis of the response pattern. The analysis of person–fit is an integral part of the application of objective measurement through Rasch models and is one of its major advantages over other forms of item-response theory (IRT).

Another way to provide evidence of validity is to follow traditional procedures for investigating concurrent, construct, and, perhaps, predictive validity. However, it is recommended that Rasch-based person measures be used instead of total raw scores. One should also produce bivariate plots for pairs of variables (i.e., tests) in correlation analysis. Useful information is often found by inspecting outliers for which the correlation fails to hold. It may be possible to explore additional information about such persons that explains their unusual performance on a scale. Finally, it is useful to plot the relationships between highly correlated concurrent measures across the entire range of the underlying variable being measured by the new test.

Step 5—Population Congruence

If one intends to use the newly developed test with only one target population, the test is now ready. However, what happens when a test is given to both Anglos and Hispanics? In such instances, one should verify that the same test may be used to measure the language variable of interest. This step requires two procedures. First, items calibrated separately in Anglo and Hispanic samples are plotted against an identity line in a bivariate graph and bounded by 95% confidence bands. Items falling within the bands are invariant and evidence the same underlying calibration of difficulty. Items outside the bands shift position and have different meanings across the two samples. For purposes of comparing Anglo and Hispanic samples, only invariant items should be used for person measurement. However, one should avoid discarding an entire set of similar items. For example, it would be problematic if an entire set of, say, comprehension items were found to be variant. (A discussion of the procedures for constructing the confidence bands is given in Wright & Stone, 1979.) Hence, the population congruence requirement is satisfied when the item calibrations are sample invariant.

Scaling Methods

Having described Rasch-based scaling methods for a single test, this section focuses on the equation of test batteries administered in both English and Spanish. In the case of language proficiency tests, the two-fold purpose of such tests is program placement (i.e., entitlement) and program evaluation (i.e., measuring growth). An example of such a test is the Language Assessment Battery (LAB), (New York City Board of Education, 1982), developed under the direction of Abbott (1982, 1985) and discussed elsewhere by O'Brien (1989).

LAB serves as a good example of the complex issues posed by language proficiency testing. It consists of two parallel forms across four vertical levels, measuring Kindergarten through 12th grade in English and Spanish. Furthermore, norms were developed based on three language-categorized populations: English proficient, limited English proficient, and Spanish proficient. This comprehensive structure of LAB necessitated the solution of a number of previously unresolved scaling design issues. For example, a vertically equated scale was developed so that scaled scores could be compared across languages. This equation, however, was based on the assumption that English and Spanish language proficiency are directly comparable. Further research is necessary to determine the criteria on which this assumption may be validated for a given test. In the case of LAB, this assumption seemed reasonable, given that items were paired by content and difficulty across English and Spanish.

It should be noted that the procedures described in this section have been modified from existing scaling techniques. Many traditional vertical scales were built on the assumption that growth follows a linear function. This was not so with the LAB, and practical work with other batteries has led to the same conclusion. That is, growth is nonlinear, particularly when looking at equal grade-level increments. The methods proposed in this chapter provide a naturalistic solution by allowing the data to inform the scaling-method user as to how the growth should be modeled. Given that the LAB data were population-based, this method ought to be replicable when the test is renormed and should be verified at such times.

The purpose of equating the LAB along a vertically scaled score system was to facilitate a meaningful quantitative evaluation of students as they progress through the academic program. With the scaled score system, it is possible to trace the growth of language proficiency for an individual or for a group of students. Most important, the vertical scale enables direct measurement of the examinee's growth regardless of the test level or form. One must only identify the grade in which the students are currently enrolled in order to ascertain their scaled scores. LAB forms A and B were horizontally equated to each other, so that the scaled score system is equated between the parallel forms. It is suggested that the English and Spanish versions of LAB be equated to the same scaled score system using the equipercentile method. For example, a scaled score of 500 on the English form B or A in grade 4 is reflective of the same language proficiency in English as a scaled score of 500 on Spanish form A or B in grade 4. One may, therefore, compare language proficiency in English and Spanish by comparing the scaled scores of the students who took either form of both tests.

The scaled score system features several types of information that are relevant to educational decision making. To summarize, the vertical scaled score system can be used to (a) measure and evaluate growth in language proficiency in either Spanish or English, (b) express scores on form A or form B on the same scale, and (c) compare a student's English language proficiency with their Spanish language proficiency.

Technical Procedures

Rasch scaling methods were applied in order to calibrate a vertically scaled score system and to equate the forms and levels of the LAB. Because the LAB was designed to measure a unidimensional language proficiency variable (with subtests), it was considered useful to model the test as a wide-range measure. Because all students in Kindergarten through 12th grade possess language proficiency in varying degrees, the levels of the LAB were designed to measure language proficiency. The Rasch psychometric model is useful for this application, because its major assumption is that, regardless of the particular items used, all test items are intended to measure a common, underlying variable, such as language proficiency. Furthermore, Rasch theory assumes that a person's total score reflects language proficiency level and is predictive of the response given to a language proficiency item of a certain difficulty level. For example, when a person whose language proficiency is b on a scale ranging from low to high proficiency attempts an item of difficulty d on a scale ranging from easy to hard, that person's response (i.e., either right or wrong) is predicted using probability by comparing the difficulty level with the person's proficiency level. When the item is equal to the person's language proficiency (i.e., when $b = d$), the person has a 50% chance of getting that particular item right (or any other language proficiency item of the same difficulty). Similarly, persons tend to miss items that are too hard for their proficiency level and succeed on items that are easy for them. Thus, the Rasch model can be used to measure language proficiency, and it facilitates the development of parallel forms as well as the meaningfulness of scores from different test levels that measure the same underlying language-proficiency variable. For the general form of the Rasch model, refer to the earlier section concerning item calibration.

In order to develop a vertical scaled score system from Rasch procedures, all of the test data were analyzed using BICAL, which is a computer program for Rasch psychometric analysis. Each grade level, form, language group, and version were analyzed separately. Rasch item difficulties, d_i, were estimated for each item, and a Rasch language proficiency level, b_n, was estimated for every possible raw score (i.e., number-of-right score).

The vertical scale was then calibrated using the BICAL analyses for each grade level on the English version, form B, limited-English speaking sample. The scaling unit of Rasch estimates of d_i and b_n, respectively, is the "logit" or log-odds unit. Logits can range from negative infinity to positive infinity. Negative values indicate easy items or low ability; positive values reflect hard items or high ability. The item and person estimates are thus reflected by a common logistic scale. The general form of the logit scale is depicted below.

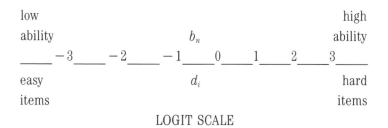

LOGIT SCALE

The ability estimates (b_n) were used as a basis for the initial raw score to scaled score conversion at grade 4, using the linear transformation given in (3).

$$Z = 35b + 500$$

Where Z is the scaled score and b is the Rasch ability estimate.

The development of the scaled score system was begun at grade 4, which was arbitrarily chosen as a convenient midpoint of the vertical scale. After the scaled scores were computed for grade 4, it was necessary to equate vertically all other grade levels by investigating the relative shifts of item difficulty and person ability, respectively, between adjacent grade levels. Within a test level, this comparison was easily performed by reviewing the b_n and d_i estimates for similarities and differences. Across test levels, one must assume that the vertical scale is best evidenced by comparing item d_i for those items that appeared in both adjacent levels. These items, referred to as *vertical anchor items*, should shift in d_i by a constant, V, which is then used to equate two vertically adjacent levels. V is estimated by the median shift of d_i for anchor items between test levels. Because the Rasch analysis was conducted for each grade level, it was possible to evaluate how accurately the anchor items estimated the vertical equating constant V.

An independent check on V was performed by recording the mean Rasch ability estimates, $\bar{b}$, for each grade within test level. The $\bar{b}$ estimates across grade levels within test level gave useful approximations for the V necessary to equate the highest grade level in a lower form to the lowest grade level of a higher form. Therefore, V should closely approximate the rate of change in the $\bar{b}$ values across grade levels in the two adjacent test levels. This procedure rendered convincing evidence that vertical equating with Rasch procedures was best facilitated by analyzing the data for grade level and then equating the test levels by averaging grade level $\bar{b}$ in the adjacent test levels. The resulting vertically equated $\bar{b}$ are reported in Table 1. These equated $\bar{b}$ estimates were then substituted as C (for "center") in the scaled score formula, $Z = 35b + C$ for every raw score.

The resulting vertically scaled score system applies to English, form B. In order to equate form A to form B, one can apply the equipercentile method. By matching percentile on form A with the same percentile on form B, one can convert the form A raw score to form B raw score and, hence, to the same scaled

TABLE 1

Center (C) of Vertical Scaled Score Distributions by Total Test and Subtest for Each Test Level and Grade (English LAB, Form B)

Level/Grade		Total	Writing	Reading	Listening
I	K				225
I	1	258		250	332
I	2	358		351	375
II	3	438	453	431	453
II	4	500	500	500	500
II	5	532	527	541	510
III	6	562	549	571	525
III	7	589	569	597	550
III	8	600	577	620	560
IV	9	625	595	645	575
IV	10	667	630	685	605
IV	11	683	650	700	625
IV	12	707	775	725	650

Note. Equation based on mean ability estimates and linear transformation. Zero and perfect scores were estimated from trend extrapolation from the previous three scores. Scaled scores are estimated from $Z = 35b + C$ wherein b is the Rasch measure of ability for each possible raw score, and C is the vertically equated center for the respective test at the respective grade level, beginning with a grade 4 $C = 500$. (Raw Score to b conversions were taken from the log ability maps in BICAL.) Form A should be equated to form B using equipercentiles, thus necessitating only one scaled score system per language test. A single vertical scaled score system is also possible if the Spanish score distribution is equated to the English system by use of equipercentiles.

score system, beginning with grade 4. Note that the equipercentiles must be done by grade.

It is also possible to use the vertically scaled score system for forms A and B, Spanish version. First, forms A and B, Spanish, are equated by grade using the equipercentile method. Then the Spanish horizontally equated score distribution can be equated via equipercentiles to the English distribution and, hence, to the common vertical scale–score system.

Conclusions

Developing and scaling tests used to measure psychological variables of Anglos and Hispanics should yield important benefits for research and application. The proposed procedural steps are intended to enhance rather than to replace traditional methods of test development and validation. In particular, demonstrating population congruence and using sample-free scaling seems important to meaningful comparisons of tests used with Anglos and Hispanics. For the special case of language proficiency testing, the growth-sensitive, language-free methods proposed in this chapter facilitate a relatively exciting way to scale language proficiency. Further research is needed to ascertain the stability of these methods. The suggested procedures for developing, validating, and equating tests should benefit the researcher's and practitioner's quest to understand and to scale measures given to Anglos and Hispanics in a more complete way.

References

Abbott, M. M. (1982, February). *Language Assessment Battery (LAB)—1982*. Paper presented to the Arizona State Department of Education, Tucson, AZ.

Abbott, M. M. (1985, April). *Theoretical considerations in the measurement of the English-language proficiency of limited-English-proficient students*. Paper presented at the annual meeting of the National Council on Measurement in Education, Chicago, IL.

Anastasi, A. (1988). *Psychological testing* (6th ed.). New York: Macmillan.

Masters, G. N., & Wilson, M. (1988, April). *PC-CREDIT: A microcomputer program for partial credit analysis*. Paper presented at the annual meeting of the American Educational Research Association, New Orleans, LA.

New York City Board of Education. (1982). *Language Assessment Battery*. New York: Author.

O'Brien, M. L. (1986). The development and use of structured tests. *Studies in Educational Evaluation, 12*, 1–88.

O'Brien, M. L. (1989). Psychometric issues relevant to selecting items and assembling parallel forms of language proficiency instruments. *Educational and Psychological Measurement, 49,* 347–354.

O'Brien, M. L., & Hampilos, J. P. (1988). The feasibility of creating an item bank from a teacher-made test, using the Rasch model. *Educational and Psychological Measurement, 48,* 201–212.

Rasch, G. (1980). *Probabilistic models for some intelligence and attainment tests.* Chicago: University of Chicago Press. (Original work published 1960)

Thurstone, L. L. (1927). A mental unit of measurement. *Psychological Review, 34,* 415–423.

Wright, B. D. (1968). Sample-free test calibration and person measurement. In *Proceedings of the 1967 Invitational Conference on Testing Problems.* Princeton, NJ: Educational Testing Service.

Wright, B. D., & Masters, G. N. (1982). *Rating scale analysis.* Chicago: MESA Press.

Wright, B. D., & Mead, R. J. (1976). *BICAL: Calibrating items with the Rasch model.* (Research Memorandum No. 23). Chicago: Statistical Laboratory, Department of Education, University of Chicago.

Wright, B. D., & Stone, M. H. (1979). *Best test design.* Chicago: MESA Press.

CHAPTER 5

Legal Issues in the Educational Testing of Hispanics

Thomas F. Donlon

Increasingly, since about 1960, tests and testing have been involved in litigation and in the courts. The reasons for this involvement have been explored by a number of writers (Bersoff, 1981; Lerner, 1971; Rebell, 1989). Perhaps the most succinct explanation is provided by Rebell (1989, p. 135):

> ...tests measure only limited domains of knowledge, in certain specific ways; *their accuracy and their usefulness depend on the manner in which they are constructed and on how their results are interpreted* [italics added]. This is precisely why issues of test construction and test use often become controversial public policy concerns.

Rebell is undoubtedly correct. These same limiting characteristics of tests explain not only public controversies, concerning policy, but the private debates that scholars have about tests. The processes of test construction, test use, and test interpretation are not mechanical; they require specific judgments about which even persons who share a common theoretical orientation and a common set of ethical and professional values may differ. The job is never done perfectly, and unanimity can never be achieved.

With such built-in potentials for problems, tests have often sparked controversy when applied to Hispanics and other ethnic minorities. A well-known example of this is *Larry P. v. Riles* (1979), the celebrated case in California involving the use of IQ tests in effecting placements in classes for the educable mentally retarded. The state law that led to the practices that led to the *Larry P.* case mandated use of tests, and specifically designated the tests that were to be used. The persons conducting the testing were conforming to this law. What, therefore, could provoke controversy?

The law itself provoked the controversy. More specifically, the professional measurement judgments that were embodied in that law did so. Anyone familiar with the legislative and administrative processes that lead to the creation and implementation of laws knows that the tests so mandated were not chosen by lot; they were specifically selected by persons considered on very rational grounds to be competent for their task. Accordingly, when the federal judge who decided the case, Judge Peckham, made his judgment that the tests were in fact inappropriate and, therefore, should *not* be used for Blacks and other minorities, he was in effect disputing the judgment of persons whose professional training in education and in testing far exceeded his own.

Judge Peckham was making new law—just as clearly as when the legislators of California made law by creating the basic statute or when the commissioner of education made law by creating directives concerning it. But although the judge's judicial power gave his new law its muscle, the law was not truly his in any personal sense. Like the law it supplanted, it was basically devised by a group of measurement professionals.

Judge Peckham was essentially agreeing with those measurement professionals who, appearing as expert witnesses for the plaintiffs, had disputed the judgments of the professionals who assisted in drafting the statute. It was the counteropinions of these in-court experts that came to be embodied in his decision.

This pattern is a common one. Legal controversies about testing are almost never between the informed and the uninformed. In fact, most of the "better" ones, (in the sense of more challenging or more interesting) are between two opposing camps of the very well-informed. Most legal issues concerning the testing of Hispanics are essentially measurement issues; they are problems that divide measurement professionals.

Legal controversies about tests, however, are seldom narrowly centered on specific psychometric techniques and principles. They focus instead on the proper standards of professional conduct—on problems of how much test development and validation effort is enough, for example. They arise not only from the intrinsic limitations of testing techniques, as identified by Rebell (1989), but from the political nature of the larger contexts in which tests serve. The act of testing is not something conducted in isolation; it is most often a component of a larger system or operation, such as education or the operation of a business. Testing is built into that larger system and contributes to the logic of it. The arguments about tests for Hispanics are very often merely components or subparts of larger arguments we have about how to cope with diversity in a society dedicated to equality. The legal issues may involve technical psychometrics, but they are frequently at the intersection of psychometrics and broader issues.

Testing creates or reveals differences. Dealing with differences is a persistent and perplexing challenge for a society dedicated to principles of equity. Test-based differences are particularly challenging because they often require an evaluation or scaling of quite different things. Measurement professionals do not have effective and agreed-on principles and techniques for dealing with many of these matters. In the absence of such clarity, there is a tendency for measurement decisions to reflect what are basically nonmeasurement factors such as pragmatics. Because measurement professionals differ in their perceptions of these nonmeasurement factors, practical measurement decisions can vary from professional to professional.

A good example of this, in the context of the testing of Hispanics, is *Chance v. Board of Examiners* (1971), which pitted both a Black plaintiff, Boston Chance, and a Hispanic coplaintiff, Louis Mercado, against the board of examiners of the school district of New York City. The plaintiffs asked for and were granted status as a class action. They charged that the examinations by which the New York City schools selected principals and other administrators were biased against both Blacks and Hispanics. They held that the tests were inadequate when applied to the diversity that was represented by the Black and Hispanic candidates. This controversy about the examinations was part of a larger controversy about the need to secure greater racial and ethnic diversity in the administrative leadership of the schools in New York City. The questions about the technical adequacy of the tests had to be evaluated in the context of this larger social setting.

As one part of their complaint, plaintiffs pointed to that part of the examination process that involved the use of oral testing. Plaintiffs' witnesses testified that the ratings based on oral testing were biased by negative judgments of such things as Hispanic accents.

Confirming such reports and providing complete protection against the problems is very hard to do. However, the likelihood of such problems is anticipated by the standards of sound measurement practice. If one is rating a subject on oral proficiency in English, and this person is not a native speaker of the language, he or she is almost certain to show some differences from a native speaker. The rating process, to be adequate, must anticipate and explicitly deal with such differences. Furthermore, having anticipated differences, everything that can reasonably be done to ameliorate bias must be done; one can, for example, select and train raters who are competent working with Hispanics. The record in *Chance* failed to show that all that could be done to minimize the potential for bias was done.

What made the controversy in *Chance* somewhat more complex was the accepted validity of using *some* kind of an appraisal of language or communication skills in the selection of school administrators. These are not jobs, after all, in which one would wish to see inarticulate persons. And it should not be perceived as anti-Hispanic to ask a bilingual administrator to demonstrate sufficient skills in English. Such a demonstration of reasonable proficiency in two languages is not asking more than the court did in another case, *Keyes v. School Dist. No. 1, Denver, Colorado* (1970), which is discussed later. What cannot be done, however, is to award more points for English-language ability above and beyond the levels needed for the job, or to penalize candidates too severely for minor deficits in English-language ability when these deficits do not impede effective performance on the job. In *Chance,* the test-sponsoring agency did not adequately demonstrate that it had guarded against disproportionate weighting favoring the upper levels of English-language ability.

The complexity of testing issues for Hispanics is reflected in the contrast between *Chance* and another controversy at the other end of the nation: *Contreras v. City of Los Angeles* (1981). In *Contreras,* the Hispanic plaintiff, María

Gonzalez, had passed a written examination for a position as auditor, but with a score that was not high enough on the resulting list of passing applicants to win her appointment. In her effort to discredit the examination as a violation of her rights under Title VII of the Civil Rights Act of 1964, she attempted to establish that oral testing in general had a *less* adverse impact on Hispanics, but still permitted employers to meet their needs and purposes. There is a serious paradox in these opposing postures by two Hispanic plaintiffs—one resisting oral testing and the other stating that its absence violated her rights.

Plaintiff Mercado, in *Chance*, essentially prevailed. The examination procedures were extensively modified as a result of the lawsuit. Plaintiff Gonzalez, in *Contreras*, lost. She made some headway in establishing that Hispanic candidates do better on oral examinations vis-à-vis their Anglo competitors, but she was not able to establish that oral examinations could do everything for the city of Los Angeles that written examinations could, and so failed, in the judgment of the court, to demonstrate the existence of a less discriminatory alternative assessment measure, which was required by Title VII.

These cases illustrate the intersection of psychometrics with larger issues and the rich potential that exists, in any practical application of tests, for dividing measurement professionals and creating legal issues. The professional staff of the board of examiners in New York did not believe that their oral interviews were in any way substandard; the professional witnesses for plaintiff Gonzalez in Los Angeles believed that oral interviews were a less discriminatory but equally useful alternative to the written examination. The court, in most cases, is presented with two sets of experts; thus, legal issues are measurement issues.

Measurement Standards

Obviously, there is a role here for professional measurement standards as agreed-on principles, and such standards do assist courts and do work to reduce the legal issues. But the concepts and models involved in most stated measurement standards are only a limited guide to professional conduct, and although the act of the professional societies in creating them is a useful deterrent to legal wars, this work falls far short of what would be required to remove the problems from the courts. The primary statement, the *Standards* (1985), remarked in earlier versions that its strictures were not intended to establish legal standards. This position has been improved, and the 1985 edition asserts in its preliminary prose that "The use of the standards in litigation is inevitable; it should be emphasized, however, that...professional judgment....plays an essential role in determining the relevance of particular standards in particular situations" (*Standards,* 1985, p. 2).

There would be fewer legal issues if the *Standards* were stated more vigorously with respect to expectations as to how much effort need be expended to optimize a testing operation. Much of what constitutes testing controversy regarding Hispanics grows out of different perceptions as to how much attention and care should be given to testing operations that involve this group. Because the professional standards are so broadly written, the reader is apt to pay insufficient attention. In community settings where such reduced attention is widely acceptable, the result can be poor practices—and lawsuits.

These kinds of problems occurred in *Gomez v. Illinois State Board of Educ.* (1987), a case that is exceptional among Hispanic-centered testing cases in that it included an effort by the plaintiffs to get tested. The plaintiffs in *Gomez* held that there was, in addition to problems of testing the wrong way, a problem of a failure to test at all.

The action was brought in 1985 on behalf of "all Spanish-speaking children of limited English proficiency 'who have been, are, or will be enrolled in Illinois public schools, and who have been, should have been, or should be assessed as limited English proficient'" (p. 1032, quoting plaintiffs' complaint.) Under Illinois law, every local school district in the state was required to identify limited-English-proficient (LEP) children. Such a process of identification was called a *census.* If a census identified 20 or more LEP students in a given school building, the local district was required to provide a transitional bilingual education program for these children. If, however, the census disclosed fewer than 20 such children, no state-mandated program was required.

According to the suit, the state had failed to provide the local districts with adequate, objective, and uniform guidelines to use in making the identifications. Local districts had been found to use as many as 23 different language proficiency tests, 11 different standardized English tests, 7 different standardized reading tests, and a sizable number of teacher-made tests. The validity of many of the instruments was questioned; the undoubted lack of consistency among decisions based on so many different instruments was also challenged. Furthermore, according to the plaintiffs, about 5,185 of the 38,364 Spanish-speaking children, about 14%, were in transitional bilingual programs.

The suit brought attention to the need for resolving ambiguities concerning both responsibility for the testing program and standards for its operation. There is little controversy in *Gomez* concerning the nature of specific tests. The argument was about the adequacy of the testing system as a whole, its consistency, and the propriety of the level of effort that it represented.

Gomez in Illinois is in some ways a replay of another case, *United States v. State of Texas* (1981). In the Texas case, the courts also faulted the state education agency for a failure to implement the bilingual education law adequately. The Texas court pointed to many of the same deficiencies that would be described 4 years later in the opinion in Illinois, and, in fact, the *Gomez* opinion refers approvingly to the earlier Texas case as "providing the proper accomodation of the competing concerns" (*Gomez v. Illinois State Board of Educ.*, 1987, p. 1041).

The Texas case used very broad-brush generalizations to dispose of the issues, but it clearly pointed to the need to do more than was being done. Faulting the state agency, the court wrote the following: "Moreover, there is no indication that the relative abilities of each particular student in Spanish and English are compared during the reclassification process" (*United States v. State of Texas*, 1987, p. 425; reversed, other grounds, 1982).

Professional standards (e.g., *Standards*, 1985) were difficult to create in their present form. It is hard to envision expanding them in a way that could be more useful for courts. But such expansions are, basically, what legal controversies concerning Hispanics should stimulate. The standards should not only be used in litigation; litigation should be used in setting the standards. The outcome of cases like *Chance* and *Contreras* should cause a wave of renewed energy in standard setting, with an effort made to state principles with sufficient force and specificity to help to resolve the disputes among professionals.

The setting of professional standards is already, in most contexts, deeply involved in controversy. There is a great deal of debating during the creation of the language of standards. Nonetheless, much of this argument proceeds from hypothetical cases. The tangibility of the specific, real-life issues found in lawsuits has a unique value as test cases for standards.

Better standards will not end all controversy. The *Standards* figured strongly in *Otero v. Mesa County Valley School Dist. No. 51* (1975), a Colorado case that struggled to define the kind of education that Hispanics are entitled to as a right. The court in Colorado essentially rejected the *Standards.* Gene Glass, testifying for the defendant school district, asserted that the experts who devised these standards had "a professional axe to grind"...that is, that they were creating standards with a view toward advancing their personal points of view. Because Glass was at the time serving as president of the American Educational Research Association, one of the organizational sponsors, the court was inclined to believe him. But although Glass was correct that there may be an intraorganizational political climate surrounding the development of test standards, this is not improper, and it does not lessen the Standards' value for courts. Creating standards is a better way to resolve issues, in a fundamental sense, than to settle legal cases.

The proper scope or detail for standards has much to do with their effectiveness. Test standards generally presume fairly simple models, such as, for example, a test-taking population that is without sufficient diversity to require formal test-maker attention. Such standards, in a sense, set the stage for legal problems because important test-taking populations have important must-be-attended-to diversity. The simplicity of the examples used in standards often leads them to fall short of a practical interpretation in a real-life context.

For example, where the ability under consideration is not linearly related to the performance on the job (e.g., the criterion) throughout the range of abilities that the testing procedure reflects, as in *Chance,* the appropriate practice is to demonstrate an adequately strong predictive relationship below the critically necessary level and to demonstrate an adequately strong protection against the extension of the rating into levels above the critically necessary level. Few standards, however, adequately address problems of this complexity. Almost all standards are written as if it is sufficient to make a general demonstration of relationship across the full range as the logical basis for decision making. Standards for the actual applications are rarely attempted. It is actual applications, however, that end up in courts.

Similarly, most stated measurement standards would not help plaintiff Gonzalez, or the court that she was in, because most do not envision a determination of the characteristics of a testing practice by anyone other than the proponent or user of the assessment procedure, and most do not describe a need to balance the goal of equitable treatment for the tested against the need for decisions that motivates the tester.

Properly written professional standards can assist courts in placing the burden in legal contests concerning the adequacy of testing. In Title VII cases, as instanced by plaintiff Gonzalez in *Contreras,* the plaintiff has one last chance to topple an existing practice even if the test sponsor demonstrates appropriate validity. The plaintiff has to show that there is a suitable alternate procedure that is equally as useful as the sponsor's current practice and less discriminatory.

Gonzalez, as noted, found this last hurdle insurmountable. She demonstrated to the court that oral assessments had been used successfully to pick auditors for Los Angeles in the past. But this past practice was under a different administrative alignment; the selection of auditors and the use of oral interviews had in the past been the responsibility of the mayor's office. The selection responsibility at the time of the suit was vested in the civil service department, and this arm had switched to a written examination. The court examined Gonzalez's demonstrations of the past successful application of oral testing and wrote the following: "That oral interviews were used in the past to hire auditors for the Mayor's office, a fact upon which Gonzalez relies, does not prove that such interviews would satisfy the merit hiring requirements of the new civil service division" (*Contreras v. City of Los Angeles,* 1981, p. 1281).

The decision in *Contreras* does not shed much light on what a court might accept as an adequate demonstration of an effective alternative. Also noteworthy is the fact that it was up to Gonzalez to demonstrate equal value for the oral methods, rather than a need for the city to demonstrate something uniquely valuable about its new written test. There is nothing in the professional standards that requires attention to such considerations by the test-sponsoring agency; the law, in the sense of a court, will rarely go beyond the profession.

Title VII plunges plaintiffs into *comparative validation:* a demonstration of equivalent validity across groups. Virtually all standards are written to consider only an adequate demonstration of *any* validity, without a need to demonstrate more or less validity than some other approach. The plaintiffs and the courts are essentially required to break new ground with respect to what constitutes an adequate demonstration of equivalent validity. New ground is more likely to divide professionals than familiar problems. A lawsuit becomes a parade of conflicting experts, detrimental to the profession and the decision by the court.

Good professional practice always needs to be balanced against practical considerations like the availability of resources. Courts pride themselves on practicality; they make such balances in a variety of ways in a variety of contexts every day. Accordingly, although it is a thesis of this chapter that legal issues are professional controversies and that explicit standards can help us to avoid cases, it is not true that informing a court about a standard that is a better theoretical way of doing things will alter the decision.

A case in point is *Rivera v. City of Wichita Falls* (1982), in Texas, where one of the charges by Mexican-American plaintiffs was that procedures for selecting police officers were inappropriately biased against them. The components of the selection process were a successive hurdles series of four tasks, of which only the first, BOLPO (described in the next paragraph), was considered to offer the requisite prima facie demonstration of discriminatory impact.

BOLPO stands for Basic Occupational Language for Police Officers. In the words of the court, it is a test of "the ability of an applicant to comprehend the type of reading material encountered in a police training academy" (*Rivera v. City of Wichita Falls,* 1982. p. 537). Almost 100% (94.6 %) of all Anglo applicants passed the test; only 60% of all Mexican Americans passed it. The court reviewed the content validity, the reliability, and the criterion-related validity of BOLPO. The reading selections were derived from "standard training materials used in police academies in Texas," so the content validity was deemed to have been established. An internal consistency reliability coefficient of .92 had been calculated using data derived from Wichita Falls incumbent police officers; the reliability was therefore judged adequate. Finally, the test had shown a criterion-related validity of .66 at two other Texas police academies; thus, the test was judged valid.

The samples being used to generate the validation data were almost entirely Anglo. The court seemed conscious of this limitation and of the possible need for a differential validity study. The total Hispanic sample, however, was composed of 35 individuals—a very small number—the implications of which were not lost on the court. It noted that "A differential validity study, in which the results of tests compared with job performance are separately reported for minority groups, was not feasible and therefore not undertaken here because there was not a sufficient sample size for protected classes" (*Rivera v. City of Wichita Falls*, p. 537).

Thus, a differential validity study was recognized as the appropriate model, but when it could not be conducted, the existing validity studies on Anglo samples were accepted and generalized.

Tests as Differentiators

Issues of professionalism and bias may be found in almost all controversies about the testing of Hispanics. Given the societal goals of equity and equality, a natural suspicion about differential treatment resulting from testing is inevitable. Accordingly, tests have frequently been involved in cases concerning charges of both de facto segregation and de jure, or mandated by law, segregation. Tests *can* produce or sustain segregation if the outcomes (i.e., scores) are correlated with group status: if the average scores attained by Group A differ from those of Group B.

Establishing illegal de facto segregation requires a demonstration of intentionality, as the language of Justice Powell in *Keyes v. School Dist. No. 1, Denver, Colorado* (1973) indicates: "The Court has come a long way since Brown I....the new formulation...is that desegregation will be ordered despite the absence of any segregatory laws if...(i) segregated schools in fact exist; (and) (ii) *a court finds that they result from some action taken with segregative intent by the school board* [italics added]" (*Keyes v. School Dist. No. 1, Denver, Colorado*, 1973, p. 230).

Testing can be the "some action" that produces the segregatory assignments. Furthermore, if the use of the tests is glaringly inappropriate, the testing practices can be held to be evidence of the necessary intent to segregate.

The testing of Hispanics is not always repudiated in these cases. *Morales v. Shannon* (1975) was a case in Texas in which it was claimed by plaintiffs that the schools were wrongfully segregated and that ability grouping, test-based in part, was unlawful. The federal district court that heard the case ruled that there was no segregatory intent with respect to student assignments. The fifth circuit court of appeals reversed this decision, holding that the racial–ethnic patterns in the schools clearly indicated segregation. However, when the appellate court specifically considered the question of the constitutionality of the use of tests and other measures to make assignments to ability groups, it sustained the lower court. It held the following:

> There was a dearth of proof as to discrimination in assignment, or in effect, either as a matter of direct proof or by inference. The groupings were made on the basis of language and mathematics test scores, academic grade performance and teacher recommendations. Given that ability groupings are not unconstitutional per se, the statistical results of the groupings here are not so abnormal or unusual in any instance as to justify an inference of discrimination. The record shows no more than the use of a non-discriminatory teaching practice or technique, a matter which is reserved to educators under our system of government. (*Morales v. Shannon,* 1975, p. 414)

Thus, both a general use of tests and the specific pattern of ability groupings in *Morales* were approved as failing to establish an intent to segregate. As *Morales* indicated, however, the evaluations of tests by courts are often oblique or implicit, rough and broad-brush. Courts will not hesitate to reach conclusions about tests on the basis of data that would not satisfy a measurement professional. The court in *Morales* did not debate validity or reliability as it assessed the ability groupings of the Hispanics. It based its decision instead on the summative effect of all the elements in the decision process. In effect, it reasoned that if the total outcome could be endorsed, the individual elements were not so bad as to distort the summative outcome, and the total set of elements could be endorsed.

The fact that the use of tests to form ability groups was not rejected by this court does *not* establish, in the usual professional measurement sense, that the tests used were actually appropriate (or valid) for their purposes. The court reached its judgment by a kind of outcomes test, an examination of the distributions of students in different categories that resulted from the operations of ability grouping. It decided that there was little abnormal in the distributions at which it was looking, and it concluded that there was nothing unacceptable in the individual components of the processes that led to the distributions.

The court was restricting its attention to the pragmatic considerations. Courts will not find issues that center on the nature of tests when applied to Hispanics, even when the potential importance of these issues is fairly obvious to an observer. To the extent that the issues are complex and time consuming to resolve, or need extensive additional information, courts will essentially go around them if the parties or the law will let them.

These observations have obvious implications for the capacities of courts to resolve legal issues. Rebell (1989, p. 137) wrote "In the testing context...courts can be highly effective in detecting and eliminating gross abuses, and in clarifying basic principles and standards." He also wrote, virtually in the same breath, "...there is a danger that...judges' lack of expertise may cause them to issue rulings that, from a professional perspective are ill conceived or erroneous" (p. 139).

On balance, it would appear that courts do not handle well the complex issues of psychometrics that are required in evaluating the equitable use of tests in assessing Hispanics. Courts pound out pragmatic and socially acceptable solutions to complex controversies, but they seldom do so by elucidating the nature of tests. A court does not speculate about or investigate possibilities; it does not go further than the record. As the *Morales* court noted, "Given that ability groupings are not unconstitutional per se,...*this record shows no more* [italics added] than the use of a non-discriminatory teaching practice or technique, a matter which is reserved to educators under our system of government" (*Morales v. Shannon*, 1975, p. 414).

Thus, the proceedings of the litigation, summarized as the record of the trial, determined the actions of the court. This record is determined by the energy or strategy of the litigants, not by the logical diligence of the court. If plaintiffs had advanced their claims through an offer of more test data, or if defendants had resisted in this manner, the record thus developed might have drawn the court more deeply into the questions of how the tests actually functioned. In the absence of such triggers for this action and in the absence of any concern for the constitutionality of ability grouping, the court simply left the matter alone.

Could a court do more? Rebell (1989, p. 139) said "...courts are highly efficient fact-finding vehicles....Probably the most exhaustive analyses of psychometric issues undertaken anywhere occur in class action litigations of controversial tests." With all due respect to one of the best writers and thinkers in this area, establishing the intrinsic properties of tests is not establishing facts in the conventional sense. Even allowing for semantic problems in the distinction between *fact* and *conclusion,* there is an ineluctable and irreducible core of uncertainty about all things psychometric. One does not so much establish a fact as render a practically useful judgment. Courts are more often boggled by the mass of measurement evidence presented rather than led to truth. Although Rebell may have been correct that the analyses in litigation are exhaustive, he overlooked the fact that both sides conduct such analyses...sometimes with different conclusions.

The Court as Tester

The foregoing cases center on the role of courts in reviewing the testing activities of others. But courts go beyond such judgments. Courts are not blind to the merits or value of testing, and they get involved, not infrequently, in ordering testing on their own. Although there is always tension between testing and its differentiations and ideals of equality, the complex problems of equity often require that people be adequately differentiated in order to adjust their treatment appropriately. In these contexts, with the court essentially the sponsor of the testing, the pragmatic nature of a court may lead it to adopt courses of action that could be, in the hands of others, contestable applications of tests.

One example of such judicial action and of a critical act of test interpretation figured in *Keyes*. Some of the Hispanic students who were to be considered for placement in bilingual programs were what is called "Lau C" students. These are students who comprehend and speak English although they come from a home-language background other than English. Some among these orally adequate children, however, although doing reasonably well on oral tests of English-language ability, did poorly on measures of writing and reading.

School district personnel reasoned that given the oral adequacy, the problems in reading and writing should be attributed to the same factors that determine the poor performance of any Anglo, native-speaking but low-achieving child. Therefore, they reasoned that these deficits should be addressed by the ordinary programs that any such Anglo child would receive, rather than by special language assistance. In other words, the orally adept, written-inept Hispanic child is no different from his or her Anglo counterparts, and it would be no more appropriate to establish bilingual programs for these Hispanics than for Anglos. The plaintiffs' experts held that the written-test performance deficits could be attributed to the home background and that special programs were appropriate.

The legislature of Colorado had in effect mandated the plaintiff's interpretation for one test-defined category of student and the defendant's interpretation for another category; under the Colorado English Language Proficiency Act (1981), the "Lau C" student was defined as "a student who comprehends and speaks English and one or more languages and *whose dominant language is difficult to determine,* if the student's English language development and comprehension is: I) At or below the district mean or below the mean or equivalent on a nationally standardized test; or II) Below the acceptable proficiency level on an English language proficiency test developed by the department" [Colo. Rev. Stat. 22-24, 103(4), 1981]. The court pointed to this legislation and ruled that special programs must be provided to children who met the statutory definition. Special programs were not needed for children who functioned above a certain level.

The complexity of these decisions, both in the courts and in the legislature, is clear. The logic that provides special language classes to Hispanics holds that there has been a deficit, owing to the non-English home-language background. The student is entitled to a recognition of that deficit and to special treatment. The law, however, uses the tests to restrict the application of this logic. If the student presents such a background, but is above the district mean, there will be no special treatment. The interpretation of test results thus varies the treatment by score level.

Tests offer a beguiling precision in the categorization of persons. But we do not know enough about the implications of those categorizations to base our more important decisions on them and them alone. Our best professional values hold that tests should not be used to categorize persons. No one—be they educator, judge, or legislator—should be permitted to attempt to solve the problems of the schools by basing decisions only on the apparently precise categories established by tests. Furthermore, the district mean is not an adequate foundation for equity. This mean can shift over time, altering access to educational programs for children whose test performances are fundamentally the same.

Such problems call into question Rebell's positive evaluation of the courts as fact-finding engines and as superior places to resolve issues. Courts do not debate academic propositions or keep cases going until they know enough to decide. Courts pound out decisions. Courts will not base their decisions on untruth, but they will all too readily be content with half-truths, or, even more often, with a case-dispositive decision that sheds no light on the truth at all.

The problem with tests caught up in litigation, then, is like the problem with tests caught up in the need to run the schools on a practical day-to-day basis. A seeming misuse of tests is not likely to be protested when it appears to produce a desired result. It is almost certainly contrary to the best measurement practice to infer on the basis of test scores alone, as in *Keyes*, what the nature and effect of a student's non-English, home-language background is, as the law in Colorado suggests. It is the congruence of test-based information with other information that is needed, not the test-based outcomes alone. The law in Colorado brings to mind the much publicized controversies about cutting scores that have occurred in recent years, such as the National Collegiate Athletic Association (NCAA) cutoff on the SAT, or the use of test-only information to award entitlements to consideration in the context of the National Merit Scholarship Program.

The use of tests in the *Keyes* case is not essentially different from the use described in *Aspira of New York, Inc. v. Board of Educ. of City of New York* (1975). Two test systems for describing Hispanics were introduced in the *Aspira* consent decree. Judgments about performance were to be reached by rules that combined information from appraisals using both English and Spanish testings. It was essentially the same logic that later came to be embodied in the *Keyes* case and other opinions: because the student's ability is reflected in the outcomes of testing in two languages, English and Spanish, it is most reasonable to base decisions on both assessments. The specific rule in *Aspira* was as follows: "...Hispanic-surnamed students who scored below the 20th percentile on the L.A.B.-English will take the L.A.B.-Spanish. Those whose scores on the latter exceed their scores on the former are to be in plaintiff class" (*Aspira of New York, Inc. v. Board of Educ. of City of New York*, 1975, p. 1166).

Such a rule is certainly definite. However, there are significant aspects of such an approach that can make a knowledgeable measurement person more than a little uncomfortable. It is not surprising, then, to read in the *Aspira* opinion a description of the then director of the office of educational evaluation of the New York City Board of Education, reflecting his evident concern. In the words of the court, the director

> stresses persuasively that the Board has been called upon for a "pioneering" endeavor; that assessing comparative language skill in the fashion that our decree requires has not heretofore been attempted on anything like the scale involved in this case; and that key requirements of information and analysis (for example, finding

measures of equivalency or comparability between the Spanish and the English L.A.B. tests) remain unsupplied as the time to move speeds for all of us. (*Aspira of New York, Inc. v. Board of Educ. of City of New York,* 1975, pp. 1163–1164)

Federal Judge Frankel, in *Aspira,* confessed in print that he was not measurement trained. He began one footnote explanation of what the "10th percentile of the norming group" meant by saying that he was doing this "For those not more comfortable than the court with such conceptions..." (p. 1162).

Furthermore, he was reasonably conscious of the limitations of what he was doing. He wrote the following of the decree:

> The crudity of this formulation is acknowledged on all sides. It is not possible to say with precise and certain meaning that an English version score at a given percentile is similar to the same percentile score on the Spanish version. Certainly distinctions between students separated by a percentile will produce results that must seem capricious at the points of division. But we are merely a court, consigned to the drawing of lines, and we do the best we can. (pp. 1165–1166)

And then, in what must constitute one of the strongest appeals for help directed at measurement professionals by any court, Judge Frankel noted in conclusion the following:

> ...all that we do today is surely open to improvement as the parties and their experts acquire—and may manage to infuse the court with—the wisdom available from further experience. (p. 1166)

The words were written in 1975. Today, 15 years later, the *Aspira* decree remains in place essentially as it was written. If professional measurement advances have improved the ability of experts to counsel the court on assignments for Hispanic children, the improvement has not led to any significant change in practice. The "crudity" of the judge's system remains in place.

Courts have reinstated fundamental insights into the proper testing of Hispanics. Testing cannot treat Hispanics and Anglos in the same way without differentiation. Almost no psychometric operation will have the same meaning for the two groups. Fortunately, the ideal in equity is not to achieve equal treatment in the sense of identical treatment. It is to achieve something recognizably different, but comparable, something equivalent in the context of the natures of the parties among whom equitable treatment is sought.

Courts have in numerous contexts rejected decision making about Hispanics based on English-language testing alone. In *Rios v. Read*, (1978) plaintiffs were Puerto Rican children in a school system on Long Island, about 60 miles from New York City. Of approximately 11,000 students, about 800 were Hispanic. The court, in reviewing school practices, wrote the following: "Students are exited from the bilingual or ESL program...without any objective or validated test. Students have been found to have reached the level of competency that qualifies them for instruction in English by retesting on the Stanford Achievement Test. The test is not valid for that purpose" (p. 23).

Only two subtests of the Stanford Achievement Test were being used. They had been introduced by the school system about 2 years prior to the suit in response to the advice of an expert consultant that the system assess "the ability of these children to comprehend spoken English." When called as a witness by the school district, this same expert testified that "the score on the Stanford test alone is an unreliable test for eliminating a student from a bilingual program" (*Rios v. Read*, 1978, p. 20).

Clearly, something is wrong in a world in which school systems introduce additional testing practices aimed at serving Hispanics, drawing on the advice of experts, only to hear the same experts fault the tests chosen when called by the schools to testify in litigation involving the practices. It seems most likely that there was a second professional rendering an opinion, a professional judgment that differed from the judgment of the first expert.

The *Rios* case emerged in 1977. By 1985, the *Standards* had been made much stronger and clearer in response to these problems, with the development of a specific section, Section 13, devoted to the topic of testing linguistic minorities. These are the questions: Could the newer, stronger standards have kept this legal issue from developing? Could the court have been spared the work of developing as a judicial finding what apparently was the viewpoint of the very expert on whose guidance the schools relied on in introducing testing?

Possibly. Standard 13.7 states clearly, "English language proficiency should not be determined solely with tests that demand only a single linguistic skill" (*Standards*, 1985, p. 75). The comment to this Standard adds, "...In making placement decisions, for example, a more complete range of language skills needs to be assessed" (p. 75). (See Geisinger's chapter in this volume for a listing of the standards from the "Testing Linguistic Minorities" section of the *Standards*.)

It is doubtful that the testing practices in *Rios* could have been established in good faith if these guidelines had been in place.

The *Standards* observed, in prefatory language to the standards of Section 13, "In some situations giving tests both in English and in the native language may be necessary to determine the kind of instruction likely to be most beneficial" (*Standards*, 1985, p. 73). This recommendation seems consistent with the statement by the court in *Texas* that "...the relative abilities of a student in Spanish and English are relevant to determining whether that student can achieve his learning potential in an English-only classroom" (*Texas and Pac. Ry. v. Behmyer*, 1903, p. 427).

Measurement theories can generate mathematical formulas for assessing the equality of quantities if these two quantities measure the same thing. Equating theory is derived from and based on such formulas. But measurement theories cannot provide operations for achieving comparability in the service of equity without some sort of logical basis derived from a judgment as to what constitutes equity. Measurement theories are not strangers to problems such as the *Aspira* problem in the context of education. The achievement testing programs of the college board provide numerous practical examples of equitable testing at work. Candidates prepared in quite different ways present themselves to colleges for admission, essentially in a competition for places. These candidates differ in academic preparation and in the specific patterns of test results presented. There is a need for an equitable system for comparing these diverse performances. Testers have provided what Angoff (1971) called "systems for expressing the comparability of tests." The problems of equitable treatment for science majors and humanities majors are not equivalent to the problems of comparing Hispanics and Anglos, but it is possible to develop testing procedures that recognize the differences in the groups and that appropriately equalize access to education.

Courts are not generally antitest. Particularly in the cases centered on issues of segregation or bilingual education in the schools, courts are fully inclined to mandate testing as a solution to problems. A good example is the opinion of the appellate court in *Keyes v. School Dist. No. 1, Denver, Colorado:*

> The key to an effective elementary bilingual classroom is the ability of the teacher to communicate with the children...[In Denver, however, teachers] are designated as bilingual in Spanish and English based on an oral interview. There are no stan-

dardized testing procedures to determine the competence of the bilingual teacher...Accordingly, it is inappropriate to assume that effective communication is taking place....(1983, p. 1516)

That is, if the goal is to provide Hispanic children with instruction that is equal to that of Anglos, one must have teachers who can communicate with them as effectively as they can with Anglos. The proper way to ensure this goal, in the opinion of the court, is not through informal or unsystematic appraisals; it is through adequate testing.

The court in *Keyes* also made calls for additional testing in the evaluation of the total program. It held that the failure of the school district to implement such testing on its own was unreasonable: "The defendant's program is also flawed by the failure to adopt adequate tests to measure the results of what the district is doing...The lack of an adequate measurement of the [program's] effects...is a failure to take reasonable action to implement the transitional bilingual policy" (p. 1518).

This call for extensive additional testing was unequivocal. It is echoed in this summary provided by the court in *Keyes*:

> Such changes must remedy...the lack of adequate...testing of the qualifications for bilingual teachers, ESL teachers, tutors and aides; the lack of adequate tests for classifying...students;...the lack of adequate testing for effects and results of the remedial program provided to the students; and the absence of any standards or testing for educational deficits resulting from their lack of participation in the regular classrooms. (p. 1520)

This overt reliance on tests to monitor educational progress by the court in *Keyes* is in one sense paradoxical. The court itself shied away from evaluating the schools by means of testing outcomes. The defendant school district had put forward extensive test results in support of its view that its programs of transitional bilingual education had achieved satisfactory results. The court wrote the following:

> This is the most difficult question in the Castaneda case analysis...It is beyond the competence of the courts to determine appropriate measurements of academic achievement, and there is damage to the fabric of federalism when national courts

dictate the use of any component of the educational process in schools governed by elected officers of local government. (p. 1518)

The issues relating to Hispanics are not, and probably cannot fully be, unique to this group. Hispanics have too much in common with other minority groups within the culture. Accordingly, some of the most meaningful cases involve these other groups. A good example is the case of *Lau v. Nichols*, which dealt with Chinese-American children in San Francisco and established the legal foundations for much of what emerged in bilingual education. The relationship, of course, works both ways; the *Morales* case is a good example of a case arising in a Hispanic context that makes a point about testing in general. As this case indicated, in evaluating legal issues it must be kept in mind that many Hispanic issues are more generally minority issues. Although there are clearly specific differences between Hispanics and other minority groups, there are, from the standpoint of the law, abstract similarities arising most often from a common special status outside the mainstream. This generalization means, also, that legal issues involving the testing of Hispanics will be instanced or clarified in cases that primarily center on some other group. Most of the discussion of *Larry P.*, for example, referred to the case as a controversy about Black children, which it was, but it was much more. The law that provoked the case of *Larry P.* mandated the testing of children in their primary language, a consideration that had much greater relevance for Hispanic children than for African-American children.

Conclusion

This chapter has not attempted to provide a comprehensive review of all cases that have involved the testing of Hispanics. Its purpose has been to describe the factors that underlie the legal issues in such testing and to discuss the complex interplay of professional standards and the capacities of the courts. A number of well-known cases, such as *Diana v. State Board of Educ.* (1973), have not been discussed. *Diana* was a California case that actually preceded *Larry P.* In it, Hispanic students won important agreements in a court-approved settlement. The settlement called for mandatory testing of bilingual children in both of the languages. In some ways, *Diana* was more significant for Hispanics than was *Larry P.*

The chapter has also not attempted to review the complex issues concerning bilingual education. Testing figures in such issues, but primarily as a means to an end. That is, testing can assist in making placement decisions with respect to bilingual programs, but it cannot define the proper nature or scope of the programs or resolve questions about the proper place for a minority language or culture in instruction. Such issues are essentially educational, rather than testing, issues.

The testing of Hispanics seems likely to continue to produce legal contests simply because it is not always easy to do it properly. Furthermore, testing is the kind of activity that can always be improved by the addition of resources and effort; because both resources and the capacity for effort are not limitless, there will always be a potential for contoversy over decisions as to what constitutes an acceptably adequate job. But the testing of Hispanics seems likely to improve in the decades ahead. The use of Spanish within the nation and culture is destined to endure in a way that was not true of the languages of the European immigrant minorities of a century ago. This very need to cope with the reality of a continuing Spanish-language presence will lead to improvement in testing. These adaptations will work to reduce the need for court interventions, and the resolution of differences at law should be a much less common event in the future.

This chapter has stressed the nature of legal issues as measurement issues that spill over into courts. It has further emphasized the role of professional standards in keeping such transfers from occurring. Two quotations seem germane in closing. The first quotation is from Justice Oliver Wendell Holmes on the dangers of setting standards by the level of energy that is ordinarily expended by those in a profession or calling: "What usually is done may be evidence of what ought to be done, but what ought to be done is fixed by a standard of reasonable prudence, whether it is complied with or not" (*Texas and Pac. Ry. v. Behmyer*, 1903, p. 470).

If I interpret this correctly, it points to the dangers of the members of a profession relying on each other to set the standard; it urges instead for a reliance on *prudence*, which my dictionary, *Websters*, defined as "the ability to govern and discipline oneself by the use of reason." (Justice Holmes's "reasonable prudence", then, is a redundancy; great dead justices, however, should be held safe from the quibblings of lesser living lawyers.)

The second quotation is by David V. Tiedeman, a prominent measurement psychologist, from the foreword to the *Eighth Mental Measurement Yearbook.* Thinking of all the legal activity that was emerging, Tiedemann wisely wrote the following:

> Today, tests stand on trial before many courts of public and legal opinion. Many persons consider themselves unfairly treated by tests and test users...Test equity seems to be emerging as a criterion for test use on a par with the concepts of reliability and validity, by which we professionally measure tests so assiduously at present. (1978, p. xxviii)

The full measure of Tiedeman's vision has not emerged. Reliability and validity remain the touchstones of our evaluations. But as we grope with the many problems that confront us in testing, and particularly in the testing of Hispanics, we will do well to keep his words in mind. The tests we want will be reliable, valid, and equitable.

References

Angoff, W. H. (1971). Scales, norms and equivalent scores. In R. L. Thorndike (Ed.), *Educational measurement* (2nd ed.). Washington, DC: American Council on Education.

Aspira of New York, Inc. v. Board of Educ. of City of New York, 394 F. Supp. 1161 (S.D. N.Y. 1975).

Bersoff, D. N. (1981). Testing and the law. *American Psychologist, 36,* 1047–1056.

Chance v. Board of Examiners, 330 F. Supp. 203 (S.D. N.Y. 1971), aff'd 458 F. 2d 1167 (2d Cir. 1971).

Civil Rights Act of 1964 (Title VII), 42 U.S.C. §2000e.

Colorado English Language Proficiency Act of 1981, Colo. Rev. Stat. §§22-24-101 to 22-24-106.

Contreras v. City of Los Angeles, 656 F. 2d 1267 (1981).

Diana v. State Board of Educ., C-70-37 RFP (N.D. Cal. June 18, 1973) (stipulated settlement).

Gomez v. Illinois State Board of Educ., 811 F. 2d 1030 (7th Cir. 1987).

Keyes v. School Dist. No. 1, Denver, Colorado, 313 F. Supp. 61 (D. Colo. 1970); 313 F. Supp. 90 (D. Colo. 1979), modified 445 F. 2d 990 (10th Cir. 1971), modified and remanded 413 U.S. 189 (1973); 368 F. Supp. 207 (D. Colo. 1973); 380 F. Supp. 673 (D. Colo. 1974), modified 521 F. 2d 465 (10th Cir. 1975) cert. den. 423 U.S. 1066 (1976) on remand 576 F. Supp. 1503 (D. Colo. 1983).

Larry, P. v. Riles 343 F. Supp. 1306 (N.D. Cal. 1979), aff'd. 502 F. 2d (9th Cir. 1974); 495 F. Supp. 926 (N.D. Cal. 1979), aff'd. in part and rev'd. in part, 793 F. 2d 969 (9th Cir. 1984).

Lau v. Nichols, 414 U.S. 563, 94 S. Ct. 786, 39 L. Ed. 2d 1 (1978).

Lerner, B. (1971). The Supreme Court and the APA, AERA, NCME test Standards. *American Psychologist, 33*, 915–919.

Morales v. Shannon, 516 F. 2d 411 (1975).

Otero v. Mesa County Valley School Dist. No. 51, 408 F. Supp. 162 (1975).

Rebell, M. A. (1989). Testing, Public Policy, and the Courts. In B. R. Gifford (Ed.), *Test policy and the politics of opportunity allocation: The workplace and the law* (pp. 135–162). Boston: Kluwer Academic Publishers.

Rios v. Read, 480 F. Supp. 14 (E.D. N.Y. 1978).

Rivera v. City of Wichita Falls, 665 F. 2d 531 (1982).

Standards for educational and psychological testing. (1985). Washington, DC: American Psychological Association.

Texas and Pac. Ry. v. Behmyer, 189 U.S. 468 (1903).

Tiedemann, D. V. (1978). In O. K. Buros (Ed.), *The eighth mental measurements yearbook.* Highland Park, NJ: Gryphon Press.

United States v. State of Texas, 506 F. Supp. 405 (E.D. Tex. 1981), rev'd 680 F. 2d 356 (5th Cir. 1982).

CHAPTER 6

Reactions to Technical and Societal Issues in Testing Hispanics

Cynthia Board Schmeiser

The preceding three chapters by Donlon, Geisinger, and O'Brien have examined issues associated with testing Hispanic students from three different perspectives: from a validity perspective, a methodological perspective, and a legal perspective. At first glance, one might conclude that these chapters represent independent perspectives that collectively examine the major issues associated with the testing of Hispanics. On further reflection, however, there appear to be three common themes that link these perspectives together. I would like to discuss these chapters in the context of the themes as follows:

Theme 1—First, there appears to be a common theme focusing on the fair and equitable use of test results.

Theme 2—The second theme that arises is an acknowledgment that test use and interpretation do not occur in a vacuum: sociopolitical, legal, economic, and other factors have a direct and oftentimes substantial effect on how test scores are actually interpreted and used.

Theme 3—The third theme focuses on the comparability of tests for minority and nonminority group members and the importance of obtaining validity evidence supporting test use and interpretation for each of these groups.

I examine each of these three themes as they have been addressed in the three chapters below.

Theme 1

First, there appears to be a common theme focusing on the fair and equitable use of test results.

Permit me to make a distinction between the concepts of fairness and bias. In my opinion, fairness is not the converse of bias. Rather, fairness relates to the equity of the uses made of a test rather than referring to the absence of bias. A test free of bias can be used unfairly. The lack of bias does not necessarily imply that a test is fair, because fairness depends on how the test results are used. A test, then, is not fair per se; a given use of that test is fair. One can imagine the possibility of a test being used fairly in one way and the same test being used unfairly in another way. From this vantage point, fairness has different definitions depending on the particular uses made of a test.

What role, then, does fairness play in the testing of Hispanics and other minorities? Clearly, fairness is an important consideration in our courts. Donlon made an important point about test equity and, if I may, I would like to extend that concept to include fairness of test use: "The ideal in equity, or fairness, is not to achieve equal treatment in the sense of identical treatment, but to achieve something recognizably different, but comparable." Test equity is emerging as a criterion for evaluating test use—perhaps, as Tiedeman (1978) suggested, on a par with reliability and validity. I believe that equity is and should be a relevant and critical criterion, both in and out of the courts, for evaluating test use. Testing professionals and test users need to be acutely aware of the importance of evaluating the fairness of test uses when tests are applied to make decisions about Hispanics or any group.

Theme 2

The second theme that arose from the three preceding chapters is an acknowledgment that test use and interpretation does not occur in a vacuum: sociopolitical, legal, economic, and other factors have a direct and oftentimes substantial effect on how test scores are actually interpreted and used.

In a number of instances, Geisinger has referred to various factors that influence whether or not a test has been used fairly. For instance, Geisinger made the point that "Values should guide both test use and test evaluation and, hence, such factors need to be considered in evaluating the use of tests and other measurement procedures." I think this is an important point. Messick (1980, 1989) included values and evidence about the consequences of testing in his broadly defined validation concept. Cronbach (1976) also noted the importance of values to considerations of test use.

Let's look at how the courts have dealt with these issues. Donlon stated in this volume that legal concerns have arisen not only from the intrinsic limitations of testing techniques, but from the political nature of the larger context in which tests serve. The legal issues, he stated, are most often at the intersection of psychometric and societal issues.

In the *Keyes v. School Dist. No. 1, Denver, Colorado* case, Donlon reported that a district mean was used to determine whether Hispanic children would be placed in special education programs. The educational environment within which the tests were being used was a complicated one, but one that needed to be analyzed carefully to determine what the consequences of testing were and whether the tests were being used appropriately. The *Morales v. Shannon* case, where plaintiffs claimed schools were wrongfully segregated, serves as an excellent example of the need to evaluate test use within the environmental context to examine the consequences of test use. Unfortunately, one of the problems facing the court, Donlon so articulately pointed out, is it rarely has analyzed psychometric issues in the context of the environment at the level that is required to be able to evaluate the equitable use of tests to assess Hispanics. Donlon appears to be somewhat skeptical of the court's ability to deal with these issues at all.

In practice, though, we are confronted daily with the challenge of ensuring that tests are being used properly in the context of the social, political, and cultural environment. In a sense, we end up with two definitions of bias—one that is a technical definition (the same score interpretations are not appropriate for different groups of concern) and the other a bias definition that associates values with the consequences of testing. This latter definition involves social justice concerns.

For instance, in the example Geisinger cited, a test is used to select insurance salespeople using the criterion of sales volume in dollars of insurance sold. The environment, however, within which insurance is sold differed for minority group members who worked in poorer communities from those of others who worked in more affluent settings. The volume of sales was directly related to the affluence of the communities, resulting in a biased criterion measure for those minority group members who were situated in the poorer communities. Had the environment been taken into consideration when the criterion was selected, it is likely that this criterion would not have been chosen. In this case, the criterion used to obtain validity evidence for the selection test was biased, resulting in an unfair test use.

Clearly, concerns about the consequences of test use require value judgments, and these value judgments raise important social policy concerns of fairness for Hispanics and other groups.

Is revising the professional *Standards for Educational and Psychological Testing* (*Standards*, 1985) a means for effectively dealing with these complexities?

Donlon called for more explicit standards and expectations that will "state principles with sufficient force and specificity to resolve disputes among professionals." He appears to believe that more specific standards will help reduce the legal controversies surrounding the testing of minorities. (Given his vast experience in the legal system, he also acknowledged that better standards will not end all disputes.)

Donlon and I may disagree as to whether more explicit standards will help to reduce the legal issues. I would argue that it is unlikely that standards can ever be stated in a way that will accommodate the tremendous diversity of environmental factors that have a dramatic impact on how well tests are used. I profess to some skepticism. Because of this diversity and because of the value judgments made about the consequences of test use, we are not able to prescribe specific standards that clarify the legal issues. In fact, it is more likely that as the standards become more specific and applicable to specific cases, we would find ourselves needing more and more standards to cover all of the various contexts, and we would lack universal standards that would be more generally applicable to a variety of situations. I am not sure that more specific standards will ever address the complicated interaction between psychometric issues and societal concerns.

Theme 3

The third theme focused on the comparability of tests for minority and nonminority group members and the importance of obtaining validity evidence supporting test use and interpretation for these groups.

O'Brien addressed the comparability of tests for Hispanics and Anglos. He described a process using the Rasch model for scaling and equating the New York City Language Assessment Battery (LAB). O'Brien proposed a process for developing comparable tests and then scaling them in a way that is sensitive to growth, but is comparable across English and Spanish test versions. This approach is an exciting one that helps to verify that performance on English and Spanish items is invariant across languages and groups.

I might first state that I agree with O'Brien about the need to ensure that a common construct is measured by the English and Spanish batteries. This commonality is a critical element for this approach to work. In addition, this construct, as O'Brien pointed out, must be unidimensional in character for the Rasch model to work well. I am somewhat concerned about whether the unidimensional requirement might be a limitation of this approach. The evidence about whether tests of language proficiency are unidimensional or multidimensional in character is contradictory (Bachman & Palmer, 1981; Oller, 1979; Scholtz, Hendricks, Spurling, Johnson, & Vandenburg, 1980; Swinton & Powers, 1980). Regardless of whether there is a consensus about the dimensionality of language proficiency in the literature, one nevertheless needs to verify the dimensionality of the construct being measured for this approach to be effective.

The approach, then, involves calibration, which is a process used to verify that the test measures the same language trait when taken by Anglo and Hispanic students. By plotting item calibrations against an identity line bounded by confidence bands, those items that are invariant for the two samples can be identified (i.e., items that fall within the bands). O'Brien recommended using only invariant items in the test for Anglos and Hispanics. It appears to me that another critical step in the process is to examine these remaining invariant items to determine if they still measure the same intended construct—language proficiency. That is, are the remaining items a content-valid representation of the domain to be measured? It is important to make sure that items measuring part of the original construct (e.g., grammar) have not been eliminated through this procedure, thereby changing the construct being measured and hampering the validity of the test.

The approach described by O'Brien emphasizes the need for constant, vigilant attention to the validity of the test throughout the test development process regardless of the methods used to scale and equate batteries of different languages.

Donlon cited several court cases dealing with a slightly different aspect of the comparability of tests for minority and nonminority group members—that is, the language in which to test. Two cases dealt with tests administered in the examinee's primary language or in English. The ruling *Larry P. v. Riles* mandated that children should be tested for ability in their native language. *Aspira of New York, Inc. v. Board of Educ. of City of New York* mandated assessments in both English and Spanish. The complexities of these cases seem to reaffirm the need for an approach like the one cited by Geisinger, whereby the choice of the language in which to test is determined by the purposes of the test and how the scores are to be used. The *Standards for Educational and Psychological Testing* (*Standards*, 1985) provided helpful guidance in this regard.

Summary

All three of these themes—fairness in testing, importance of the context of test use, and the comparability of tests for Hispanic and non-Hispanic students have a basic foundation in validity. Amassing validity evidence is essential for proper test use and interpretation. It prescribes many aspects of the technical process used to develop tests, and validity evidence is almost universally at issue in legal challenges. These three chapters clearly demonstrate that the validity issues surrounding the testing of Hispanics are complicated and difficult. We have not solved these issues in terms of either how we develop tests that result in fair and equitable uses for Hispanics, how we should interpret and use test results for minorities in practical, but complex settings, or how we should evaluate the consequences of testing as they affect minority group members. We clearly have a lot of work to do.

References

Bachman, L. F., & Palmer, A. S. (1981). A multitrait-multimethod investigation into the construct validity of six tests of speaking and reading. In A. S. Palmer, P. M. Groot, & G. A. Trosper (Eds.), *The construct validation of tests of communicative competence* (pp. 149–165). Washington, DC: Teachers of English to Speakers of Other Languages.

Cronbach, L. J. (1976). Equity in selection: Where psychometrics and political philosophy meet. *Journal of Educational Measurement, 13,* 31–41.

Messick, S. (1980). Test validity and the ethics of assessment. *American Psychologist, 35,* 1012–1027.

Messick, S. (1989). Validity. In R. L. Linn, (Ed.) *Educational measurement* (3rd ed., pp. 13–103). New York: American Council on Education & Macmillan.

Oller, J. W. (1979). *Language tests at school.* New York: Longman.

Scholtz, G., Hendricks, D., Spurling, R., Johnson, M., & Vandenburg, L. (1980). Is language ability dividable or unitary: A factor analysis of 22 English language proficiency tests. In J. W. Oller & K. Perkins (Eds.), *Research in language testing* (pp. 24–34). Rowley, MA: Newbury House.

Standards for educational and psychological testing. (1985). Washington, DC: American Psychological Association

Swinton, S. S., & Powers, D. E. (1980). *Factor analysis of the Test of English as a Foreign Language for several language groups* (TOEFL Research Report No. 6). Princeton, NJ: Educational Testing Service.

Tiedeman, D. V. (1978). Foreward. In O. K. Buros (Ed.), *Eighth mental measurement yearbook* (p. xxviii). Lincoln, NE: Buros Institute of Mental Measurements.

PART TWO

Educational Issues in the Testing of Hispanics

CHAPTER 7

Overcoming Bias in Educational Assessment of Hispanic Students

Giuseppe Costantino

Historical Overview

The 1990 advance census estimated the Hispanic population at 20.8 million, which represents approximately a 14.3% increase over the 1987 census figure (Rogler, Malgady, & Rodriguez, 1989). The annual growth rate of the Hispanic community has been estimated at 4.8%, compared with 1.8% for Blacks and .06% for Whites (U.S. Bureau of Census, 1990). Accordingly, school-age Hispanic children may be the largest growing group in the United States. Migration, acculturation, language, and socioeconomic and educational barriers have been associated with drug and alcohol abuse, delinquency, lower self-esteem, and, above all, the highest high school dropout rate of all ethnic–racial groups (Aspira of New York, 1983; Rogler et al., 1989). This alarming dropout rate has been associated with poor school achievement, which in turn has been linked to cognitive–intellectual deficits or biased standardized tests and discriminatory assessment, depending on whether one reads the research literature of the proponents of genetic determinants of lower academic achievement (e.g., Dunn, 1987; Jensen, 1969) or the critics of standardized tests (e.g., Costantino & Malgady, 1983; Mercer, 1988; Olmedo, 1981; Padilla, 1979; Padilla & Ruiz, 1973).

The nature–nurture versus test bias controversy has persisted for over a half century. Padilla and Ruiz (1973) reported that Garth (1923) used group mean differences in IQ to emphasize evidence of the superiority of White children over Mexican-American children. This kind of research literature progressed to the deficit hypothesis in the early 1960s, which posited that minority youngsters, especially Blacks and Hispanics, grow up in environments that engender serious verbal–cognitive deficits (Bernstein, 1962; Deutsch, 1965; John, 1963). This hypothesis led to the belief of lower intellectual abilities of Black individuals (Jensen, 1969) and to the more recent statement by Dunn (1987) that emphasized that minority youngsters, especially those who are Black, Hispanic, or American Indian–Alaskan, achieve much lower grades in reading, science, and mathematics than their nonminority counterparts.

The research literature emphasizing biased assessment of minority groups, especially Hispanics, has been fragmented (Olmedo, 1981). Early attempts to assess cognitive functions in Hispanic children by taking into consideration the level of acculturation and bilingualism were made by Anastasi and Cordova (1953) and Anastasi and deJesús (1953). These studies indicated that Puerto Rican children did not differ significantly from White and Black children in mean sentence length and in maturity of language structure. Subsequently, various social scientists and educators argued that the low performance of minority children on standardized tests was associated with biased tests and discriminatory assessment. Various scientists have also presented evidence that when minority children were tested with nontraditional instruments and assessed or taught by racially–ethnically congruent examiners and teachers, students performed within the normal range of intelligence and academic achievement (e.g., Cole & Bruner, 1971). Unfortunately, the research literature criticizing standardized tests has had very little impact on reducing the placement of a disproportionately high number of minority children into special education classes, in preventing minority children from dropping out of high schools, or conversely, in facilitating admission of minority students to colleges and universities. Placement of minority children in special education classes reached such a dramatic level by the mid-1970s that Oakland (1977) lamented, "It is perplexing and disturbing that black, Hispanic and other minority children are over-represented in classes for mentally retarded while underrepresented in classes for physically handicapped and gifted. Many persons attribute this situation to discriminatory assessment practices and suggest that their flaws are so widespread that formal assessment practices should be discontinued altogether" (p. iii). Public outcry about these types of conditions has even promoted legal actions as in the case of *Diana v. State Board of Educ.* (1973). In this case, the plaintiffs were nine Mexican-American pupils who complained that, as students, they were placed in special education programs because they were tested in English with biased instruments. Although this case was settled out of court, it was mandated that those children be retested in Spanish. Following retesting seven of the nine pupils showed an increase of 15 points in IQ and, therefore, were declassified and removed from classes for the mildly mentally retarded. Consequently, the court mandated that the California Department of Education retest all Mexican-American and Chinese-American pupils in special classes for the mildly mentally retarded (Olmedo, 1981). Because of numerous legal actions against what was seen as discriminatory assessment, in 1975, a California court banned the use of standardized IQ tests for placement of children in special education programs. However, the ban had very little impact on the number of referrals and placements of minority children in special classes. Hence, in 1979, the court established a rigid quota for minority pupil placement in special education (Reschly, 1981). Even with these protective measures, the increased awareness of what might constitute biased assessment, and the requirement that linguistic minority children be tested in their dominant language, minority children, especially children who are Hispanic or Black, continued to be overrepresented in special education classes during the 1980s in several states, such as New York and New Jersey (Reschly, 1981) and persist in being overrepresented today. Unfortunately, although the controversy among (a) the defenders of standardized tests (e.g., Gutkin & Reynolds, 1980; Jensen, 1980), (b) the critics (e.g., Costantino, Malgady, & Rogler, 1988; Malgady, 1990; Oakland & Laosa, 1977; Padilla, 1979), and (c) the defenders–critics (e.g., Cole, 1981) is continuing, minority individuals go on to experience strong barriers in educational settings, thus fulfilling the old Spanish proverb—while the donkeys fight, the barrels get squashed. The problem seems unsolvable.

Overcoming Test Bias

Several behavioral scientists and educators have been endeavoring to resolve this problem at theoretical or operational levels. As a result of litigation stemming from discriminatory assessment in the public school systems, the Office of Civil Rights in 1975 mandated that assessment of linguistic minorities be conducted in the dominant language of the students. Furthermore, the U.S. Department of Education formulated and implemented plans for bilingual education, which were phased out in 1980 (Olmedo, 1981). Recent analysis of the bilingual education controversy indicated that linguistic minority children in the public school system are optimally educated through an early intervention of bilingual education, for it has been argued that bilingual education appears to overcome language and educational barriers (Padilla et al., 1991). Notwithstanding the contrary arguments of ineffectiveness of bilingual education, several innovative bilingual programs have shown that students enrolled in those programs showed significantly increased academic achievement (e.g., Baca & Amato, 1989; Cummings, 1986; Kerman, 1979). Mercer, an advocate of the educational rights of minority students and a strong critic of standardized IQ tests since the early 1970s (1972), developed the System of Multicultural Pluralistic Assessment (SOMPA) in order to assess the intelligence of low socioeconomic status (SES) minority children in a nonbiased manner (Mercer & Lewis, 1977). This culturally sensitive technique had a wide appeal until the early 1980s, when it was strongly criticized on conceptual and psychometric grounds (Reynolds, 1985). Examiners also discovered the poor predictive validity of the testing system with educationally deprived, minority children, who scored within the average level of intellectual functioning on the SOMPA, but who were still unable to function in regular classes. However, the SOMPA seems to have adequate predictive validity with bright minority students. In fact, this testing system is used to assess minority students, primarily Hispanic, for magnet class placement in the Dade County (Florida) Public School System. When tested with the SOMPA, a large percentage of minority students reach an IQ of 125 and, therefore, become eligible for gifted classes. However, when tested with other standardized instruments, the majority of minority students fail to achieve the superior IQ category, thus, are excluded from those gifted classes (Costantino, 1990; J. Jackson & M. Madera, personal communication, 1990). Notwithstanding its psychometric flaws, the SOMPA shows some educational utility with academically proficient minority students.

Another attempt to overcome test bias was made with the development of Tell-Me-A-Story (TEMAS), a multicultural thematic apperception test (Costantino, 1978). This projective test was developed as a culturally sensitive instrument to facilitate accurate personality, cognitive, and emotional assessment of minority children. The TEMAS comprises 23 chromatic pictures depicting Hispanic and Black characters (on the minority version) and White characters (on the nonminority version). The pictures portray culturally congruent characters, culturally relevant themes, and settings familiar to the examinees in order to promote identification with the main characters and provoke greater verbal fluency and pull for greater self-disclosure (Costantino, Malgady, & Rogler, 1988). Because verbal fluency is the sine qua non for the validity of the clinical analysis of projective protocols (McClelland, Atkinson, Clark, & Lowell, 1953/1976), the early TEMAS psychometric research was conducted to dispute the verbal deficit hypothesis with respect to minority children. Two studies indicated that Hispanic examinees were significantly more verbally fluent in response to the TEMAS stimuli than to the traditional Thematic Apperception Test (TAT) stimuli (Costantino & Malgady, 1983; Costantino, Malgady, & Vazquez, 1981). The test, which is now being used in several public school systems throughout the United States to provide nonbiased cognitive, affective, and personality profiles, may contribute to reducing the unjustified placement of minority children in special education classes.

Additional research on the importance of fostering educational achievement and providing educational opportunities for Hispanic students has been conducted by Durán and Pennock-Román. A noteworthy technique, which departs from traditional assessment, is a form of curriculum-based assessment described by Durán in this volume. This clinical assessment of instructional performance in the classroom appears to overcome the discriminatory assessment by using observable learning behaviors and, at the same time, linking assessment to instruction and promoting optimal cooperative learning. However, a conceptual and theoretical framework needs to be developed, and psychometric studies assessing its validity should be conducted. Standardized aptitude tests, such as the SAT, have been criticized for being biased against minority students (e.g., Durán, 1983; McClelland, 1973). The chapter that follows by Pennock-Román focuses on the relationship between language proficiency and mean differences of SAT and GRE scores among linguistic minority groups, with an emphasis on Hispanics. This research shows that Hispanics who score poorly at the end of high school on the SAT, score much higher at the end of the 4 years of college on the GRE. This improvement suggests that linguistic-minority and limited-English-proficiency (LEP) students should be given the opportunity to be admitted to colleges, even if their scores are below required admission norms.

Conclusions

A half century of debate has not resolved the controversy over inherent deficit versus test bias in the psychological testing of Hispanics. However, I have documented some endeavors to overcome discriminatory assessment during the last 2 decades and would like to conclude this chapter by citing the relevant work of a collaborator who has written pointedly on test bias (Malgady, 1990; Malgady, Rogler, & Costantino, 1987; Malgady, Rogler, & Costantino, 1988).

The status quo hypothesis concerning minorities is that there is no bias. Research on test bias does not provide sufficient evidence—largely because of either inconsistent findings or a lack of findings—to contradict this status quo hypothesis on an empirical basis. That is, we cannot accept the statistical alternate hypothesis that there is minority test bias. Traditional statistical reasoning leads to posing no bias as the null hypothesis in minority assessment research.

Given the equivocal findings of empirical research on assessment of Hispanics, we cannot reject the null hypothesis of no bias simply because the research does not justify a contradiction of the status quo. If the null hypothesis is traditionally formulated as a no-bias condition, contrary to many hypothesis testing situations, the consequences of a Type II error may be more serious than a Type I error. (Type I error is incorrectly rejecting the null hypothesis of nondifference. Type II error is incorrectly failing to reject the null hypothesis of nondifference.) If new evaluation and dispositional procedures or criteria are developed, and a Type I error is committed, economic and research resources will have been misspent. If a Type II error is committed, Hispanics will end up being unfairly evaluated by standardized psychological and educational tests. Hence, a Type I error would impose an unfair burden on the school system because special considerations of culture are unjustified, whereas a Type II error would mean unfair special education class placement and inability to attend colleges which would be detrimental to Hispanic individuals.

Because the second type of error seems to be more serious for Hispanic students, traditional hypothesis posing may be questionable. The *Standards for Educational and Psychological Testing* (*Standards*, 1985) include numerous cautions against using norms, item content, and validity and prediction estimates with demographically, linguistically, and culturally different populations. Some of these standards are found in Geisinger's chapter earlier in this volume.

Thus, it may be wiser to change the status quo: Traditional assessment procedures would be presumed guilty of bias against other cultures unless proved innocent. Therefore, standardized instruments should be used with extreme caution, and culturally sensitive tests and assessments with Hispanics should be increasingly used.

References

Anastasi, A., & Cordova, F. (1953). Some effects of bilingualism upon the intelligence test performance of Puerto Rican children in New York. *Journal of Education Psychology, 44*, 1–19.

Anastasi, A., & deJesús, C. (1953). Language development and non-verbal IQ of Puerto Rican preschool children in New York City. *Journal of Abnormal and Social Psychology 15*, 357–366.

Aspira of New York. (1983). *Racial and ethnic high school drop-out rates in New York City: A summary report 1983*. New York: Author.

Baca, L., & Amato, C. (1989). Bilingual special education: Training issues. *Exceptional Children, 56*, 168–173.

Berstein, B. (1962). Social class, linguistic codes and grammatical elements. *Language and Speech, 5*, 221–240.

Cole, M., & Bruner, J. S. (1971). Cultural differences and inferences about psychological processes. *American Psychologist, 26*, 867–876.

Cole, N. S. (1981). Bias in testing. *American Psychologist, 36*, 1094–1102.

Costantino, G. (1978, November). *Preliminary report on TEMAS: A new thematic apperception test to assess ego functions in ethnic minority children*. Paper presented at the Second American Conference on Fantasy and the Imaging Process, Chicago, IL.

Costantino, G. (1990, January). *Training school psychologists in the use of the TEMAS test, a multicultural thematic apperception test*. Workshop presented at the Dade County Public Schools, Miami, FL.

Costantino, G., Malgady, R., & Rogler, L. (1988). *TEMAS (Tell-Me-A-Story) manual*. Los Angeles, CA: Western Psychological Services.

Costantino, G., & Malgady, R. G. (1983). Verbal fluency of Hispanic, Black and White children on TAT and TEMAS. *Hispanic Journal of Behavioral Sciences, 5*, 199–206.

Costantino, G., Malgady, R. G., & Vazquez, C. (1981). A comparison of the Murray-TAT and a new thematic apperception test for urban Hispanic children. *Hispanic Journal of Behavioral Sciences, 3,* 291–300.

Cummins, J. (1986). Empowering minority students: A framework for intervention. *Harvard Educational Review, 56,* 18–36.

Deutsch, M. (1965). The role of social class in language codes and grammatical elements. *Language and Speech, 5,* 221–240.

Diana v. State Board of Educ. C-70-37 RFP (N.D. Cal. June 18, 1973) (stipulated settlement).

Dunn, L. M. (1987). *Bilingual Hispanic children on the U.S. mainland: A review of research on their cognitive, linguistic, and scholastic development.* Circle Pines, MN: American Guidance Service.

Durán, R. P. (1983). *Hispanics' education and background: Predictors of college achievement.* New York: College Entrance Examination Board.

Garth, T. R. (1923). A comparison of the intelligence of Mexican and mixed and full blood Indian children. *Psychological Review, 30,* 388–401.

Gutkin, T. B., & Reynolds C. R. (1980). Factorial similarity of the WISC-R for Anglos and Chicanos referred for psychological services. *Journal of School Psychology, 18,* 34–39.

Jensen, A. (1969). How much can we boost IQ and scholastic achievement? *Harvard Educational Review, 39,* 1–23.

Jensen, A. (1980). *Bias in mental testing.* New York: The Free Press.

John, V. (1963). The intellectual development of slum children: Some preliminary findings: *American Journal of Orthopsychiatry, 33,* 813–822.

Kerman, S. (1979). Teacher expectation and students achievement. *Phi Delta Kappan, 60,* 41–42.

Malgady, R. (1990, May). *Overcoming obstacles in minority research: Issues of bias assessment.* Paper presented at the meeting of the American Psychiatric Association, New York City.

Malgady, R. G., Rogler, L. H., & Costantino, G. (1987). Ethnocultural and linguistic bias in mental health evaluation of Hispanics. *American Psychologist, 42,* 228–234.

Malgady, R. G., Rogler, L. H., & Costantino, G. (1988). Reply to the empirical basis for ethnocultural and linguistic bias in mental health evaluations of Hispanics. *American Psychologist, 43,* 1097.

McClelland, D. C. (1973). Testing for competence rather than for "intelligence." *American Psychologist, 28,* 1–14.

McClelland, D. C., Atkinson, J. W., Clark, R. W., & Lowell, E. L. (1976). *The achievement motive.* New York: Irvington. (Original work published 1953).

Mercer, R. (1972, May). I.Q.: The lethal label. *Psychology Today,* 44–97.

Mercer, J. R., (1988). Ethnic differences in IQ scores: What do they mean? (A Response to Lloyd Dunn.) *Hispanic Journal of Behavioral Sciences, 10,* 199–218.

Mercer, J. R., & Lewis, J. F. (1977). *System of multicultural pluralistic assessment (SOMPA).* New York: The Psychological Corporation.

Oakland, R. (Ed.). (1977). *Psychological and educational assessment of minority children.* New York: Brunner/Mazel.

Oakland, T., & Laosa, L. M. (1977). Professional, legislative, and judicial influences on psychoeducational assessment practices in schools. In T. Oakland (Ed.), *Psychological and educational assessment of minority children*. New York: Brunner/Mazel.

Olmedo, E. L. (1981). Testing linguistic minorities. *American Psychologist, 36*, 1078–1085.

Padilla, A., Lindholm, K. L., Chen, A., Durán, R., Hakuta, K., Lambert, W., & Tucker, R. G. (1991). The English-only movement: Myths, reality and implication for psychology. *American Psychologist, 46*, 120–130.

Padilla, A. M. (1979). Critical factors in the testing of Hispanic Americans: A review and some suggestions for the future. In R. W. Tyler & S. H. White (Eds.), *Testing, teaching and learning: Report of a conference on testing*. Washington, DC: National Institute of Education.

Padilla, A. M. & Ruiz, R. A. (1973). *Latino mental health: A review of literature* (DHEW Publication No. HSM 73-9143). Washington, DC: U. S. Government Printing Office.

Reschly, D. J. (1981). Psychological testing in educational classification and placement. *American Psychologist, 36*, 1094–1102.

Reynolds, C. R. (1985). Review of "System of Multicultural Pluralistic Assessment." In J. V. Mitchell, Jr. (Ed.), *The ninth mental measurements yearbook* (1519–1522). Lincoln, NE: The Buros Institute of Mental Measurements.

Rogler, L., Malgady, R., & Rodriguez, O. (1989). *Hispanics and mental health: A framework for research*. Malabar, FL: Robert E. Krieger Publishing Co.

Standards for educational and psychological testing. (1985). Washington, DC: American Psychological Association.

U. S. Bureau of the Census (1990). *The Hispanic population in the United States: March 1990*. (Serial P-20 No. 449). Washington, DC: U. S. Government Printing Office.

CHAPTER 8

Interpreting Test Performance in Selective Admissions for Hispanic Students

María Pennock-Román

I n this chapter, the major focus is on the question, "What meaning can be inferred from scores on tests used for selective admissions to higher education for Hispanic students?" Two kinds of meaning for scores are discussed: how well they reflect cognitive skills (as distinct from other factors influencing test performance) and how well they predict future academic performance. The two types of score interpretation reflect different and important uses of tests.

Much of the miscommunication and disagreement that exists between measurement specialists and those outside the field can be traced to differences in values concerning what inferences are critical when evaluating aptitude tests used in selective admissions. Whereas measurement specialists have traditionally stressed predictive validity (e.g., Anastasi, 1984; Schoenfeldt, 1984), psychologists in other specialties emphasize construct-related concerns. For example, cognitive

The writing of this chapter was supported by the National Science Foundation's Program of Visiting Professorships for Women and the Educational Testing Service and was completed while Pennock-Román was on leave from the Educational Testing Service at Princeton University.

psychologists evaluate tests on the basis of how well they reflect examinees' level of underlying competence in cognitive processes such as mathematical problem solving, reading comprehension, and verbal reasoning (e.g., Sternberg, 1984).

In this chapter, investigations of several variables other than "pure" cognitive abilities that influence test performance and academic achievement are examined. First, proficiency in English and other home languages (mostly Spanish), family and educational background, and test speededness are considered. Second, the relationship of test scores and the aforementioned variables to the prediction of academic achievement is examined. Third, a few studies that have investigated the prediction of academic achievement in an English-language environment using aptitude tests administered in Spanish are reviewed. Some research on foreign students is included in order to confirm findings where studies on Hispanic groups are few. (Investigations of language proficiency and academic achievement in higher education for foreign and Hispanic students often address parallel issues and obtain similar findings.) Nevertheless, studies on Hispanic groups predominate. The material is organized around questions needing to be addressed. The answers that follow cannot be viewed as definitive because no one issue has been researched sufficiently to justify such conclusions. Implications of the findings are discussed in light of the relevance of the variables to the measurement of cognitive abilities and to the short-term prediction of academic achievement.

On Guard Against the Charge of Obviousness

This review has been influenced by Gage's (1991) essay in defense of social and educational research against the charge of obviousness in results. Although there are cases in research where the direction of an association between variables and outcomes is predictable, Gage pointed out that the strength of association is not knowable ahead of time. Furthermore, one cannot anticipate factors and contingencies that influence the magnitude of effects and associations without research-based knowledge. "Even if [a] broad generalization is a truism...to enhance the truism with the specifics that make it have value for theory and practice...research does become necessary" (Gage, 1991, p. 13).

Taking this perspective one step further, Gage's paper implied that a review of social science research that merely repeats the broad generalizations and conclusions from original studies is vulnerable to charges of obviousness of the findings. Hence, there is an effort here to include where possible the magnitude of associations, necessary contingencies, and any important, specific details that may impact theory and practice.

Background Variables Influencing Test Performance

The major focus in this section is on the extent to which proficiency in English and Spanish affects scores at the level of both the total test and individual items. In addition, family socioeconomic status, educational background, and test speededness are briefly reviewed.

For the study of Hispanic subgroups in the United States, research on monolinguals or bilinguals with high proficiency in English is most directly relevant when considering selective admissions at the college or graduate and professional school level. With the exception of Puerto Rican students educated in Puerto Rico, the majority of Hispanic students in the United States taking tests such as the Scholastic Aptitude Test (SAT) and Graduate Record Examination (GRE) report that English is their best or preferred language, even if many may have spoken Spanish or another language in the home. The percentages of English-dominant students are more than 93% for Mexican Americans, 90% for Puerto Ricans (state resident), and 84% for "Other Hispanic/Latin American" students (Arbeiter, 1984; College Board, 1982; Educational Testing Service, 1988; Ramist & Arbeiter, 1982, 1984, 1986; Smith, 1986).

Despite the much greater size and, hence, interest in samples with high English proficiency, it is useful, nevertheless, to begin the discussion with a consideration of test scores for persons having low levels of English proficiency. In these samples, the effects are more dramatic and trends are easier to detect.

Low English Proficiency and Aptitude Test Scores

At first reading, many of the research findings regarding the aptitude test performance of students with low English proficiency appear to reveal mostly truisms that are knowable without research. Consider Alderman's (1982) study, where Puerto Rican students ($N = 411$) were administered the SAT; the Prueba de Aptitud Académica (PAA), a college admissions test in Spanish; and the Test of English as a Foreign Language (TOEFL); among other measures. Alderman found, not surprisingly, that for students with low TOEFL scores (below 344), there was essentially no relationship between aptitude measured in Spanish and aptitude measured in English. Instead, he found that across the sample of nonnative speakers varying in English proficiency, there was a very high correlation ($r = .83$) between the TOEFL and SAT verbal subtests (SAT-V). This result is confirmed by other studies showing high correlations between the TOEFL and measures such as the GRE Verbal subtest and the Graduate Management Admissions Test (GMAT) with nonnative speakers (Angelis, Swinton, & Cowell, 1979; Powers, 1980; Wilson, 1982).

Hence, for nonnative speakers having a low level of proficiency in the language of the test, scores on the test do not reflect the intended aptitude. Rather, low verbal-aptitude scores in a nonnative language reflect mostly examinees' limited proficiency in the language of the test. This result can be deduced a priori. If we consider persons at the extreme end with virtually no comprehension of the language of the test, we can predict that all would obtain randomly achieved, near-zero scores regardless of aptitude.

We could also foresee without research that quantitative tests would be less influenced by language proficiency than verbal tests, thus coming closer to measuring the targeted skills in nonnative speakers. These results are indeed found. Studies on this topic have demonstrated that the correlations between a quantitative test administered in English and a measure of English proficiency were smaller than the TOEFL–verbal-aptitude correlations (e.g., Alderman, 1982; Angelis et al., 1979; Powers, 1980; Wilson, 1982). Furthermore, the correlations between the SAT mathematics subtest and the PAA mathematics subtest in Spanish were higher than the correlations between the SAT-V and the Spanish verbal-aptitude scores for the same sample (Alderman, 1982).

Taking a closer look at these studies, however, we find important practical information about the degree of relationship among variables. We can obtain answers to specific questions pertaining to score interpretation for nonnative speakers, such as the degree of overlap between verbal tests in English and language-proficiency measures, between two aptitude tests in different languages, and between an achievement test and language-proficiency measures.

How much shared variance or association exists between verbal and quantitative tests administered in English and English-language proficiency measures (such as the TOEFL) for samples of nonnative speakers?
Studies have shown that about 27% to 58% of the variance for verbal tests ($r = .52$ to $.76$, Angelis et al., 1979; Ayers & Peters, 1977; Powers, 1980; Schrader & Pitcher, 1970; Sharon, 1972; Wilson, 1982) and about 4% to 30% for quantitative tests ($r = .20$ to $.55$, Ayers & Peters, 1977; Powers, 1980; Wilson, 1982) is shared with English-proficiency measures like the TOEFL.

One caveat in interpreting these findings is that we cannot make an absolute distinction between verbal aptitude and English proficiency, despite considerable efforts in the construction of language-proficiency measures. Thus, some of this overlap between the aforementioned tests and the TOEFL, or any other language-proficiency test, reflects a combination of both general verbal aptitude and proficiency in the specific language it is designed to measure. Although language-proficiency tests also tap cognitive aptitudes, their level of difficulty is less than for tests such as the American College Test (ACT), SAT-V, and GRE-V tests, and they do not discriminate well among native speakers of English (Angoff & Sharon, 1971; Clark, 1977). The distinction between cognitive-aptitude and language-proficiency tests rests primarily on difficulty. Hence, aptitude variance not reflected in proficiency tests is referred to here as *aptitude beyond* or *over and above* proficiency.

How strong a relationship exists between aptitude tests in two languages?

There are several studies, mostly on Puerto Rican and Hispanic students from Florida, where correlations between aptitude tests in both the first (Spanish) and second (English) languages are available. In these investigations, we find slightly different results according to the time interval between tests. When tests in the two languages are administered close together in time, verbal tests share about 49% to 64% of the variance ($r = .70$ to $.80$; Alderman, 1982; Boldt, 1969; Educational Testing Service, 1988) and quantitative tests about 64% ($r = .80$, Alderman, 1982; Boldt, 1969). Slightly lower correlations ($r = .30$ for verbal tests and $.70$ for quantitative tests) were found by Bornheimer (1984) using college records where time intervals between testings in the two languages tended to be longer. By themselves, the two kinds of study have identified two partially overlapping influences on the scores in an aptitude test given in a nonnative language: language proficiency and aptitude as measured in the native language. We can integrate these findings for a sample that has taken the two aptitude tests and a measure of English proficiency, and then we can decompose the percentages of variance attributable to each component.

For nonnative speakers, what percentage of the variance in verbal and quantitative test scores in the examinee's weaker language can be said to be aptitude over and above proficiency in that language?

In the aforementioned (p. 101) study by Alderman (1982), when students in Puerto Rico were grouped across all TOEFL-score levels, the variance overlap in SAT-V scores was broken down into 36% English-language proficiency (main effect and interactive terms related to TOEFL scores) versus 44% PAA V aptitude scores. In the same sample, the variance in quantitative SAT scores overlapped 15% with English proficiency and 63% with PAA mathematical-aptitude scores (in Spanish).

However, an important issue is the influence of the level of English proficiency in the sample on the strength of this relationship. One would expect that the degree of overlap would increase with the level of competence in the student's weaker language. This effect has indeed been found, and it can be quantified when there are both proficiency tests and aptitude tests in the two languages involved, as in Alderman's study.

How does the relationship between aptitude tests in two languages vary according to language proficiency?

In Alderman's study (1982), the relationship between aptitude in the first language (Spanish) and aptitude in the second language (English) was moderated by the level of proficiency in the second language. For Puerto Rican SAT test takers with TOEFL scores of 344 and lower (at least one standard deviation below the mean), the raw regression weight of SAT-V on PAA-V was essentially zero (.02). When TOEFL scores were within one standard deviation of the sample mean (435), the raw regression weight of SAT-V on PAA-V was .20. For examinees with TOEFL scores of at least 527 (one standard deviation above the sample mean), the raw regression weight was .47. This moderator effect meant that the prediction of SAT-V from TOEFL scores and PAA-V scores in the whole sample was improved by including an interactive term (TOEFL × PAA-V), which accounted for 6% of the variance in SAT-V scores. For the prediction of the quantitative SAT-M, the moderator effect (variance accounted for by the interactive term TOEFL × PAA-M) was equally large. These results demonstrate that the level of overlap between aptitude tests in two languages varies according to the level of proficiency in the examinees' second language and by the type of test content (verbal vs. quantitative). However, the exact percentages reported in Alderman's study are not necessarily generalizable to samples having average TOEFL scores lower or higher than Alderman's sample mean (435), to other tests with different verbal demands, or to other language groups.

The moderating effect of proficiency is crucial in terms of practical issues in test use and score interpretation, because it can help us to identify at what level of English proficiency we can expect an aptitude test in English to become a useful measure for nonnative speakers.

At what TOEFL score do aptitude tests in English begin to reflect aptitude as measured in the native language?

For students taking the SAT in Puerto Rico, the correlations between SAT-V and verbal aptitude measured in Spanish begin to be nontrivial at about a score of 500 on the TOEFL (Alderman, 1982), although the SAT-V may still underestimate verbal skills at this level. By contrast, for quantitative tests in the two languages, correlations are nontrivial at lower TOEFL scores. Nevertheless, the TOEFL–quantitative-test-score correlations do suggest some degree of underestimation of mathematics scores for nonnative speakers with low levels of English proficiency.

By how much do tests in the weaker language underestimate the abilities of language-minority students?

Undoubtedly, the scores of students tested in a nonnative language are depressed by the language handicap and do not reflect their true cognitive abilities in their native tongue. Although test users would like to correct for the student's language handicap in interpreting scores, research thus far has not addressed how to measure the degree of underestimation of abilities when examinees are tested in their weaker language. If one could theoretically derive what a score on, say, the SAT should be for individuals with given scores on an aptitude test in their native language, assuming perfect proficiency in English, one would be able to compare actual versus theoretical SAT scores for those persons. Such a comparison would provide a measure of the underestimation of abilities on the SAT due to the language handicap.

However, this comparison would be difficult to do because one would need to have tests of abilities in two languages that were psychometrically parallel and equated to the same scale. There are many complex problems involved in adapting and translating tests to different languages and cultures (Laosa, 1973). (One may also consider O'Brien's chapter within this volume with regard to this problem.) Angoff and Cook (1991) attempted to establish a theoretical conversion between the PAA and the SAT using translations. Their aim was to provide admissions committees with useful information on the interpretation of PAA scores as an adjunct to the SAT. Angoff and Cook were cautious in their recommendations on how to use the scale conversion because some bias may be introduced by nonequivalences in translations, and the normative samples for the SAT and PAA are different and essentially nonoverlapping. Nevertheless, it would be interesting to compare actual SAT scores for students taking the PAA and the SAT with the theoretically predicted SAT score derived by Angoff and Cook's scale equivalence. Based on Alderman's (1982) correlational evidence of moderator effects, one would expect greater divergence the lower the English proficiency of the test taker.

Achievement (Subject-Matter) Tests for Specific Subjects and Low English Proficiency

Do subject-matter tests have lower or higher correlations with English proficiency than with general verbal-aptitude tests? Does the degree of overlap depend on the degree to which the test is quantitative versus verbal? These issues have not been addressed in Hispanic samples, but research with foreign nationals gives interesting, relevant findings. In answer to the first query, Wilson (1987) considered a variety of approaches including correlations between GRE Subject Test scores, GRE General Test scores, and self-rated English proficiency among foreign nationals. The self-rating was dichotomous based on the question, "Do you communicate better in English than in any other language?" He concluded that "scores on GRE Subject Tests appear to be less sensitive to differences in general English proficiency than scores on tests involving more general English language content" (p. S-13).

These results were not predictable a priori, but they do make sense after the fact. For foreign students, technical terms in their own field of study (e.g., macroeconomics and ribosomes) may be much more familiar than words less likely to be learned from textbooks or journals and may appear on the GRE General Test verbal analogies (e.g., mosaic *tile,* a ship's *galley,* or *hackles* in the neck of fowl).[1]

In terms of the second query, there was a trend in the expected direction—a positive relation between the amount of verbal content in the subject matter and the size of the correlation with self-rated proficiency. For example (Wilson, 1987), the median correlation between self-rated English proficiency and subject tests in the quantitative fields (e.g., engineering, economics, and geology) was essentially zero (− .02), similar to the − .02 obtained with the quantitative GRE General Test, and much lower than the .38 obtained with the verbal GRE

---

[1] *Taken from items in sample tests provided in the 1987–1988 and 1988–1989 GRE Information Bulletins which are retired, formerly administered GRE-V forms.*

General Test for students in those fields. In contrast, among students in fields with more verbal emphasis (e.g., literature, music, history, and psychology), the median correlations with proficiency were .31 for subject tests, .43 for the GRE-V, and −.04 for the GRE quantitative subtest. However, some surprises occurred; for some highly verbal fields, sociology and political science, the correlation with English proficiency was essentially zero, whereas more substantial correlations were found for geology (.29) and biology (.18).

Moderate to High English Proficiency and Total Test Scores

Correlations between self-rated proficiency in English and SAT verbal and mathematics scores among Hispanic students in the United States who have moderate to high proficiency in English show trends similar to those found with low proficiency samples. However, correlations are generally of slightly lower magnitude than the aforementioned findings reported by Wilson (1987) with foreign students and the GRE General Test. Durán, Enright, and Rock (1985) found that a dichotomous classification of English as the best language correlated .19 with the SAT-V, .09 with the SAT-M, and .25 with the Test of Standard Written English (TSWE), which covers grammar and composition. Higher correlations (.29 to .35) with the verbal SAT were found with specific self-ratings of proficiency in understanding spoken English, in speaking, in reading, and in writing. Corresponding correlations were also higher for the TSWE (.31 to .39) and the SAT M (.10 to .15).

Pennock-Román (1990) found correlations between the SAT subtests, the TSWE, and self rated proficiencies in English for Hispanic students at six U.S. universities that were similar in magnitude to the correlations found by Durán et al. (1985). In addition, a cloze test of proficiency in reading English was found to correlate .25 to .58 with the SAT-V, .22 to .49 with the TSWE, and −.08 to .45 with the SAT-M, depending on the university. (For further information on the cloze procedure of measuring reading, see Bormuth, 1967, 1968.)

The lower test performance of bilingual Hispanic students is also clearly evident when we consider mean SAT scores for students classified by language background. For example, Pennock-Román (1988) used College Board data on recent cohorts of college-bound seniors to show that Mexican-American and Puerto Rican students who learned English first in the home had mean SAT-V scores roughly 50 to 80 points higher than those learning a first language other than English in the home. Mean quantitative scores for corresponding groups differed by roughly 20 to 30 points. Pennock-Román found that the differences in SAT verbal-score means between White, non-Hispanic students and Hispanic students were substantially reduced when language background was held constant.

Extent to Which Scores Are Depressed by Limited Language Skills

Although it is plain that test scores underrate abilities for bilinguals with low levels of English proficiency, little research has addressed the size of the systematic error or at what level, if any, of language proficiency the underestimation becomes trivial. Alderman's (1982) study suggested that underestimation of abilities varies by level of proficiency in the language of the test and that it is largest for students low in proficiency.

What cannot be predicted is whether the systematic error becomes negligible at high levels of proficiency or if it is merely reduced, but still appreciable. It is possible that bilinguals who are so proficient that they may be indistinguishable from monolingual native speakers still may be underrated. One could argue, for example, that their vocabulary breadth in any one language is an underestimate because it probably excludes a portion of the lexicon in the other language. Hence, it is possible that assessment of verbal skills in the native tongue may be useful in the evaluation of talent for bilinguals.

A partial answer to the estimation of the systematic depression of scores may be approached by considering how well test scores predict a criterion (e.g., college grades in an English environment) for bilinguals in comparison to monolinguals. If bilinguals' performance on the criterion variable exceeds that of monolinguals with comparable test scores, then we have clear evidence that the test underestimates ability. The problem with this approach is that the criterion is also subject to language-proficiency effects, as is evident in the results reviewed in the section on prediction of academic achievement. Hence, no criterion can reflect ability in the abstract, but only ability in an environment with a particular language.

Spanish Proficiency and Total Test Scores

If we assume that language proficiency has a simple relationship to immigration history, one would expect two patterns of findings in the relationships among Spanish proficiency, English proficiency, and aptitude test scores: (a) that English and Spanish proficiency would be negatively associated, and (b) that high Spanish proficiency would imply low test performance in English (because of the language handicap). That is, one could expect that recent immigrants would favor Spanish, they would be less proficient in English, and they would be poor test takers in English.

The results show a trend in this direction, but it is very weak and inconsistent across samples in different regions of the country. For example, correlation coefficients between proficiency ratings in the two languages among college students in the Pennock-Román (1990) study typically ranged from −.20 to +.10. That is, proficiencies in the two languages were largely unrelated to each other, but there was perhaps a very weak trend toward a slightly lower proficiency in Spanish when proficiency in English was high.

Also, the relationship between proficiency in Spanish and aptitude test performance was *not* necessarily a strong negative one. In absolute value, the correlations were smaller than in the relationship between English proficiency and test performance in English. In the Durán et al., (1985) study, correlations between self-rated proficiency in Spanish and test scores on the SAT ranged from −.26 to −.12 (the negative sign indicates that high Spanish proficiency implies lower test scores in English).[2] However, in the Pennock-Román (1990) study, the range included some positive correlations (−.27 to +.23), and these positive correlations occurred more often for students in New York and Florida.

The inconsistency in the correlations may reflect a more complex relationship between immigration history and maintenance of the Spanish language. There are some long-settled families and residents of certain regions of the United States. (e.g., New Mexico; San Antonio, TX) who have stressed retention of Spanish for many generations. Furthermore, there are geographical regions in the United States (e.g., Miami, parts of New York City and Los Angeles, and along the U.S.–Mexican border) where the concentration of recent immigrants and Spanish speakers is high, and where back-and-forth migration is common. In those areas, subsequent generations are exposed to Spanish in the neighborhood and encouraged to learn it even when they are born in the United States.

Among families who make an effort to retain cultural traditions and in the previously mentioned geographical areas, it is not unusual to find bilinguals who

---

[2] *Durán, Enright, and Rock (1985) reported positive correlations because the proficiency scale was reversed from the direction used in Pennock-Román's (1990) study. That is, in the former study, the scale had the lowest values for the highest levels of proficiency. Here, the signs were reflected to simplify comparisons between findings in the two studies.*

are proficient in both languages. Consequently, a high proficiency in Spanish does not necessarily imply a handicap in English or on test scores in English.

Linguistic Features Influencing Test-Item Scores in Spanish-Speaking or Spanish-Origin Samples

At the item level, several studies on both foreign and native-born U.S. students have found a relationship between linguistic features of test items and differential item functioning for Spanish-speaking foreign students and Hispanic students compared with non-Hispanic White students (Alderman & Holland, 1981; Breland, Stocking, Pinchak, & Abrams, 1974; Chen & Henning, 1985; Schmitt, 1988; Schmitt & Dorans, 1990). *Homographs*—words having more than one meaning for the same spelling—were differentially more difficult for Mexican-American and Puerto Rican students. Also, *false cognates*—words of Latin origin that may be similar in appearance or origin yet have different meanings in English and Spanish—were differentially more difficult for Hispanic examinees. In contrast, words that were *true cognates*—having similar meanings in both Spanish and English—were sometimes differentially easier for Hispanic students (e.g., melodious and melodioso). This effect emerges more often when the word is frequently used in Spanish and infrequently used in English. Also, some items are differentially easier for Hispanic students when the content of the item is of special interest to Hispanic groups (Schmitt, 1988).

Thus, bilingualism was either an advantage or a disadvantage depending on the test item. Such linguistic effects were seen more often in vocabulary items such as antonyms and analogies. Moreover, the size of the effect was larger for Puerto Rican students than for Mexican-American students (Schmitt, 1988). This result may reflect the lower frequency of Spanish use in the home in the latter group, at least in college-bound samples (Pennock-Román, 1988).

Quality of Educational Background and Total Test Score

There is an extensive body of research demonstrating that performance on aptitude tests is strongly related to examinees' socioeconomic background, quality of schooling, and types of courses taken. Specific demonstrations of this relationship between coursework and scores on the American College Tests (ACT) is found in Laing, Engen, and Maxey (1987) and in the *Preliminary Technical Manual for the Enhanced ACT Assessment* (American College Testing Program [ACT], 1989). The *Profiles of College Bound Seniors* (Arbeiter, 1984; College Board, 1982; Ramist & Arbeiter, 1982, 1984, 1986) and the *College Bound Seniors Ethnic/Sex*

Data for recent years show mean scores for various race–ethnic groups when classified by parental education, numbers of courses taken, and types of courses taken in high school. For students of all groups, those who took more coursework in high school scored higher on the relevant test. This relationship tends to be stronger in the areas of mathematics and natural sciences. There is reason to believe that the relationship should *not* be interpreted to mean that causality is unidirectional, that is, that taking more courses increases scores. At least part of this association reflects self-selection in that the higher scoring students are more likely to choose greater numbers of courses and more advanced material in a given area. However, the increase in scores across cohorts of 10th to 12th graders additionally suggests an effect in the other direction—that taking more courses may raise scores on relevant tests (ACT, 1989). Angoff and Johnson (1988) have also shown longitudinal gains or decreases in quantitative skills associated with curricular choices during the undergraduate college years.

When one controls for differences in numbers of courses taken and the type of academic preparation received in high school, the discrepancy in mean scores between Hispanic and non-Hispanic White students on tests such as the SAT and ACT is greatly reduced (Chambers, 1988; Pennock-Román, 1988). Pennock-Román (1988) found that 20% of Mexican-American high school students tended to take fewer than 15 courses of academic subjects, whereas only 12% of non-Hispanic White students took this few. Also, only 16% of Mexican-American high school students attempted 20 or more year-long academic courses, whereas 35% of the non-Hispanic White students took that many. Hence, at least part of the score discrepancy between Hispanic and non-Hispanic White students is associated with differences in course-taking patterns in high school.

The influence of prior academic preparation on group differences in test performance has also been documented in studies of differential item functioning. Loyd (1982) found that reading comprehension items that were differentially more difficult for Hispanic students tended to require background knowledge not presented in the item itself.

Test Speededness, Test-Taking Strategies, and Total Test Scores

The issue of test speededness deserves special attention in the study of the test performance of Hispanic students and linguistic minorities. There is evidence from experimental studies that decoding time for verbal materials is longer when presented in a bilingual's weaker language (Dornic, 1980). Furthermore, Dornic's review showed that the difference in performance for individuals working on tasks in two languages increased under conditions where subjects were asked to work as quickly as possible. This line of research indicates that bilinguals and nonnative speakers of English take longer to process and complete the same test items than monolingual English speakers.

Llabre (1991) has recently reviewed research on test speededness, test-taking preparation, and test performance of Hispanic students. Studies on test speededness are relatively few and are often based on samples with less than 100 Hispanic subjects. Most investigations contrasting scores under varying time limits indicate that increasing time limits would differentially enhance the performance of Hispanic students relative to non-Hispanic students (Knapp, 1960; Llabre & Froman, 1987; Llabre & Froman, 1988; Younkin, 1986). On the other hand, some studies have shown no greater improvement for Hispanic students than for other groups when time limits are extended (Rincón, 1979; Wright, 1984). Nevertheless, Rincón found an interaction between speededness and test anxiety for Hispanic students that was not present for non-Hispanic White students.

Under normal time conditions for standardized aptitude tests, Hispanic and foreign students tend to complete verbal sections of aptitude tests less often than non-Hispanic U. S. citizens. On the SAT, Schmitt and Dorans (1990) reported that Hispanic students tend to reach fewer items at the end of verbal sections when compared with non-Hispanic White students with comparable total scores.

Llabre (1991) attributed the difference in speed of completion of tests for Hispanic examinees to a lack of test sophistication and unfamiliarity with budgeting time in tackling items, rather than to difficulties with the English language. Her studies with Froman (Llabre & Froman, 1987, 1988) showed that time spent on individual items correlated less with item difficulty for Hispanic test takers than for non-Hispanics. On the other hand, presenting items one at a time with a standard time length did not differentially improve performance for Hispanic students (Llabre & Froman, 1988). Rivera and Schmitt (1988) found evidence that Hispanic students omitted test items more frequently on the SAT than did Hispanic non-White students with the same overall score. Studies of test sophistication with Hispanic groups are relatively few in higher education, but the studies that exist (mostly on younger children) suggest substantial score gains for Hispanic examinees receiving test preparation instruction (Benson, Urman, & Hocevar, 1986; Dreisbach & Keogh, 1982; Goldsmith, 1979; Maspons & Llabre, 1985;

Oakland, 1972). Hence, more research on test time limits and the factors influencing slower test taking for Hispanic students is needed.

Sources of Variation in Scores and Their Effect on Validity

Many of the same factors shown here to be associated with test scores for Hispanic students—quality of educational background, parents' socioeconomic status, familiarity with tests, experience with time limits and test-taking strategies—are also related to the test performance of other ethnic groups and races. In addition, for Hispanic students and linguistic minorities, language background is an important influence on scores. Hence, most, and perhaps all, aptitude tests cannot be considered "pure" measures of cognitive abilities for any students. Differences in educational opportunities and language background between Hispanic students and non-Hispanic White students suggest that the relationship between scores on tests and underlying cognitive abilities are not equal for the two groups.

However, the College Board and the Graduate Records Examination Board, for example, justifiably argue that the aim of tests in selective admissions is not to assess cognitive abilities in the abstract; rather, these tests are supposed to be measures of "developed" aptitudes necessary for competent performance in higher education. Therefore, evidence that these educational history and language background variables are correlated with scores does not rule out tests as useful measures in terms of forecasting performance in college—the main function of tests used in selective admissions.

What is needed is an evaluation of the extent to which the aforementioned variables influence how accurately we can estimate future academic performance for Hispanic students using these tests. Another issue is whether scores for Hispanic students can be interpreted in the same way as are scores of non-Hispanic White students. Hence, the usefulness of test scores for selective admissions depends in part on the effects these variables have on college achievement. That is, in terms of forecasting performance in higher education, can tests be said to be on the same scale for Hispanic students as they are for non-Hispanic White students?

A partial answer to these questions may be approached by considering how well test scores predict a criterion (e.g., college grades in an English environment) for Hispanic students and linguistic minorities in comparison with majority students. If language background and test speededness affect the precision with which abilities are estimated in Hispanic and linguistic minority groups, then the accuracy of prediction will be lower for these groups in comparison with non-Hispanic White students. If the performance of Hispanic examinees and foreign nationals on the criterion variable exceeds that of non-Hispanic White examinees with comparable test scores, then we have clear evidence that the test is under-estimating developed abilities in Hispanic and foreign students. Of course, such analyses would assume that the criterion variable is scaled in commensurate units for the groups that are contrasted.

Background Variables and the Prediction of Academic Achievement

This section focuses on the accuracy of predicting academic achievement in higher education with aptitude tests in both Spanish and English and how this prediction is affected by English and Spanish proficiency. Additional variables such as family socioeconomic status, educational background, and test speeded-ness are also briefly considered.

Prediction of Academic Achievement, English Proficiency, and Aptitude Tests

From the perspective of educators interested in predicting academic achieve-ment, score variation reflecting familiarity with the language of the test is not necessarily a source of invalidity. Obviously, proficiency in the language prevalent in the targeted academic environment has to predict success in that environ-ment. In the extreme case, consider a newly arrived cohort of geniuses who know no English. Despite their talent in their native languages, they cannot begin to understand lectures, take classroom tests, or do homework in English. Hence, the issue is not whether English proficiency as measured by tests such as the TOEFL is important for success in U. S. institutions of higher education, but to what degree it forecasts academic performance or to what degree it modifies the pre-dictive validity of tests designed to discriminate aptitudes at the highest levels. Answers to these questions are detailed later.

In reviewing these findings, we should remind ourselves that proficiency tests cannot be viewed as pure measures of language knowledge separate from underlying verbal aptitude. Measures of cognitive aptitudes and language profi-ciency overlap considerably because proficiency tests include reading comprehen-sion and vocabulary. Rather, the following analyses illustrate how well tests of listening skills or functional literacy in English (that are easy for native speakers) can predict academic achievement for bilingual students.

To what degree do English-proficiency tests predict Hispanic students' academic performance in an English-language environment?
Answers to this question vary according to Hispanic students' length of residence in the continental United States. In a study of 47 Spanish-dominant Puerto Rican graduate students who received their undergraduate training in Puerto Rico, Bornheimer (1984) found a correlation of .54 between the English-language section of the *Prueba de Aptitud para Estudios Graduados* (PAEG) and grades at New York University.

For Hispanic students who are native-born or long-term residents of the continental United States, the correlations between English proficiency and academic performance at U.S. colleges and universities tend to be lower. Pennock-Román's (1990) study included several measures of English proficiency, including a cloze test of reading comprehension that has been shown to have high correlations with the TOEFL (Hale et al., 1988). Pennock-Román found that the correlations of the cloze test with academic achievement in the freshman year varied from .11 to .25 at four institutions.

The wide range of correlation coefficients for these two investigations is consistent with research on foreign students. Most of the studies on this topic with foreign students, however, are flawed by very small samples and a failure to keep the criterion of grades on the same scale. Typical problems in design include the merging of institutions that vary in selectivity, the combining of different graduate fields of study that vary in grading standards, the lack of separation of graduate and undergraduate grades, and the use of sample sizes less than 45. Given these problems, it is not surprising that results are quite variable, with correlations ranging from $r = -.17$ to .58 (Hale, Stansfield, & Durán, 1984; see studies listed under section D, the relation of TOEFL to later academic performance, p. 12).

The value for the Bornheimer (1984) study fell within the upper part of the range of correlations in studies on foreign students, whereas the Pennock-Román (1990) results fell within the lower part of this range. There was considerable restriction of variance in cloze test scores due to the high English proficiency of the Pennock-Román samples, which probably attenuated correlations. Nevertheless, the results support the view that English proficiency, that is, functional literacy in the language of the academic environment, is related to academic achievement even among long-term residents. One caveat is that this conclusion is based on only two studies (albeit, involving six independent samples) of Hispanic students.

Given these findings, one would expect that the predictive validity of aptitude tests for both foreign and native-born bilingual students would not necessarily be moderated by the influence of English-language proficiency on aptitude test scores.

English-Language Aptitude Tests

This section considers various findings about the prediction of academic achievement for Hispanic students versus non-Hispanic White students using aptitude tests administered in English. The issues involved are the size of correlations, under- or overprediction, and the relationship to English proficiency.

To what degree can aptitude tests in English predict Hispanic students' grades in U.S. institutions, and how does this compare with findings for non-Hispanic White students?

In the 16 separate analyses from studies of Hispanic students at U.S. institutions reviewed by Durán (1983), the median correlations between college admissions tests and college achievement were .25 for verbal tests and .23 for quantitative tests. Pennock-Román (1990) found that correlations for SAT-V varied from .13 to .37, and the correlations for SAT-M varied from .13 to .30 at four institutions, but lower values were found elsewhere.[3]

Although Durán's review of 16 separate analyses found that correlations between test scores and freshman-year college grades tended to be slightly lower for Hispanic groups than for non-Hispanic White groups, the differences were rarely statistically significant. Pennock-Román (1990) found that the standard errors of estimate were essentially equal for Hispanic and non-Hispanic White students at six universities.

---

[3]*Correlations are shown for two institutions in California, one in Texas, and another in Florida. Lower values were found at the New York institution where none of the typical predictors, including high school grades, had strong relationships to freshman-year grades. Also, correlations between predictors and freshman-year grades in Massachusetts were very low because of widely varying grading standards by college major.*

Maxey and Sawyer (1981) reported the effectiveness of the ACT tests in predicting college performance of Mexican-American students ($n = 3,717$) and other groups at 172 institutions in the academic year 1977–1978. A regression equation was developed for each college, based on the most recent data available from either the 1973–1974, 1974–1975, or 1975–1976 academic years. They found that the prediction of Mexican-American students' grades was only very slightly less accurate than the prediction of non-Hispanic White students ($n = 89,804$). That is, 52% of the Mexican-American students' predicted grade averages were within .50 grade units of their earned grade averages, compared with 57% for non-Hispanic White students. The proportion was obtained by looking at the distribution of differences in grades pooled across universities.

Thus, the results from relatively few studies on Hispanic students who took the SAT (22 independent analyses in Pennock-Román, 1990, and Durán, 1983) and on less than 4,000 Hispanic students who took the ACT provide little evidence of differential validity for Hispanic versus non-Hispanic White students when variability in undergraduate college grades is controlled. It appears that the lower correlations sometimes found in Hispanic samples may reflect lower variance in freshman grades for Hispanic groups at the undergraduate level.

There is also little evidence of differential validity in the prediction of law school grades for Hispanic groups using the Law School Admissions Test (LSAT). Comparing Chicano groups with non-Hispanic White groups, Powers (1977) found slightly higher correlations for the Chicano groups at 7 out of 10 law schools, but the differences were not statistically significant. Wightman and Muller (1990) also found slightly higher validities for Hispanic groups (apart from Chicano groups) than for non-Hispanic White groups at 8 of 13 law schools. Chicano groups had slightly higher validities than non-Hispanic White groups at three out of seven law schools. As in Powers' study, none of the contrasts in validity coefficients in 20 law schools were statistically significant. Both studies attributed the slightly higher validities for Hispanic groups to differential range restriction. There was greater variability in LSAT scores and 1st-year grades among Chicano and other-Hispanic groups than among non-Hispanic White groups.

However, these findings give us only a partial evaluation of tests as predictors for Hispanic students and nonnative speakers, because the accuracy of prediction involves other considerations besides the degree of correlation between course grades and test scores. We are also concerned with the extent to which tests in a second language may underpredict performance on classroom tests and on homework as reflected in grades.

To what extent do aptitude test scores underestimate the future academic achievement for Hispanic students as compared with non-Hispanic White students?

Pennock-Román (1990) showed that instead of underestimating future academic achievement, test scores tended to give a slight overestimation. That is, at most universities, Hispanic students had slightly lower grades than non-Hispanic White students with the same test scores. Specifically, regression equations based on non-Hispanic White samples using the SAT alone (without high school record) tended to overpredict the college grades of Hispanic students at four of six universities. The differences between actual and predicted grades (in grade point units) ranged from -0.25 (lower grades than predicted) to $+.09$ (higher grades than predicted). This difference in the direction of overprediction exceeded $\frac{1}{10}$ of a grade point at three out of six universities.

The two institutions with the largest overprediction had relatively more Hispanic students than non-Hispanic students majoring in the sciences, where grading standards tend to be stricter than in other fields (Elliott & Strenta, 1988; Strenta & Elliott, 1987). Hence, at least part of the overprediction at these institutions was due to artifactual differences in the scale of college grades across subject areas.

Unfortunately, most of the studies reviewed by Durán (1983) did not compare the regression equations for Hispanic and non-Hispanic students using test scores as the only predictors. When regression equations were contrasted, they usually combined both test scores and high school grades as predictors. These studies showed only subtle differences in regressions. A few studies found a small trend in the direction of overprediction, with Hispanic students having slightly lower grades than expected based on a combination of test scores and high school records. Pennock-Román (1990) also found that the combination of test scores and high school record tended to overestimate college grades for Hispanic students at five out of six universities. This overestimation was greater than that found for tests alone. The range of differences between actual grades and predicted grades were from $+.08$ (better grades than predicted) to $-.31$ (lower grades than predicted).

Maxey and Sawyer (1981) found that on the average, across all the 172 institutions considered, Hispanic students' grades in 1977-1978 were neither over-predicted nor underpredicted by regression equations based on the total group from earlier academic years.

Powers (1977) and Wightman and Muller (1990) consistently found that both LSAT and undergraduate grades tended to overpredict 1st-year law school grades for Chicano and other Hispanic groups as compared with non-Hispanic White groups, although the differences were not large.

In sum, the pattern of regression differences more often reveals that His-panic students receive actual grades that are slightly lower than the grades pre-dicted from previous academic performance and test scores. However, in addition to the issue of underprediction and overprediction, another important matter is the extent to which academic achievement can be predicted more accurately by incorporating measures of proficiency in English in the regression analyses.

Does taking into account the level of English proficiency in addition to aptitude test scores improve the prediction of Hispanic students' academic achievement?

One way to combine English proficiency with aptitude test scores in regression equations is to evaluate its incremental prediction of academic performance over and beyond test scores, that is, as an independent variable or main effect. (If a main effect is found, it would indicate that aptitude test scores would systemati-cally under- or overpredict performance in college for students at low levels of English proficiency, depending on the direction of the effect.) This effect would occur if, for example, nonnative speakers perform better on homework or class-room assignments where unlike test administrations, time limits are more gener-ous, and dictionaries are readily available.

Pennock-Román (1990) considered English proficiency as a main effect. She found that adding English proficiency to the regression (whether the cloze test or self-reported proficiencies) did not improve the prediction over the accu-racy attained with SAT scores. That is, the college performance of Hispanic stu-dents with relatively lower English proficiency was not systematically better or worse than their aptitude scores would predict.

A limitation is that these findings may only apply to students with high lev-els of proficiency because the samples in Pennock-Román's study attended at least 2 years of high school in the United States. Research on foreign students suggests that her findings may not generalize to samples with lower English proficiency. For example, Wilson (1985) and Stolzenberg and Relles (1991) found that the prediction of 1st-year grades for foreign students in business schools increased (multiple R^2 increment greater than .015) when TOEFL scores were added as predictors to the regression that included GMAT. However, this effect varied by level of proficiency in the sample: The increase in R^2 was trivial for students with high TOEFL scores (above 602). The Pennock-Román (1990) and Wilson (1985) studies both concluded that for high-proficiency students, there is little improvement in the prediction of academic achievement when measures of English proficiency are factored in.

Another possibility in combining English proficiency with aptitude test scores in regression equations is to evaluate proficiency as a moderator variable, that is, as a variable that interacts with test scores. (If an interaction effect is found, it means that the slope or degree of relationship in the regression of college grades on test scores varies according to English proficiency.) A moderator effect would be expected if aptitude tests are too difficult at very low levels of English proficiency, producing little discrimination among ability levels (i.e, a floor effect). If so, this restriction in discrimination would result in lower correlations between aptitude tests and academic performance. As English proficiency increases, correlations would be expected to rise until they reach values typical for native speakers of English.

The issue of English proficiency as a variable that moderates predictive validity for aptitude tests has not received adequate attention with Hispanic samples. Evidence from studies with foreign students (Sharon, 1972; Wilson 1985, 1986) shows that correlations between 1st-year grades in graduate school and GRE or GMAT scores vary by level of English proficiency, although not for all majors and not consistently for both verbal and quantitative subtests. Hence, it would be informative to extend this line of research to Hispanic samples.

Achievement Tests and Predicted Grades

The prediction of academic achievement using subject-matter tests has not been adequately studied with Hispanic samples. However, some interesting findings with foreign nationals suggest the possible usefulness of this approach at the graduate level. Wilson (1979) found that the GRE-Advanced tests in specific subject areas nearly always had higher correlations with graduate performance than either of the GRE General Tests. In verbal areas, the median correlation for advanced tests was .35 as compared with .31 for GRE-V. In quantitative areas, the median correlation for advanced tests was .34 as compared with .31 for GRE-Q. Typically, nonnative speakers of English have a smaller language handicap on subject specific tests, as discussed earlier and shown here. Subject-matter tests may, therefore, have slightly higher validity.

Use of Aptitude Tests Administered in Spanish to Predict Academic Achievement in an English-Language Environment

Given the limitations of aptitude tests administered in English for students more proficient in Spanish, several researchers have investigated how well aptitude tests administered in Spanish predict academic performance at U.S. institutions. The *Prueba de Aptitud Académica* (PAA), developed by the College Board in Puerto Rico, has been used to predict high school and college grades at the undergraduate level, whereas the *Prueba de Aptitud para Estudios Graduados* (PAEG), another test developed in Puerto Rico, has been used to predict graduate-level grades at New York University.

Gannon, Oppenheim, and Wohlhueter (1966) and Carlson (1967) used the PAA to predict college grades in California and Texas. Gannon et al. (1966) found that the multiple R for a regression based only on the Spanish tests was .46 at the University of the Pacific ($n = 77$; other universities had less than 20 cases). At the Texas Western University where both the SAT and PAA tests were available ($n = 73$ for 1964–1965, and $n = 85$ for 1965–1966), the best combination of predictors of college grades were the quantitative test in Spanish plus the verbal test in English (multiple $R = .50$ and .26, respectively for each academic year). The Spanish verbal test added little to prediction when combined with SAT scores and PAA-M. Unfortunately, Carlson (1967) did not report regression results with just the Spanish tests for the Texas Western University data.

Boldt (1969) tried all possible dyads of verbal and quantitative PAA and SAT tests as predictors of high school grades among students in Dade County, FL. He found that there was no clear-cut choice among pairs of predictors. Based on his complete sample of 140 bilingual students who varied in language preference, zero-order correlations for SAT-V and PAA-V with high school grades were similar (.42 and .36, respectively). The correlations between grades and the quantitative tests were .46 for SAT-M and .43 for PAA-M. Among the subsample of students preferring Spanish ($n = 55$), he found that the tests in Spanish taken together predicted high school grades with a multiple R of .62; the regression of grades on combined SAT tests had a nearly identical multiple R of .59.

Boldt (1969) attempted to identify the level of English proficiency at which the Spanish-language tests were more accurate predictors of grades than the English-language tests. He classified students according to the number of questionnaire responses answered in English versus Spanish and found that language preference moderated the degree to which English-language tests should be weighted more than the Spanish-language tests. However, the differences in regressions were quite subtle.

Bornheimer (1984) looked at zero-order correlations between test scores and grades in graduate education and found that English-language verbal tests were clearly superior to a verbal aptitude test administered in Spanish for predicting performance in an English-language environment. The correlations between grades and GRE-V ($r = .39$) and the English subtest of the PAEG ($r = .54$) far exceeded the correlation between grades and the PAEG-V ($r = .26$). Quantitative tests in either language had low correlations with grades ($r = .17$ to .18).

The limited evidence available thus far suggests that at very low levels of English proficiency, language skills are the best predictor of grades in an English-language environment where fields of study are not heavily quantitative. At moderate levels of proficiency, the Spanish-language tests are useful predictors, but they are not necessarily more highly correlated with grades than are tests in English such as the SAT and the GRE.

The majority of these studies suggest that Spanish-language quantitative aptitude tests can indeed predict academic performance in an English-language environment at least as well as aptitude tests in English. However, there are no well-established guidelines (outside of Puerto Rico) on which to base admissions criteria for these Spanish-language tests. Although Angoff and Cook (1991) tried to establish a conversion in scales between the PAA and the SAT, this predicted correspondence rests on the adequacy of translations and needs further study. No efforts along these lines have been carried out with the PAEG. Thus, the only alternative at this time is for universities to examine the regression of college or graduate school grades on Spanish-language tests individually at each institution.

Because these studies have shown nearly equal results for Spanish versus English tests, they could also be taken to support the use of the SAT and GRE. However, investigators did not contrast the regression of grades on these tests with regressions based on native speakers of English at U.S. institutions. Therefore, at this point, it is not clear if selective admissions test scores give essentially equal predictions for Spanish-dominant students and non-Hispanic White students.

Research on foreign students suggests that intercept differences may be large and that the regression for Spanish-dominant students would differ substantially from that of native speakers of English. Specifically, the pattern of means for grades and test scores suggest that verbal tests such as the SAT-V and GRE-V typically underpredict substantially the academic performance of foreign students. For example, in studies by Shay (1975) and Wilson (1986), foreign students had mean 1st year grades that were comparable with those of nonforeign students despite having significantly lower GRE-V scores. However, it appears from these investigations that the underprediction by the GRE-Q is much less marked.

Studies are needed to see if underprediction of academic achievement occurs for Spanish-dominant students as compared with non-Hispanic White students with the same SAT or GRE scores. If underprediction occurs, each institution would have to set admissions criteria for Spanish-dominant students based on a regression separate from that for native speakers. The aforementioned studies on foreign students suggest that the determination of criteria for admissions purposes and the interpretation of scores on the SAT and GRE for Spanish-dominant samples could deviate substantially from the use of these tests with native speakers of English. Those studies suggest that students with very low verbal test scores in English may perform adequately in college or graduate school, particularly if they major in quantitative or technical fields.

Prediction of Academic Achievement and Proficiency in Spanish

Pennock-Román (1990) examined the relationship between academic achievement and proficiency in Spanish, which in her sample was only very weakly related to English proficiency. One reason for this procedure was to examine whether Spanish-language measures were assessing additional dimensions of aptitude not reflected in English-language aptitude tests such as the SAT. Another reason was to explore whether the relationship between SAT scores and academic achievement varied according to family language background.

The analyses examined whether Spanish proficiency acted as a main effect in the regression of grades on aptitude tests and other predictors. Proficiency was measured both by a reading comprehension test in Spanish (available at four universities) and by self-reported ratings of Spanish proficiency (available for most cases at five universities). There was agreement between the self-reported and objective measures of proficiency within each of the four universities where the objective test was given. On the other hand, the results varied across the five universities that had enough cases with data on Spanish proficiency. At two institutions, the more highly proficient students did have higher grades than less proficient students, other things being equal. However, at two others, the results were in the opposite direction, and at the fifth institution, there was no difference according to Spanish proficiency. This pattern did not consistently support the view that Spanish measures would reflect additional relevant aptitudes for college work.

A variety of explanations were suggested for the pattern of results, including campus variability in the numbers of Spanish speakers who took remedial courses or who chose to major in Spanish. Pennock-Román also proposed that the two universities where Spanish-proficient students performed better than predicted may have been more supportive environments for Spanish-speaking students. She noted that these schools had larger proportions of Hispanic students or were located close to a city where there were many Hispanic students at other nearby universities. Thus, Pennock-Román favored the view that the variations of geographical location and the proportional representation of Hispanic students on campus may have been related to the schools' climate in terms of acceptance of culturally different students. However, specific information on course taking, majors, and students' perceptions about the college environment were not available to verify these possibilities.

Quality of Educational Background and Prediction of Academic Achievement

Although the relationships of school and family background with test performance are well known, few researchers have considered the interplay among these variables as they affect academic achievement in college. The influence of background on college preparation would be reflected in test scores, so that the scores may capture most of the information about student background that is relevant to predicting college achievement. On the other hand, background variables may influence academic achievement independently of test scores if they are related to dimensions of college readiness not reflected in multiple-choice aptitude test scores.

Pennock-Román (1990) included the type of high school program (whether academic or general), the number of academic high school courses in humanities, the number of academic courses in mathematics and science, and the father's level of education in the regression of college grades on test scores and other predictors. She found a small but significant improvement in R^2 at the majority of institutions, as compared with regression models without these background variables as predictors.

The regression weights for these predictors were not always in the direction one would expect. For example, the number of mathematics and science courses in high school was negatively related to college grades when other variables were controlled. It is possible that this effect is an artifact of different grading standards across fields of study. That is, students with many courses in these fields may have received lower grades because they were more likely to choose scientific areas of study.

The most important effect, however, was the reduction of Hispanic and non-Hispanic White differences in regressions. At the three universities where Hispanic students tended to be overpredicted by the equation for non-Hispanic White students, all but a trivial amount of overprediction was eliminated when the background variables were added. Although these background variables are important in understanding differences in regression equations between Hispanic and non-Hispanic students, the effects were too small for practical use in college admissions.

Test Speededness, Test Expertise, and Prediction of Academic Achievement

On the one hand, one could argue that student test-taking speed and test sophistication could be a source of error variance in dealing with multiple-choice tests, an artifact not related to later college achievement. On the other hand, test-taking speed and test sophistication may actually be components that improve predictive validity. In special circumstances, such as law school or air traffic control training, speed on reading and perceptual tasks may be an asset for handling the high volume of reading and perceptual demands placed on students. In those cases, speed is a legitimate source of variance in test scores that would increase the predictive validity of the test. Furthermore, speed in executing tasks may also be a valid component of test scores if it reflects how well integrated and accessible knowledge is for students in a given content domain. Test sophistication can also be a predictively valid component of test scores if it reflects how savvy a student is at finding shortcuts to real-life problems and identifying a teacher's priorities in grading tests and papers.

Not much research examining the relationship between speededness and the criteria against which tests are typically evaluated with Hispanic and other linguistic minority students has been done. One exception is a study by Wilson (1990) who looked at the predictive validity of less speeded and more speeded sections of a regular administration of the GRE-V, using 1976 data. He created two scores from one section of the GRE-V: the sum of first half of the reading section items and the sum of the second half of the items. Naturally, the first half was assumed to be less speeded than the second half (although both sections could be said to be speeded if students limit their time per item equally for both parts of the test). Wilson grouped individuals in the sample in a variety of ways and correlated the two scores with self-reported grades within groups.

The results varied across groups, but they supported the view that speed is a source of irrelevant error variance for Hispanic students and linguistic minorities. However, all of the differences in correlation coefficients between grades and the less speeded versus the more speeded sections were small (about .01 to .04). Wilson found that the less speeded section was more valid for foreign students, U.S. citizens who indicated that English was not their preferred language, and Hispanic students (differences of .03 to .04). In contrast, the speeded section was relatively more valid (differences of .01 to .02) for other groups.

Because both half tests were administered together under the same total time limit, any variation between sections obtained by Wilson should be considered a lower bound estimate of the differences one would find in tests that had more sharply contrasted time limits and that were separately timed. The evidence from this exploratory study suggests that speed may be a valid component for some groups, but a source of error for Hispanic and bilingual examinees. Wilson recommended having two reading comprehension scores, one to reflect speed and level and the other to reflect level without speed. The relative validity of the two types of components for bilingual examinees deserves further investigation.

Research on test preparation by Maspons and Llabre (1985) supported the view that test sophistication is a source of error variance for Hispanic examinees. Students at a community college were divided into control and experimental groups before taking a placement examination. The experimental group received a 30-minute training session that included a practice test, and the control group received a college orientation session. Subsequent grades in courses for which subjects later enrolled correlated much more highly with test scores for the trained groups ($r = .66, .67$; $n = 32, 44$) than for the control groups ($r = .13$, $.39$; $n = 42, 42$). Thus, predictive validity was enhanced for students receiving instruction in test preparation.

These few studies suggest that speededness and test sophistication may influence the test performance of Hispanic students, but more research needs to be done that takes into account the level of acculturation and language background of examinees.

Summary of Findings

The Relationships of Test Scores to Background Variables and Test Characteristics

The evidence thus far has demonstrated that many factors—language background, quality of educational experience, parental education, and ease in dealing with speeded tests—are reflected in the test performance of Hispanic students and linguistic minorities. Most of the studies on foreign nationals and on educationally disadvantaged students have come to similar conclusions.

Despite the higher English proficiency of Hispanic samples as compared with foreign nationals of different countries, there are many parallel findings in the two groups concerning linguistic variables that affect test performance. Limited skills in English are associated with lower verbal scores and longer completion times for timed tests, but the language handicap is much smaller for quantitative tests and some achievement tests. The degree to which an aptitude test reflects talent in bilingual examinees varies according to the examinee's proficiency in the language of the test, the degree of difficulty of verbal content of the test, and the specificity of the test vocabulary to a subject domain familiar to examinees. As proficiency in the language of the test increases, the extent to which abilities are reflected by the test increases, and scores rise. Clearly, tests (in English or the second language) are less pure measures of cognitive skills for language minority students than they are for monolingual English-speaking students.

Although it is plain that test scores underestimate cognitive abilities for bilinguals with low levels of English proficiency, estimation of the size of the systematic error at different levels of proficiency has not been attempted. Use of Angoff and Cook's (1991) conversion between SAT and PAA scores could prove useful for this purpose with Spanish-dominant students.

Investigations of group differences in test-item performance has also revealed consistent patterns across linguistic minorities and Hispanic groups. In responding to English vocabulary test items, knowledge of a language related to Latin (such as Spanish) is sometimes an advantage and sometimes a disadvantage, depending on whether the word is a homograph, a true cognate, or a false cognate.

Prediction of College Achievement, Background Variables, and Test Characteristics

Research on the relationship between college achievement and some variables that influence test performance other than "pure" cognitive abilities indicates that some of the variables are valid components of scores in the predictive sense. English proficiency is moderately related to college achievement, although the strength of the relationship declines at the upper levels of proficiency. Quality of educational background and parental education, also reflected in test scores, adds relatively little to the prediction of college achievement when added to test scores. These results suggest that lower test scores associated with disadvantaged educational background validly reflect less adequate preparation for college.

On the other hand, there is evidence that test scores of foreign nationals should be interpreted differently from the scores of native speakers of English. In quantitative fields, the academic potential of students with low levels of English proficiency is substantially underestimated by verbal tests. Furthermore, taking into account both verbal aptitude and English proficiency improves prediction; the relative weighting of these variables depends on the level of proficiency of the student.

The relationship among Spanish proficiency, test performance, and academic achievement have been less well studied, and results so far are inconclusive.

Relatively few studies have examined the effects of test speededness and examinees' test sophistication on test performance and academic achievement. The limited evidence suggests that speededness and test sophistication are minor sources of invalidity for linguistic minorities and Hispanic students. That is, less speeded tests were slightly more highly correlated with undergraduate grades for nonnative speakers of English and Hispanic examinees. Furthermore, training in test taking improved the ability of tests to predict college grades in specific subjects.

Differences between Hispanic and non-Hispanic White groups in accuracy of predicting college achievement using aptitude tests are subtle, usually not statistically significant, and associated with restricted variance in college grades. However, at the graduate level, there is evidence that achievement tests in specific subject areas have higher predictive validity for all groups. Because these tests are less influenced by language proficiency, the results suggest that admissions committees should place greater reliance on such tests than on general aptitude tests, at least at the graduate level.

The use of aptitude tests administered in Spanish is another promising alternative to the exclusive use of English-language aptitude tests in the prediction of academic achievement for Spanish-dominant students. Quantitative tests in Spanish have typically predicted college or graduate grades in an English environment about as well as the English-language tests. Their use may be perceived by students as more fair. The evidence suggests, however, that a measure of proficiency in English is also necessary to achieve the best prediction of grades. Some studies showed that the best pair of predictors was a verbal test in English and the quantitative test in Spanish.

Conclusion

Major research findings on selective admissions tests in higher education for Hispanic students and other linguistic minorities have been summarized after classifying studies according to the variables studied, the English proficiency of the sample, and the analysis of scores at the level of the item or total score.

Two kinds of score interpretation are considered. The first is the type of inference that lay persons, many educators, and psychologists outside the field of psychometrics emphasize in the evaluation of scores. That is, it is the degree to which scores reflect cognitive abilities, uncontaminated by other variables such as education and language background. The second type reflects the pragmatic concerns of measurement specialists who evaluate how well scores on tests designed for college admissions predict future achievement.

The evidence supports the view that some types of inferences are more valid than others across varying levels of examinee proficiency in the language of the test (usually English). The adequacy and interpretation of scores can vary depending on which purpose we consider—the measurement of level of cognitive skills or the prediction of academic achievement in the short term.

In general, we are on fairly safe ground when making inferences about short-term predictions of academic performance (at U.S. institutions) for students at moderate to high levels of English proficiency. Pennock-Román's (1990) and Wilson's (1985) findings suggested that for bilinguals with moderate to high levels of English proficiency, aptitude tests predict about as well as they do for native speakers and that there is little difference in prediction accuracy according to level of English proficiency.

However, the interpretation of scores for making other types of inferences (e.g., talent identification and level of cognitive abilities in general) is troublesome for all test takers, but especially for bilingual ones, particularly when English is their weaker language.

The interpretation of scores as measures of cognitive skills for students who lack essential coursework or experience in test taking is also problematic. Research suggests that differences in mean test scores between Hispanic and non-Hispanic students reflect variations in the quality and quantity of courses taken, especially in mathematics.

The linguistic and educational diversity of Hispanic students forces to the surface the relevance of the verbal, educational, and speed demands of situations and contexts in which the criterion is measured. In other words, criterion variables are themselves reflections of several underlying constructs corresponding to the aforementioned demands. These considerations suggest that a more theoretical framework needs to be developed that examines the match between the constructs measured in the test and the variables of relevance to the targeted behavior. Such a framework would transcend research on Hispanic samples because it would provide a clearer theoretical basis for score interpretation and the evaluation of validity for students in general.

References

Alderman, D. L. (1982). Language proficiency as a moderator variable in testing academic aptitude. *Journal of Educational Psychology, 74,* 580–587.

Alderman, D. L., & Holland, P. W. (1981). *Item performance across native language groups on the Test of English as a Foreign Language* (TOEFL Research Rep. No. 9). Princeton, NJ: Educational Testing Service.

American College Testing Program (1989). *Preliminary technical manual for the enhanced ACT assessment.* Iowa City, IA: Author.

Anastasi, A. (1984). Aptitude and achievement tests: The curious case of the indestructible strawperson. In B. S. Plake (Ed.), *Social and technical issues in testing: Implications for test construction and usage* (pp. 129–140). Hillsdale, NJ: Erlbaum.

Angelis, P. J., Swinton, S. S., & Cowell, W. R. (1979). *The performance of non-native speakers of English on TOEFL and verbal aptitude tests* (TOEFL Research Rep. No. 3, ETS Research Rep. RR-79-7). Princeton, NJ: Educational Testing Service.

Angoff, W. H., & Cook, L. L. (1991). Equating the scores of the College Board Prueba de Aptitud Académica and the College Board Scholastic Aptitude Test. In G. Keller, J. Deneen, & R. Magallán (Eds.), *Assessment and access: Hispanics in higher education* (pp. 133–166). New York: SUNY Press.

Angoff, W. H., & Johnson, E. G. (1988). *A study of the differential impact of curriculum on aptitude test scores* (ETS Research Rep. No. RR-88-46). Princeton, NJ: Educational Testing Service.

Angoff, W. H., & Sharon, A. T. (1971). A comparison of scores earned on the Test of English as a Foreign Language by native American students and foreign applicants to U.S. colleges. *TESOL Quarterly, 5,* 129–136.

Arbeiter, S. (1984). *Profiles, college-bound seniors, 1984.* New York: College Entrance Examination Board.

Ayers, J. B., & Peters, R. M. (1977). Predictive validity of the Test of English as a Foreign Language for Asian graduate students in engineering, chemistry, or mathematics. *Educational and Psychological Measurement, 37,* 461–463.

Benson, J., Urman, H., & Hocevar, D. (1986). Effects of testwiseness training and ethnicity on achievement of third and fifth-grade children. *Measurement and Evaluation in Counseling and Development, 18,* 154–162.

Boldt, R. F. (1969). *Concurrent validity of the PAA and SAT for bilingual Dade County High School volunteers* (College Entrance Examination Board Research and Development Rep. RDR-68-9, No. 3, Statistical Rep. SR-69-31). Princeton, NJ: Educational Testing Service.

Bormuth, J. R. (1967). Comparable cloze and multiple-choice comprehension test scores. *Journal of Reading, 10,* 291–297.

Bormuth, J. R. (1968). Cloze test readability: Criterion scores. *Journal of Educational Measurement, 5,* 189–196.

Bornheimer, D. G. (1984). Predicting success in graduate school using GRE and PAEG aptitude test scores. *College and University, Fall,* 54–62.

Breland, H. M., Stocking, M., Pinchak, B. M., & Abrams, N. (1974). *The cross-cultural stability of mental test items: An investigation of response patterns for ten sociocultural groups* (ETS Project Rep. 74-2). Princeton, NJ: Educational Testing Service.

Carlson, A. B. (1967). *Further results on the validity of the Prueba de Aptitud Académica in United States Colleges and Universities* (Statistical Rep. SR-67-67). Princeton, NJ: Educational Testing Service.

Chambers, G. A. (1988). *All of America's children: Variants in ACT Test Scores—What principals need to know.* Paper presented at the convention of the NASSP, Anaheim, California.

Chen, A., & Henning, G. (1985). Linguistic and cultural bias in language proficiency tests. *Language Testing, 2,* 155–163.

Clark, J. L. D. (1977). *The performance of native speakers of English on the Test of English as a Second Language* (TOEFL Research Rep. No. 1). Princeton, NJ: Educational Testing Service.

College Entrance Examination Board. (1982). *Profiles of College Bound Seniors, 1981.* New York: Author.

Dornic, S. (1980). Information processing and language dominance. *International Review of Applied Psychology, 29,* 119–140.

Dreisbach, M., & Keogh, B. K. (1982). Testwiseness as a factor in readiness test performance of young Mexican-American children. *Journal of Educational Psychology, 74,* 224–229.

Durán, R. P. (1983). *Hispanics' education and background: Predictors of college achievement.* New York: College Entrance Examination Board.

Durán, R. P., Enright, M. K., & Rock, D. A. (1985). *Language factors and Hispanic freshmen's student profile* (College Board Rep. No. 85-3). New York: College Entrance Examination Board.

Educational Testing Service. (1988). *Examinee and score trends for the GRE general test: 1977-78, 1982-83, 1986-87, and 1987-88. GRE general test data summary report for 1987-88, Vol. 1* (Report No. 297986). Princeton, NJ: Educational Testing Service.

Educational Testing Service. (1988). *Guide to the Prueba de Admisión para Estudios Graduados, 1988–89.* Princeton, NJ: Author.

Elliott, R., & Strenta, A. C. (1988). Effects of improving the reliability of the GPA on prediction generally and on comparative predictions for gender and race particularly. *Journal of Educational Measurement, 25,* 33–347.

Gage, N. L. (1991). The obviousness of social and educational research results. *Educational Researcher, 20,* 10–16.

Gannon, F. B., Oppenheim, D., & Wohlhueter, J. F. (1966). *A validity study of a Spanish language scholastic aptitude test in United States colleges and universities* (Statistical Rep. SR-66-2). Princeton, NJ: Educational Testing Service.

Goldsmith, R. P. (1979). *The effect of training in test-taking skills and test anxiety management on Mexican American students' aptitude test performance.* Unpublished doctoral dissertation, University of Texas at Austin.

Hale, G. A., Stansfield, C. W., & Durán, R. P. (1984). Summaries of studies involving the Test of English as a Foreign Language (TOEFL Research Rep. No. 16). Princeton, NJ: Educational Testing Service.

Hale, G. A., Stansfield, C. W., Rock, D. A., Hicks, M. M., Butler, F. B., & Oller, J. W. (1988). *Multiple-choice cloze items and the Test of English as a Foreign Language* (TOEFL Research Rep. No. 26, ETS Research Rep. RR-88-2). Princeton, NJ: Educational Testing Service.

Knapp, R. R. (1960). The effects of time limits on the intelligence test performance of Mexican and American subjects. *Journal of Educational Psychology, 51,* 14–20.

Laing, J., Engen, H. B., & Maxey, J. (1987). *Relationships between ACT Test Scores and High School Courses* (ACT Research Rep. Series 87-3). Iowa City, IA: American College Testing Program.

Laosa, L. M. (1973). Cross-cultural and subcultural research in psychology and education. *Interamerican Journal of Psychology, 7,* 3–4.

Llabre, M. M. (1991). Time as a factor in the cognitive test performance of Latino college students. In J. Deneen, G. Keller, & R. Magallán, (Eds.), *Assessment and access: Hispanics in higher education* (pp. 95–104). New York. SUNY Press.

Llabre, M. M., & Froman, T. W. (1987). Allocation of time to test items: A study of ethnic differences. *Journal of Experimental Education, 55,* 137–140.

Llabre, M. M., & Froman, T. W. (1988). *Allocation of time and item performance in Hispanic and Anglo examinees* (Final report). Institute for Student Assessment and Evaluation, University of Florida.

Loyd, B. H. (1982, March). *Analysis of content-related bias for Anglo and Hispanic students.* Paper presented at the annual meeting of the American Educational Research Association, New York.

Maspons, M. M., & Llabre, M. M. (1985). The influence of training Hispanics in test taking on the psychometric properties of a test. *Journal for Research in Mathematics Education, 16,* 177–183.

Maxey, J., & Sawyer, R. (1981). *Predictive validity of the ACT Assessment for Afro-American/Black, Mexican-American/Chicano, and Caucasian American/White Students* (ACT Research Bulletin, 81-1). Iowa City, IA: American College Testing Program.

Oakland, T. (1972). The effects of test-wiseness materials on standardized test performance of preschool disadvantaged children. *Journal of School Psychology, 10,* 355–360.

Pennock-Román, M. (1988). *The status of research on selective admissions tests and Hispanic students in postsecondary education* (Research Rep. RR-88-36). Princeton, NJ: Educational Testing Service.

Pennock-Román, M. (1990). *Test validity and language background: A study of Hispanic American students at six universities.* New York: College Entrance Examinations Board.

Powers, D. E. (1977). Comparing predictions of law school performance for Black, Chicano, and White law students. Report LSAC 77-3. In Law School Admission Council's (Eds.), *Reports of*

LSAC sponsored research: Vol. III, 1975–1977 (pp. 721–776). Princeton, NJ: Law School Admission Council.

Powers, D. E. (1980). *The relationship between scores on the Graduate Management Admission Test and the Test of English as a Foreign Language* (TOEFL Research Rep. No. 5, ETS Research Rep. RR-80-31). Princeton, NJ: Educational Testing Service.

Ramist, L., & Arbeiter, S. (1982). *Profiles of college-bound seniors, 1982.* New York: College Entrance Examination Board.

Ramist, L., & Arbeiter, S. (1984). *Profiles of college-bound seniors, 1983.* New York: College Entrance Examination Board.

Ramist, L., & Arbeiter, S. (1986). *Profiles of college-bound seniors, 1986.* New York: College Entrance Examination Board.

Rincón, E. T. (1979). *Test speededness, test anxiety, and test performance: A comparison of Mexican-American and Anglo-American high school juniors.* Unpublished doctoral dissertation, University of Texas at Austin.

Rivera, C., & Schmitt, A. (1988). *A comparison of Hispanic and White students' omit patterns on the Scholastic Aptitude Test* (ETS Research Rep. RR-88-44). Princeton, NJ: Educational Testing Service.

Schmitt, A. P. (1988). Language and cultural characteristics that explain differential item functioning for Hispanic examinees on the Scholastic Aptitude Test. *Journal of Educational Measurement, 25,* 1–13.

Schmitt, A. P., & Dorans, N. J. (1990). Differential item functioning for minority examinees on the SAT. *Journal of Educational Measurement, 27,* 67–81.

Schoenfeldt, L. F. (1984). The status of test validation research. In B. S. Plake (Ed.), *Social and technical issues in testing: Implications for test construction and usage* (pp. 61–86). Hillsdale, NJ: Erlbaum.

Schrader, W. B., & Pitcher, B. (1970). *Interpreting performance of foreign law students on the Law School Admission Test and the Test of English as a Foreign Language* (Statistical Rep. No. 70-25). Princeton, NJ: Educational Testing Service.

Sharon, A. T. (1972). English proficiency, verbal aptitutde, and foreign student success in American graduate schools. *Educational and Psychological Measurement, 32,* 425–431.

Shay, H. R. (1975). Affect [sic] of foreign students' language proficiency on academic performance. *Dissertation Abstracts International, 36,* 1983A–1984A. (University Microfilms No. 75–21, 931).

Smith, H. R. (1986). *A summary of data collected from Graduate Record Examinations test takers during 1984–85* (Data Summary Rep. No. 10). Princeton, NJ: Educational Testing Service.

Sternberg, R. J. (1984). What cognitive psychology can (and cannot) do for test development. In B. S. Plake (Ed.), *Social and technical issues in testing: Implications for test construction and usage* (pp. 39–60). Hillsdale, NJ: Erlbaum.

Stolzenberg, R. M., & Relles, D. (1991). Foreign student academic performance in U.S. graduate schools: Insights from American MBA programs. *Social Science Research, 20,* 74–92.

Strenta, A. C., & Elliott, R. (1987). Differential grading standards revisited. *Journal of Educational Measurement, 24,* 281–291.

Wightman, L. F., & Muller, D. C. (1990). *An analysis of differential validity and differential prediction for Black, Mexican American, Hispanic, and White law school students* (Law School Admission Council Research Rep. 90-03). Newtown, PA: Law School Admission Services.

Wilson, K. M. (1979). *The validation of GRE scores as predictors of first-year performance in graduate study: Report of the GRE cooperative validity studies project* (GRE Board Research Rep. GREB No. 75-8R). Princeton, NJ: Educational Testing Service.

Wilson, K. M. (1982). *GMAT and GRE aptitude test performance in relation to primary language and scores on TOEFL* (TOEFL Research Rep. No. 12). Princeton, NJ: Educational Testing Service.

Wilson, K. M. (1985). *Factors affecting GMAT predictive validity for foreign MBA students: An exploratory study* (ETS Research Rep. RR-85-17). Princeton, NJ: Educational Testing Service.

Wilson, K. M. (1986). *The relationship of GRE General Test scores to first-year grades for foreign graduate students: Report of a cooperative study* (GRE Board Professional Rep. GREB No. 82-11P, ETS Research Rep. 86-44). Princeton, NJ: Educational Testing Service.

Wilson, K. M. (1987). *The GRE Subject Test performance of U.S. and non-U.S. examinees, 1982–84: A comparative analysis* (GRE Board Report No. 83 20P, ETS Research Rep. No. 87 4). Princeton, NJ: Educational Testing Service.

Wilson, K. M. (1990). *Population differences in speed versus level of GRE reading comprehension: An exploratory study* (GRE Report No. 84-09). Princeton, NJ: Educational Testing Service.

Wright, T. (1984). *The effects of increased time limits on a college level achievement test* (Research Rep. No. 84-12). Miami, FL: Miami-Dade Community College.

Younkin, W. (1986). *Speededness as a source of test bias on the College Level Academic Skills Test.* Unpublished doctoral dissertation, University of Miami.

CHAPTER 9

Clinical Assessment of Instructional Performance in Cooperative Learning

Richard P. Durán

Testing and assessment play a prominent role in the current educational reform movement, but the contributions that they make to educational outcomes are indirect at best. Research on the educational performance of Hispanic and other underserved ethnic minority students suggests that existing standardized achievement and aptitude tests are likely to have limited effectiveness in guiding the actual delivery of improved instruction to students. This claim has two bases.

Users of existing standardized tests presume an underlying static model of cognition and learning that is not well suited to improving the actual process of instruction of subject matter and skills that are targets of existing assessments. Tests are intended to assess what students know and not how they can learn

Research was sponsored by the Center for Research on Effective Schooling for Disadvantaged Students, Johns Hopkins University.

what they don't fully know. This problem is further compounded by sociolinguistic and ethnographic research findings that the classroom learning behavior of language-minority students is mediated by students' cultural, social, and linguistic background. The results of existing standardized tests do not help us to understand whether instructional practices intended to teach target subject matter and thinking skills are compatible with students' cultural and social perceptions.

Alternative assessment methods are needed to help teachers analyze language-minority student's interaction and concomitant learning behavior in classroom instruction. Instruction is inherently a social communication process as well as a cognitive process. For this reason, new forms of assessment that evaluate instruction as a process may not be altogether individualized assessments. An individual student's ability to learn in interactive settings is a function of the student's own previous learning, but it is also influenced by interaction with the teacher and other students. Accordingly, new clinical assessment methods of learning as a process should be sensitive to the ways in which language-minority students use their communicative competence in classrooms given their cultural, social, and linguistic backgrounds.

In this chapter, as an alternative to the exclusive use of standardized tests, I will discuss a way in which to begin the design of a clinical assessment of students' instructional interaction that permits in situo assessment of students' ability to teach and learn reading-comprehension skills within a cooperative learning curriculum. The curriculum I am studying is known as Cooperative Integrated Reading and Composition (CIRC; Stevens, Madden, Slavin, & Farnish, 1987). The assessment method I am proposing focuses on identifying interactional strategies used by students during instruction and analyses of how these strategies might affect acquisition and mastery of target content materials and skills. I chose a question-asking and -answering activity within the CIRC curriculum for assessment because it has specific learning objectives and because it depends on students' intercommunication and their active monitoring of problem-solving behavior. A further advantage of developing an instructional assessment method for cooperative learning activities such as CIRC is that such activities can permit students to take more active control of their own learning than would typically occur in whole-group instruction. Thus, in theory, it should be possible to devise assessments that address the metacognitive learning skills possessed by or being acquired by students. If this goal is attainable, we could assess how students learn to learn as well as how they converge on solutions to instructional problems.

The assessment approach I propose is exploratory and draws on cognitive-science accounts of situated cognition and activity theory and on Vygotskian-based notions of teaching and learning. By exploratory, I mean that the approach can only be partially sketched out at present and partially supported by example analyses of students' interactions. Many conceptual and measurement problems would need to be resolved before the method could be used in practice. Nevertheless, the assessment approach is substantiated by accumulating research on learning as the active construction of knowledge by learners.

The theoretical perspective underlying the assessment approach assumes that classrooms are organized into activities that mirror those in everyday life and culture. Students and teachers are presumed to share relatively compatible perceptions about how to behave and interact while engaging in classroom activities. It is also assumed that social interaction in the classroom serves as the foundation for learning and eventual internalization of cognitive skills. From a neo-Vygotskian view of learning, it is hypothesized that knowledge is first shared via communication among individuals and that this knowledge gradually becomes internalized within each individual. The main goal of the clinical assessment approach described here is to interpret the occurrence of specific kinds of teaching and learning strategies evident in the discourse of students as they attempt to acquire new knowledge through instruction. This information could help teachers and school staff understand how students respond to everyday instruction of target subject matter and cognitive skills. The information could also help teachers in adjusting instructional practices so that students would progress more quickly and systematically toward learning objectives. Most important, this information could be used to help students improve control of their own learning.

The goal of devising a procedure to assess instructional interaction of language-minority students clinically can be better understood by seeing how it contrasts with existing attempts to improve tests in light of the current education reform movement. This discussion is followed by citations of specific research on cognition, learning, and sociolinguistics in the classroom that are stimulating the development of the current assessment approach.

Testing and Educational Reform

Since the release of a *Nation at Risk* (National Commission on Excellence in Education, 1983), much of the burden for the improvement of schooling has been placed on improvements that might be made in testing as a means of increasing accountability for educational practices. Over the past decade, there has been a rise in state-level, student-achievement testing programs and in teacher-aptitude and competency-testing programs (National Commission on Testing and Public Policy, 1990). The reform movement's emphasis on testing appears grounded in the belief that student achievement and teacher effectiveness need to be measured against well-conceived and well-articulated standards of knowledge and desirable teaching practices. This reconceptualization of educational standards has led to suggestions on how to improve existing standardized multiple-choice testing practices based on refined descriptions of school curricula, but it has also given rise to the exploratory development of alternative forms of assessment that go under the rubric "authentic assessment" or "performance-based assessment" (e.g., Linn & Dunbar, 1990).

The movement to create authentic assessment has been greatly influenced during the past decade by concern for improving the higher order thinking skills of students. Attention has been called to the limitations of basic-skills-oriented instruction emphasizing the mastery of lower level mathematics and language-arts skills. The assumption that mastery of lower level skills is a prerequisite for mastery of higher level skills is no longer universally accepted. Instead, it is believed by many educators that students need intensive exposure to complex learning tasks requiring more active reasoning and integration of skills early on in their schooling. The upshot of this concern has not been as evident in instruction as it has been in testing. State-level and national-level testing programs have begun to explore the creation and use of new materials that do not rely on traditional single-answer, multiple-choice test questions and that require more active problem solving and construction of answers.

The efforts underway to reform testing have included exploring a large range of possible item types and response formats, such as item types that involve passage-length stimuli, open-ended problem scenarios, and response formats that involve multiple acceptable-answer possibilities. Alternatives to single-answer, multiple-choice responses have included, for example, essay responses, construction of learning products and portfolios, and performance of complex behaviors in authentic or simulated real world contexts. It is not possible to discuss these new developments in depth in this chapter. Although these new methods of assessment represent a significant improvement in conceptualizing learning competence, they have yet to broach the gap between test performance and the actual conduct of instruction. They share this limitation with existing standardized, multiple-choice testing methods.

Test items and response formats may be improved under authentic assessment, but the design of these and traditional assessments is not tied theoretically to an understanding of how to help students learn from their performance on test items. The act of testing is viewed as separate from the act of teaching the skills that are assessed. Recent theoretical work in cognitive science and test theory questions the value of this separation and points to the possibility of directly connecting assessment with instruction (Frederiksen & Collins, 1989; Lidz, 1987; Mislevy, in press). This new approach proposes that we go beyond whether a student picks a correct answer to a test-item question. When students answer test items incorrectly, their incorrect answers and reasons for making them are likely to contain valuable information for teaching students those skills under assessment. This position, however, has an important caveat. Diagnostic information can be useful for instruction only if testers and teachers have available an underlying model or theory about how content and skills are acquired and then revealed by students' test performance. Using such a model permits the identification of the extent of progress that students are making in acquiring the content or skills in question and also permits the development of a training regime that further advances the progress of individual students. The training provided to students can be combined directly with testing as part of a dynamic assessment (Durán, 1989; Lidz, 1987).

Situated Cognition and Activity Theory

Theoretical research in cognitive science on situated cognition bolsters an argument for creating tests and assessments that are directly connected to instruction. As mentioned earlier, it is proposed that learning is inherently a constructive activity on the part of students and that it is possible for an external observer to infer clinically the interactional strategies that students use as they construct their own learning.

Although there is no single theory of situated cognition, proponents of this view hold that cognitive theories of higher order learning and mental functioning need to be based on everyday (and sometimes not-so-everyday) cultural perceptions of behavioral activity settings and their demands on the individual (Brown, Collins, & Duguid, 1989). From this perspective, learning and thinking are always grounded in the here-and-now perception of a behavioral setting by individuals and on individuals' social negotiation of mutually expected behaviors. Classroom settings are no exception.

Some cognitive researchers have analyzed classrooms in terms of scripts guiding the behavior of students and teachers in various activities (e.g., Fivush, 1982). When students and teachers are engaged in classroom learning, they participate in activities that have a shared cultural and mental meaning that has been constructed and mutually negotiated over the history of the classroom. Each participant in a classroom learning activity anticipates playing a role or range of roles as a learning activity proceeds, and each role is tied to rights and obligations for behavior that others expect or come to expect. As the sociolinguist Erickson (1982) noted, there are different ways to analyze students' perceptions of a classroom learning activity. An academic learning activity can be viewed in terms of its participation structures or socially shared norms for communication in the activity in question. For example, a reading lesson may require students to discuss and answer questions based on a story that they have read. The participation structure of students' interaction while discussing questions and answers represents students' shared and negotiated knowledge about how to talk to each other for the purpose of analyzing and answering questions. In addition, learning activities may also be viewed in terms of their organization of cognitive-learning goals for the participants. On the other hand, the cognitive structure of a learning activity represents the understanding that students have about how to evaluate progress and how to accomplish a learning task. For example, in the case of story-question answering, the cognitive goals might include the ability to understand the requirements of a good answer and to know how to find information in a text to support an answer.

The importance of analyzing how participation structures and perception of cognitive goals affect the instructional behavior of language-minority students has been documented repeatedly in classroom ethnography and sociolinguistic studies of classroom behavior (e.g., Cazden, 1988; Green & Wallat, 1981; Philips, 1983). Research on Hawaiian children enrolled in the Kamehameha Early Education Program (KEEP) is especially relevant to the present chapter because it involved analyzing the communication patterns of students working in collaborative learning groups during reading-comprehension and language-arts instruction. KEEP researchers investigated specific discourse strategies that elementary school children used in exploring the topic of story texts and the answers to story questions arising in small group instruction (Au et al., 1986). Observation of the children discussing a story showed that they relied on a participation structure known as "talk story" that was followed by adult Hawaiian community members when they told stories to each other. In discussing a story, students often interrupted each other and the teacher to add new and valuable insights, similar to the way adult community members participate in story telling interactions. Children found it natural to use Creole Hawaiian English as they discussed a story, and teachers found that this stimulated rather than inhibited students' discussion of a story.

Ethnographic observation of KEEP children's behavior across a wide range of reading-curriculum activities proved insightful. Careful analyses of the children's interaction in a variety of reading-lesson activities reveal a number of general strategies that appear to guide students' joint accomplishment of problem-solving tasks in the classroom. Jordan (1980) found that KEEP students used the following strategies: a) seeking and giving immediate feedback about small segments of performance; b) scanning for and using multiple sources of help and information; c) scanning for evidence that other children need help and information; d) volunteering to help others; e) switching between learner and teacher roles; f) using modeling and intervention as major teaching and learning devices; and g) working jointly on tasks.

Although the strategies identified by Jordan (1980) are not tightly specified, they exemplify ways in which classroom small-group instruction can manifest learning and teaching strategies that fuse social interaction with a shared cognitive analysis of task demands.

Research on the technique of "reciprocal teaching" (Palincsar & Brown, 1984) is also relevant because it involves collaborative learning in reading instruction and highlights the importance of interactional strategies in helping students to gain competencies. The reciprocal teaching method begins by having an adult reading instructor model different high-level reading strategies for a small group of students in the context of a daily reading lesson. The strategies modeled include the following: a) summarizing important ideas in a passage, b) generating informative questions that might be asked about a passage, c) clarifying passage elements when breakdowns in understanding occur, and d) predicting in advance what may occur next in a passage. As the instruction proceeds, individual students are asked to model each reading strategy for other students in the group. The adult instructor then assesses student performance using the different strategies. That is, the reading instructor immediately provides students with feedback on how well the reading strategies are carried out and includes advice on how to improve them. Students exposed to the reciprocal teaching method showed significant gains in standardized reading test scores relative to comparison-group children not exposed to the program. The results also showed that students participating in the program transferred the higher order comprehension strategies they had learned in the reading lessons to other classroom reading activities in a variety of subject-matter areas.

Padrón (1986, 1987) investigated the effectiveness of the reciprocal teaching procedure and a questioning procedure to train third-, fourth-, and fifth-grade Hispanic bilingual children in English-language reading-comprehension skills. The questioning procedure involved training students to understand how questions about ideas in a reading passage require different kinds of analyses. The results of the study showed that fourth and fifth graders receiving both forms of training earned significantly higher reading test scores than two comparison groups of students who had not received the training in comprehension skills. Third graders receiving one form of reading training also earned higher reading test scores than the comparison groups, but these differences did not attain statistical significance. Padrón (1986), in her summary of these findings, suggested that future studies should investigate the effectiveness of the two comprehension training procedures in the first (non-English) language of students.

A Neo-Vygotskian Account of Teaching and Learning

Tharp and Gallimore (1988) put forth a neo-Vygotskian model of teaching and learning that helps to identify more concisely the interactional strategies that undergird effective instruction, which may occur in KEEP, reciprocal teaching, and other learning settings. These investigators claim that effective teaching can only occur when a teacher or other more capable person actively assists a student in accomplishing a learning task that the student could not accomplish independently. Students possess a zone of proximal development for any given learning task. The zone of proximal development represents the capacity that students have for accomplishing a task independently. The wider the zone, the better able students are to accomplish a task with minimal help and cues from a more capable other or learning partner. Students with a narrow zone of proximal development for a given learning task need more help in performing a task.

The effective teacher goes beyond assuring that students get active help in extending their immediate ability to perform problem-solving tasks. They also provide assistance to learners that helps them to gradually internalize their mastery of tasks so that they can do them on their own.

Tharp and Gallimore (1988) distinguished six strategies that good teachers commonly use with students. They include the following:

- *modeling*—offering behavior for imitation;
- *contingency management*—arranging rewards or punishments depending on whether behavior is desired;
- *feeding back*—providing information on the suitability of behavior relative to a performance standard;
- *instructing*—directing a student on how to accomplish a task;
- *questioning*—asking for information activating more competent task behavior;
- *cognitive structuring*—providing explanatory and belief structures that organize and justify problem representations and solutions.

To this list we may add a seventh category representing a teacher's sharing of new information with a learner in a manner that may be distinguished from modeling behavior per se:

- *informing*—giving factual or conceptual information to a student.

The aforementioned categories of teaching strategies provide a useful framework for characterizing how teachers help students learn. These categories can also be applied to describing how students help each other in collaborative and cooperative learning. The categories are used as part of the assessment framework for instruction proposed in this chapter. They are a useful beginning point for inferring what strategies students use to help each other learn, but they need to be augmented. The seven strategies focus on forms of help that students may give to each other with and without the assistance of a teacher, but they need to be complemented by identification of strategies that students use to guide their own learning as they interact during instruction. The following learning strategies are proposed to begin this augmentation (Durán, 1990):

- *asking for help*—students ask questions of other students or a teacher as a means of aiding their own problem solving;
- *demonstrating knowledge*—students produce verbal responses or behaviors that they judge as appropriate to problem-solving activities;
- *testing a hypothesis*—students produce verbal responses or behaviors that signal a test of whether a response is appropriate or not;
- *challenging*—students express beliefs that a knowledge claim or behavior by a student or the teacher is inappropriate;
- *acknowledging information and feedback*—students verbally or paralinguistically signal comprehension or else uncertainty about assistance provided by other learners or a teacher.

The seven teaching strategies and five learning strategies outlined here constitute the assessment framework proposed in this chapter for assessing students' instructional interaction. Application of the framework is demonstrated by analyzing the discourse of two Hispanic fourth-grade students engaged in question asking and answering and prediction making within the context of a CIRC treasure hunt activity.

Dyadic Question Answering and Prediction Activity in CIRC

The CIRC curriculum is intended to help students in the early grades acquire a variety of reading and literacy skills. The curriculum centers around treasure hunt units, each lasting 5 or more days, which are focused on the reading of a narrative story presented in two successive segments. Following an introduction of key vocabulary terms and an exploration of the relevance of terms to a potential story, students are asked to read a story segment silently and then aloud in pairs. Next, student dyads are required to discuss and answer a set of questions developed for each passage segment. Questions for the first segment end with a question asking students to predict what will happen next in the story; these questions are known as *prediction questions.*

Students in dyads are at about the same reading level, although it is often advantageous to pair a more capable reader with one who is less capable. When presented with a question, students are expected to discuss ways in which it may be answered. When they have completed this discussion, each student writes his or her answer down on a sheet designed for this purpose. Answers must be in complete sentences.

Questions are intended to stimulate children's comprehension of a story and not just to assess what they comprehend. Typically, the questions are about story grammar elements. These elements are the essential ingredients of a story such as the identity of the characters, the setting, the activities and motives of story actors, and the outcome of the story.

Appendix A displays a sample story titled "A Hike in New York City," which is read by fourth-grade students in our CIRC project. Appendix B displays the key vocabulary terms taught to students before beginning the story and five treasure-hunt questions and one prediction question accompanying the reading of the first ½ of the story.

Analyzing Dyadic Interaction

Our goal in analyzing interaction among students in dyads as they answer questions is to assess ways in which the interaction stimulates comprehension and comprehension-skill development. Presumably, students should be less capable of answering questions on their own than when working in pairs. The different perspectives brought to bear by each child in answering a question should help both children evaluate their understanding of what a story actually stated and the suitability of alternative answers to a question.

Two fourth-grade bilingual students, (fictionally referred to here as) Lupe and Juan, were asked to read the first ½ of the story in Appendix A. The story is about a hiking trip to Central Park by a group of children. The first ½ of the story focuses on a mother's concern about her children making the hike. The mother repeatedly attempts to dissuade the children from taking the hike citing a number of reasons. The reasons range from the ridiculousness of the hike to a concern for the children's health and safety. The children successively address each concern raised by the mother, and they succeed in getting permission to undertake the hike by the end of the first ½ of the story.

After reading the first ½ of the story, Lupe and Juan proceeded to answer the treasure-hunt questions shown in Appendix B. The first question asked was the following: "Why does Mama ridicule the whole idea of the hike?"

Appendix C presents a transcript of Lupe and Juan's discussion of question 1 accompanied by intervening comments from Mr. S, the teacher. Appendix C also includes an assessment of teaching and learning strategies that can be inferred to guide students' interactions. Mr. S is an active participant in the early part of the discussion, but then backs off to assist other students. Question 1 is a fairly high-level question, requiring inferences about the beliefs, values, and motives of Mama and how she manifests her opposition to the hike indirectly. An appropriate answer might be something like "Mama is afraid that the children would get lost or hurt." The term *ridiculous* is critical to understanding the question, and the initial interactions between the students and Mr. S (lines 1–13) involve Mr. S's use of modeling and questioning. This interaction is accompanied by the students' use of direct and indirect questions to request help in generating the appropriate responses.

The discussion in Appendix C and the strategy assessment suggest that students actively alternate between the roles of tutor and tutee. The discussion in Appendix C is centered on answering the target question and shows noticeable cohesion across the conversational turns, although the students display difficulty in negotiating a good answer to the target question. The students do not understand the meaning of the word *ridiculous* as it occurs in the sentence: "Her method of discouraging us from venturing into the unknown was to make the entire project appear ridiculous," which was attributed to the mother at the start of the story and the meaning of *ridicule* as it occurs in question 1: "Why does Mama ridicule the whole idea of the hike?"

Although the students do not arrive at a clear understanding of the meaning of the ridiculous and ridicule, they expend a good deal of effort probing and confirming specific hypotheses about how to answer question 1. In the end (lines 27–32), they arrive at an acceptable answer to the question citing the mother's concern about the (narrator) son's safety. Although the students show an inability to understand the terms ridiculous and ridicule even with the help of the teacher, their discourse shows an active exploration of reasons put forth by the mother to oppose the children's outing.

The example discussion shows that students may engage in extensive interaction during dyad question answering, but that they might, nonetheless, need additional guidance in understanding the characteristics of good answers. However, apart from their difficulty with vocabulary, Lupe and Juan showed an understanding of a range of strategies for helping each other. They displayed a willingness to demonstrate knowledge and to guide their interactions through questioning and seeking help, and they showed an ability to evaluate each others' responses. The line-by-line assessment of strategies used by the two students shows a very active attempt to construct knowledge in a way that would be impossible to demonstrate by performance on existing tests of reading achievement.

Limitations to the Assessment Approach and Further Research

The coding of possible teaching and learning strategies used by students in Appendix C is inherently clinical and raises a number of conceptual and methodological questions. It is misleading to believe that the students necessarily thought in exactly the manner suggested by the coding. Conversational interaction is very much a process of inferring and negotiating communicative intent and meaning (Gumperz, 1981). The very acts of deciding how to interpret what others say and what to say next constitute complex forms of assessment on the part of interlocutors given their perceptions of the nature of a communicative activity (Goodwin & Goodwin, in press). Schemes of discourse assessment, such as those put forth in this chapter that evaluate how individuals assess each other, are inherently interpretive. There is no unique system for characterizing the particular speech acts underlying turns of discourse and it is quite likely that any turn of discourse may be interpreted by interlocutors as serving more than one communicative function. In addition to these concerns, it is a fact that illocutionary and perlocutionary force may be encoded in multiple communication channels in discourse. An utterance may have multiple levels of possible meaning that can be inferred by analysis of its linguistic structure and accompanying paralinguistic cues as it occurs in a communicative and behavioral context. Clearly, the ability of external observers to infer the meaning of interlocutors is affected by knowledge of the individual interlocutors and their sociocultural backgrounds, which affect their use of linguistic and paralinguistic strategies (Gumperz, in press). However, all the foregoing concerns do not automatically invalidate the development of an assessment scheme—although they do raise serious concerns that need specification and attention.

There is considerable value in diagnosing how students negotiate meaning in instruction in light of the limitations of existing achievement testing procedures. The individual turns of discourse generated by students can show a coherence with regard to topic, and they can show clear evidence of an effort to negotiate meaning toward resolving the academic task at hand. The assessment categories put forth here for analyzing students' discourse have considerable heuristic power in that they can create a descriptive map of students' ability to learn from each other and to guide their own learning. The categories also seem to be sensitive to the rapid oscillation between teacher and learner that students may show in cooperative learning activities.

Improvements in this assessment approach should address the possibility that more than one teaching and learning strategy may be operating at any one point in an interaction. Also, it may be possible that a student is simultaneously enacting teaching and learning strategies. For example, a student's utterance of "no" to a claim by another student may constitute feedback to another student (a teaching strategy), and at the same time, it may be a challenge embodying a learner's attempt to test the quality of his or her own understanding.

Another possibility to consider is that some strategies may overlap and be distributed across several consecutive turns of discourse. This is most apparent for a teaching strategy such as cognitive structuring. For example, in Appendix C, the teacher's utterances in lines 8, 10, and 13 appear to represent a failed attempt at guiding Juan and Lupe to restructure how they attack comprehending the meaning of the terms ridicule and ridiculous.

From a traditional measurement point of view, development of the clinical assessment technique described here raises some straightforward questions that need to be addressed. One obvious question is whether independent interpreters of student discourse would show high interrater agreement. The answer to this question could be broached by an appropriate set of rater reliability studies following training in the use of the discourse coding strategies. A second set of questions related to reliability is conceptually more difficult to address: To what extent are students' propensities to use various learning strategies a stable property of individuals versus a property determined by the context given the specific learning task, the interrelationships among the individual students involved, and the idiosyncratic situational factors surrounding conduct of a learning activity? As mentioned at the start of this chapter, I believe that it may not be possible or even make sense to try and answer this question. On theoretical grounds tied to analyses of situated cognition, dynamic assessment, and Vygotskian theory, it may be better to ask a different but related form of the question, namely: How can we manipulate the nature of instructional activities and their interpersonal communications demands so as to foster students' ability to learn from each other by using different forms of interactional strategies?

Traditional approaches to measurement focus on the validity of an assessment approach in terms of the ability of test users to make valid inferences based on test behavior. The present assessment approach centers on the following notion of *instructional validity*. Is the process of instruction effective in helping students master target subject-matter and thinking skills? The assessment procedure that has been sketched here, if fully developed and articulated, would potentially be able to document students' movement through their zone of proximal development for a learning task. As students progress in their learning, their performance on learning tasks should be characterized by less and less reliance on explicit help in performing problem-solving tasks and by evidence of a transfer of skills and content knowledge across learning activities and learning settings.

References

Au, K. H., Crowell, D. C., Jordan, C., Sloat, K. C., Speidel, G. E., Klein, T. W., & Tharp, R. G. (1986). Development and implementation of the KEEP reading program. In J. Orasanu (Ed.), *Reading comprehension: From research to practice.* Hillsdale, NJ: Lawrence Erlbaum Associates.

Brown, J. S., Collins, A., & Duguid, P. (1989). Situated cognition and the culture of learning. *Exceptional Researcher, 18,* 32–41.

Cazden, C. B. (1988). *Classroom discourse.* Portsmouth, NH: Heinemann.

Durán, R. P. (1989). Assessment and instruction of at-risk Hispanic students. *Exceptional Children, 56,* 154–158.

Durán, R. P. (1990). *Teaching the discourse of cooperation.* Paper presented at the annual meeting of the American Educational Research Association, Boston, MA.

Erickson, F. (1982). Taught cognitive learning in its immediate environments: A neglected topic in the anthropology of education. *Anthropology and Education Quarterly, 13,* 149–180.

Fivush, R. (1982). *Learning about school: The development of kindergartners' school scripts.* Unpublished doctoral dissertation. City University of New York, Graduate Center, New York.

Frederiksen, J. R., & Collins, A. (1989). A system approach to educational testing. *Educational Researcher, 18*(9), 27–32.

Goodwin, C., & Goodwin, M. W. (in press). Context, activity, and participation. In P. Auer & A. di Luzo (Eds.), *The contextualization of language.* Amsterdam: John Benjamins.

Green, J. L., & Wallat, C. (Eds.). (1981). *Ethnography and language in educational settings.* Norwood, NJ: Ablex.

Gumperz, J. J. (1981). Conversational inference and classroom learning. In J. L. Green & C. Wallat (Eds.), *Ethnography and language in educational settings.* Norwood, NJ: Ablex.

Gumperz, J. J. (in press). Contextualization revisited. In P. Auer & A. di Luzo (Eds.), *The contextualization of language.* Amsterdam: John Benjamins.

Jordan, C. (1980). *The culturally sensitive selection of teaching practices.* Paper presented at the annual meeting of the American Educational Research Association, Boston, MA.

Levenson, S. (1989). A hike in New York City. In J. Cassidy, K. K. Wixson, & D. Roettger (Eds.), *Find your way: Teachers' Edition—Scribner Reading Series* (pp. 126–132). New York: Macmillan.

Lidz, C. (Ed.). (1987). *Dynamic assessment.* New York: Guilford Press.

Linn, R. L., & Dunbar, S. B. (1990). *Complex, performance-based assessment: Expectations and validation criteria.* Unpublished manuscript.

Mislevy, R. J. (in press). Foundations of a new test theory. In N. Frederiksen, R. Mislevy, & I. Bejar (Eds.), *Test theory for a new generation of tests.* Hillsdale, NJ: Lawrence Erlbaum Associates.

National Commission on Excellence in Education. (1983). *A nation at risk: The imperative for educational reform.* Washington, DC: U.S. Government Printing Office.

National Commission on Testing and Public Policy. (1990). *From gatekeeper to gateway: Transforming testing in America.* Chestnut Hills, MA: Boston College.

Padrón, Y. N. (1986). *Training limited English proficient students to use cognitive reading strategies.* Paper presented at the National Reading Conference, Austin, TX.

Padrón, Y. N. (1987). *Identifying and teaching cognitive reading strategies.* Paper presented at the Third International Conference on Thinking, Honolulu, HI.

Palincsar, A. S., & Brown, A. L. (1984). The reciprocal teaching of comprehension fostering and monitoring activities. *Cognition and Instruction, 1,* 117–175.

Philips, S. (1983). *The invisible culture: Communications in the classroom and community on the Warm Springs Indian Reservation.* White Plains, NY: Longman.

Stevens, R. J., Madden, N. A., Slavin, R. E., & Farnish, A. M. (1987). Cooperative integrated reading and composition: Two field experiments. *Reading Research Quarterly, 22,* 433–454.

Tharp, R. G., & Gallimore, R. (1988). *Rousing minds to life: Teaching, learning, and schooling in social context.* New York: Cambridge University Press.

Appendix A: A Hike in New York City

At least once each summer we kids went off on a hike, but never without strong opposition from Mama. When it came to the open road, Mama had a closed mind.

Her method of discouraging us from venturing into the unknown was to make the entire project appear ridiculous:

"You're going on a what?"

"We're going on a hike."

"What's a hike?" Mama would ask.

When we started to explain it, the whole idea did in fact become ridiculous.

"We're going walking, Ma."

"Walking? For that you have to leave home? What's the matter with walking right here? You walk; I'll watch."

"You don't understand, Ma. We take lunch along."

"I'll give you lunch here, and you can march right around the table," and she would start singing a march, clapping her hands rhythmically.

"Ma, we climb mountains in the woods."

She couldn't understand why it was so much more enjoyable to fall off a mountain than off a fire escape.

"And how about the wild animals in the woods?"

"Wild animals? What kinds of wild animals?"

"A bear for instance. A bear could eat you up."

"Ma. Bears don't eat little children."

"Okay. So he won't eat you, but he could take a bite and spit it out? I'm telling you now, if a wild animal eats you up don't come running to me. And who's going with you?"

"Well, there's Georgie—"

"Georgie? Not him? He's a real wild animal!" She then went on to list all the conditions for the trip. "And remember one thing, don't tear your pants, and remember one thing, don't eat wild berries and bring me home the cramps, and remember one thing, don't tell me tomorrow morning that you're too tired to go to school, and remember one thing, wear boots, a sweater, and an umbrella, and a hat, and remember one thing, if you should get lost in the jungle, call up so I'll know you're all right. And don't dare come home without color in your cheeks. I wish I were young and free like you. Take soap."

Since the consent was specifically granted for the next day only, that night none of us slept. There was always a chance that it might rain. Brother Albert stayed at the crystal set all night like a ship's radio operator with his earphones on, listening to weather bulletins and repeating them aloud for the rest of us. "It's clearing in Nebraska. Hot air masses coming up from the Gulf. They say it's good for planting alfalfa. Storm warning off the coast of Newfoundland. It's drizzling in Montreal."

[End of first ½]

At six A.M. we were ready for Operation Hike, rain or shine, but we had to wait for Papa to get up. We didn't need his permission, but we did need his blanket.

Into the valley of Central Park marched the six hundred, bowed down with knapsacks, flashlights, a cereal box compass-mirror (so you could tell not only where you were lost but who was lost), a thermos bottle (semiautomatic—you had to fill it but it emptied by itself), and an ax. Onward! Forward! Upward! Philip was always the leader. He was the one to get lost first! Jerry was the lookout. He would yell, "Look out!" and would fall off the cliff. None of us knew how long we were supposed to march. We went on because we didn't know what to do if we stopped. One brave coward finally spoke up, "I can't go on anymore. The heat is killing me. Let's start the fire here."

No hike was complete without Georgie and his Uncle Bernie's World War I bugle. This kid had lungs like a vacuum cleaner. With him outside the walls of Jericho, they could have sent the rest of the army home. He used to stand on a hill and let go a blast that had the Staten Island ferries running into each other.

Lunch, naturally, had been packed in a shoe box—sandwiches, fruit, cheese, and napkins all squashed together neatly. The lid would open by itself every twenty minutes for air.

It happened every time—the Miracle of the Sandwiches. One kid always got a "brilliant idea." "Hey. I got a brilliant idea. I'm tired of my mother's sandwiches. Let's everybody trade sandwiches." All the kids exchanged sandwiches, and miraculously we all ended up with salami.

Albert was the true nature lover. "You know, you can learn a lot about human nature from the ants," he always said as he lifted up rock after rock to study his favorite insects. And he was right. While he was studying the ants, someone swiped his apple.

We came home with color in our cheeks—green. To make sure we could go again, we didn't forget Mama. We brought her a bouquet. She took one whiff and broke out in red blotches. Papa yelled but wouldn't come near us. He was afraid it was catching.

Appendix B

WORD MASTERY LIST

*opposition	*consent	salami
*rhythmically	*specifically	
*conditions	ferries	

TREASURE HUNT

Section I.

Stop at the end of first ½. Discuss the answers to the questions with your partner. Then, write your answers, while your partner answers separately.

1. Why does Mama ridicule the whole idea of the hike?
2. Name two of the conditions Mama sets for the hike.
3. Why does Albert listen to the radio the night before?
4. Which wild animal is Mama worried about?
5. What kind of mistake in reasoning is Mama making about the hike?

MAKE A PREDICTION:

Will the children go on the hike, or not?

Appendix C: Assessment of Discussion Between Juan (J), Lupe (L), and Teacher (Mr. S)

1. L: Now there.
2. J: Okay, number one.
3. L: Okay, why does Mama ridiculi- (pronunciation problem) the whole idea of the hike? Why does Mama ridiculis the whole idea of the hike? [**Questioning**]
4. J: Hmm, rididi- [**Testing a hypothesis**]
5. Mr. S: Ridicule. [**Modeling**]
6. L: Ridicule. [**Demonstration of competence**]
7. J: What's that? [**Asking for help**]
8. Mr. S: Remember your vocabulary word that we had yesterday? [**Questioning**]
9. L: Ridiculus? [**Testing a hypothesis**]
10. Mr. S: Uh-huh [**Feeding back**] So what does she make, doing with the hike? [**Questioning**]
11. L: She makes ridiculus? [**Questioning or testing a hypothesis**]

12. J: She thought that the wild animals—that the bear—would eat you up. [**Demonstrating competence**]

13. Mr. S: Now remember, what's this 'why does Mama'? [**Questioning**]

14. L: Because she's always thinking that they're gonna eat her, that they are going to eat her son, and that he's going to eat something that he shouldn't eat. [**Demonstration of competence**]

15. J: But, but their son, the his son—his son will—his son wanted to go too? [**Questioning**]

16. L: The son? [**Questioning**]

17. J: Yes. [**Feeding back**]

18. L: Yes? He wanted to go? [**Testing a hypothesis**]

19. J: And was Mama afraid of the—they could be lost in the jungle? [**Questioning**]

20. L: Yes. [**Demonstrating competence**]

21. J: And would they think that—would they think that—that—Did she think of this idea of the hike? [**Questioning**]

22. L: The idea of the hike? [**Asking for help**]

23. J: Yes [**Feeding back**], did she think of this idea of the hike? [**Questioning**]

24. L: No. [**Feeding back**]

25. J: Who thought of this idea? [**Questioning**]

26. L: Um, her little boy. [**Demonstration of competence**]

[A break occurs in the discussion of question 1 as the students go on to explore the remaining questions 2 through 6. Students then return to question 1 in order to write their answers.

27. J: (reading) Why does Mama ridi- [**Questioning**]

28. L: I don't understand that. [**Acknowledging information and feedback**]

29. J: Why? [**Questioning**]

30. L: Because she's always—she's always thinking wrong or that something's gonna happen to her... [**Demonstrating competence**]

31. J: her son. [**Demonstrating competence**]

32. L: son. [**Demonstrating competence**]

CHAPTER 10

Dynamic Measurement for Dynamic Education: A Call for Compatible Measurement– Learning Models

Barbara S. Plake

The Durán and Pennock-Román chapters focused on measurement issues in educational settings. Durán's chapter considered the use of testing information from a broadened conceptualization of the instructional process when applied to educational decisions. Pennock Román[1] focused her comments on the differential use of test information for making educational decisions, in particular with regard to admission into higher education programs.

I first consider these chapters separately and then attempt to synthesize the issues raised by them by focusing on their implications for measurement-based educational decisions about students.

---

[1] *These comments are being made based on recent publications, presentations, and comments to Plake made by Pennock-Román. These materials were provided to Plake by Pennock-Román. Pennock-Román's chapter for the volume was not available at the time this chapter was prepared.*

Test Utility in Dynamic Classrooms

In Durán's chapter, "Clinical Assessment of Instructional Performance in Cooperative Learning," which concerned the testing of Hispanics to improve instruction, Durán presented several important themes, including (a) a call for enhanced use of tests for making instructional decisions, (b) a concern about the quality and usability of existing standardized tests to advance the understanding of the evolving nature of learning and instruction, and (c) a recognition that classroom learning is mediated by the cultural, social, and linguistic backgrounds of students. All of the these themes have critical implications for the measurement community.

Use of Tests for Instructional Decisions

The need for test results to inform instruction has been recognized by educators for many years. Unfortunately, many of the measurement–instruction models implemented in the classroom were not sufficient for making instructional decisions from test data because of a limited perspective on what constituted *test* data. Some educators felt that only sporadically administered, formal assessments were tests. This view resulted in a limited use of data in making the myriad ongoing educational decisions necessary for instruction. Furthermore, some educators also failed to make the distinction between the uses of test data for summative and formative purposes, applying test data only for summarizing learning rather than for shaping instructional decisions.

The perception some educators had of the limited use of test data were seldom countered by educational measurement experiences available to classroom teachers. Very few teacher-education majors take a course in educational measurement as part of their coursework (Hills, 1991; Schafer & Lissitz, 1987). And of those who do take measurement coursework, some maintain that the curriculum of such courses does not satisfy the breadth of measurement training relevant to classroom teachers' instructional needs (Gullickson & Ellwein, 1985; Hills, 1991). The measurement community has been directing energies toward improving training and communication with teachers and teacher educators. One example of such activity is the joint publication by the National Education Association (NEA), the National Council on Measurement in Education (NCME), and the American Federation of Teachers (AFT) of the *Standards for Teacher Competencies in the Educational Assessment of Students* (AFT, NCME, NEA, 1990). Additionally, the Northwest Regional Education Laboratory has developed training materials designed to address classroom measurement needs of teachers (Stiggins, 1991).

Other related programs and projects have been undertaken to address the need for teachers to be able to use test data for instructional decision making. Undergraduate measurement textbooks are focusing more on the interactive nature of assessment and instruction. Teachers are being encouraged to recognize the sources of information that are relevant to educational decisions and to seek means to quantify and systematize their influences. A recognition by teachers that social, behavioral, and cultural factors influence instructional decisions will allow for the development of fairer applications of these data in instructional decisions.

Quality and Usability of Traditional Standardized Tests

While teachers are being encouraged and instructed in ways to incorporate test data in instructional decisions, a broadened perspective of what constitutes test occurrences has emerged. This evolution (some would view it as a revolution) in assessment methods is seen as a result of (a) the need to quantify behavioral observations from less formal assessment experiences and (b) the dissatisfaction over a static model of testing using objective item types. The need for a recognition and systematization of assessment experiences blends well with the previously stated goal of obtaining assessment information that will better match the myriad of instructional decisions made daily by teachers.

Objective-type tests, currently labeled "traditional tests," have been criticized recently as a limited source of information for use in making instructional decisions (Stiggins, in press). These criticisms of the limited informational quality provided by results from objective tests have led some educators to recommend substituting nontraditional or *authentic* assessment systems. While the arguments about the instructional validity–utility of objective tests continue, insufficient attention is being given to the psychometric implications of these proposed substitute assessment methods. Many of the criticisms targeted toward the objective-type tests can also be levied at the substitute approaches (Dunbar, Koretz, & Hoover, in press). More research is needed to address questions about the proposed improved information and use of test results from authentic rather than traditional assessments.

Mediation of Classroom Learning

The recognition that learning in the classroom is mediated by noninstructional factors adds even more complex demands on instructional assessment systems. Within this instructional environment, measurement can serve a multitude of functions. In addition to providing formative information for use in making instructional decisions for students and summative data regarding achievement of educational objectives, measurement can and should provide information about the social, cultural, and linguistic climate of the instructional setting. Carefully designed and implemented assessment programs could provide information to inform teachers and administrators of the qualitatively different learning environments present in instructional settings. (Moos's efforts, 1979, 1987, e.g., have shown that the instructional environment can be measured.) Thus, the measurement–assessment program could be used to enhance the instructional-assessment information.

The three themes identified in Durán's chapter have important implications for educational testing of all minority students. First, as teachers articulate and operationalize informal assessment methods, an understanding of some subtle sources of bias could become clearer. Unless these informal assessment systems are clarified, unrecognized and unintentional sources of measurement bias will likely remain. Second, the nontraditional tests have the potential to improve or erode the quality of assessment for minority groups. Although some argue that minority groups are disadvantaged by the objective types of tests, no clear evidence has been adduced to confirm that minority groups are not also disadvantaged by these nontraditional types of assessment. Research is needed in this area. Third, objective instrumentation could be used to assess the complex interactive culture of the learning environment. Problems surrounding the measurement of any dynamic system are not easily solved. Measurement of the ecology of the classroom presents even more sophisticated measurement challenges. Serious energy needs to be devoted to the measurement issues surrounding assessment of the dynamic process and personological variables relevant to classroom learning.

Test Use in Educational Decisions for Minority Groups

The topic of Pennock-Román's chapter, "Interpreting Test Performance in Selective Admissions for Hispanic Students," which described various research findings relating to the testing of Hispanics in educational admissions, is a topic that has been receiving some recent attention by the measurement community (Durán, 1983; Linn, 1990; Pennock-Román, 1988). Differential predictive validity is often found between minority and majority groups. Some studies indicate that there is a tendency for smaller predictive validities for tests when applied to Hispanic students as opposed to White non-Hispanic students. In general, however, overprediction is most typically observed for Hispanic students.

There are several possible explanations for the lower predictive validities for minority-group members. Whereas some are statistical in nature (e.g., the reliability of the criterion), others are related specifically to opportunities and experiences of the minority-group members. One aspect of the differential prediction of success in college for minority- and majority-group members may be a function of different course-taking patterns (Linn, 1990). In addition, whether or not English is the first language of persons in the minority groups has also been shown to be related to predictive validity in educational settings (Pennock-Román, 1990).

Implications for Measurement

The measurement issues raised by differential prediction of educational success for minority- and majority-group members are many and warrant enhanced and energetic attack by measurement specialists. Problems with reliability of predictor variables as well as criteria need serious attention. If variables are multidimensional (e.g., grades) or based on too few data points, the accuracy of the information on which the predictive relationship is based is questionable (Linn, 1990). An item-response, theory-based criterion that takes course difficulty into account shows promise for reducing the differences seen in predictive accuracy. (Young, 1991a, 1991b).

Future Directions for Educational Measurement Specialists

The Durán and Pennock-Román chapters highlighted areas for enhanced research and development efforts for measurement specialists. Assessment in the classroom will need to be interactive, varied, and responsive to the complex cultural interactions of multicultural education environments. Outcomes of the educational process, as indicators of learning, are also being called on to function as predictor variables of success in higher education programs. New measurement applications of item-response theory models are being developed in response to increased recognition of the impact of varied educational experiences on the prediction of educational promise.

Both the Pennock-Román and Durán chapters drew attention to the need for developing measurement systems that are sensitive to the multidimensional, complex realities of education. The classroom is a dynamic environment; measurement of such an environment requires interactive assessment technology. Prediction of educational promise, likewise, needs to be based on the measurement models that are able to reflect the nonstatic nature of educational experiences.

Some measurement specialists may bemoan the current complex demands being made on educational measurement programs. However, current educational systems have not become more complex. Complexities were there before. Measurement methods need to be developed and refined in congruence with the complexities of the variables we want, and need, to measure. The need, therefore, is for dynamic measurement finally to catch up with dynamic education.

References

American Federation of Teachers, National Council on Measurement in Education, & National Education Association. (1990). *Standards for teacher competence in education assessment of students.* Washington, DC: National Council on Measurement in Education.

Dunbar, S., Koretz, D. M., & Hoover, H. D. (in press). Quality control in the development and use of performance assessment. *Applied Measurement in Education.*

Durán, R. J. (1983). *Hispanic's education and background: Predictors of college achievement.* New York: College Entrance Examination Board.

Gullickson, A. R., & Ellwein, M. C. (1985). Post-hoc analysis of teacher-made tests: The goodness of fit between prescription and practice. *Educational and Psychological Measurement, 4,* 15–18.

Hills, J. (1991). Apathy concerning grades and testing. *Phi Delta Kappan, 72,* 540–545.

Linn, R. L. (1990). Admissions testing: Recommended uses, validity, differential prediction, and coaching. *Applied Measurement in Education, 3,* 297–318.

Moos, R. (1979). Evaluating educational environments. San Francisco: Jossey-Bass.

Moos, R. (1987). Person-environment congruence in work, school, and health care settings. *Journal of Vocational Behavior, 31,* 231–247.

Pennock-Román, M. (1988). *The status of selective admissions tests and Hispanic students in postsecondary education.* Paper commissioned by the National Commission of Testing and Public Policy, the International Development Research Association, and the Ford Foundation in San

Antonio, Texas. (Educational Testing Service [ETS] Research Rep. No. RR-88-36). Princeton, NJ: ETS.

Pennock-Román, M. (1990). *Test validity and language background.* New York: College Entrance Examination Board.

Schafer, W. D., & Lissitz, R. W. (1987). Measurement training for school personnel: Recommendation and reality. *Journal of Teacher Education, 38,* 57–63.

Stiggins, R. J. (1991). Relevant classroom assessment training for teachers. *Educational Measurement; Issues and Practice, 10,* (1), 7–12.

Stiggins, R. J. (in press). Facing the challenges of a new era in educational assessment. *Applied Measurement in Education.*

Young, J. W. (1991a). Gender bias in predicting college academic performance: A new approach using item response theory. *Journal of Educational Measurement, 28,* 37–48.

Young, J. W. (1991b). Improving the prediction of college performance of ethnic minorities using IRT-based GPA. *Applied Measurement in Education, 4,* 229–240.

PART THREE

The Testing of Hispanics in Industry and Research

CHAPTER 11

Introduction to the Testing of Hispanics in Industry and Research

Lorraine D. Eyde

Hispanics make up the second largest and fastest growing minority group in the United States (Davis, Haub, & Willette, 1983). By the year 2000, Hispanics, non-Hispanic Blacks, and other minority groups are expected to make up ⅓ of the new entrants into the labor force (Johnson & Packer, 1987). Therefore, it will be increasingly important for employers to learn to manage a multicultural workforce in which Hispanics are expected to play an important role. Applied and basic research on Hispanic samples should provide helpful information for use in selecting, placing, training, and supervising Hispanic workers and for educating students of Hispanic origin. In this introduction, I present background information on the composition of the Hispanic population and workforce, discuss variables related to educational and occupational achievement, and comment on moderator variables, such as socioeconomic level. These variables are likely to

The views expressed are those of Eyde and do not necessarily reflect those of her employer. Eyde thanks the library staff of the Office of Personnel Management and Lois Northrop for their assistance.

affect the test performance of Hispanics. Hispanic subgroups differ in their average test scores, for example, on the Scholastic Aptitude Test (Durán, 1983). Test score differences may be associated with the background differences of test takers, because the Hispanic population varies widely in its racial and national origins and in its socioeconomic and dialectal composition.

The term *Hispanic* is nebulous in its meaning (Valdivieso & Davis, 1988). Before the 1970 census, the term hardly existed (Davis et al., 1983), and definitions have changed over time (Valdivieso & Davis,1988). Some demographers who study the national origin and the sociodemographic characteristics of Hispanics question the existence of a single Hispanic population and the use of this ethnic label (Bean & Tienda, 1987). Nevertheless, Valdivieso and Davis (1988) have used Bean and Tienda's commentary to develop this definition: "The terms Hispanic or Latino generally refer to individuals whose cultural heritage traces back to a Spanish-speaking country in Latin America, but also include those persons with links to Spain, or from the southwestern region of the U.S., once under Spanish or Mexican control" (1988, p. 2).

Despite disagreement on definitions, demographers do agree that the number of Hispanics in the population has increased and that considerable growth is expected in future years. The number of Hispanics increased 34% from 1980 to 1988, whereas there has been a comparable 7% increase in the general population (Valdivieso & Davis, 1988). According to the Census Bureau, Hispanics in 1990 accounted for 9% of the U.S. population, and their growth is greater than predicted by demographers (Vobejda, 1991). In fact, the demographer Davis has predicted that "Hispanics could number some 47 million and comprise 15% of the population by the year 2020, displacing [non-Hispanic] blacks as the country's largest minority" (Davis et al., 1983, p. 3).

Hispanic immigrants have migrated from many countries. In 1989, the mainland Hispanic population continued to be represented most heavily by Mexicans (63%), Puerto Ricans (13%), Central and South Americans (10%), Cubans (6%), and other Hispanics (8%) (U.S. Bureau of the Census, 1989). It is difficult to arrive at exact figures because of illegal immigration and the movement of Puerto Ricans back and forth from the island to the mainland.

The subgroups within the Hispanic population differ in significant ways (U.S. National Commission for Employment Policy [USNCEP], 1982). They live in different parts of the country, which vary in economic growth and in the kinds of jobs available, and they attained citizenship at different times. The majority of Mexican Americans are at least second-generation Americans, whereas Central and South Americans and Cubans are recent arrivals. They vary in age with the median age of Cubans at 36—14 years above that of Mexican Americans and Puerto Ricans. There are large differences in educational attainment among Hispanic subgroups. The USNCEP reported the following statistics:

> Mexican-Americans and Puerto Ricans have a low level of education. Those over 25 years old have a median education of 9 and 10 school years, respectively. The comparable figure is about 12½ years for the total U.S. population. The low levels of education are partly due to the lack of schooling of immigrants, who comprise a larger proportion of these groups than of the non-Hispanic population. However, native Mexican-Americans and mainland-born Puerto Ricans average at least 1 year less of schooling than white non-Hispanics of the same age. By contrast, Cubans are a well-educated group. Their median formal education is about the same as that of the non-Hispanic population. (1982, p. 11)

The Congressional Research Service prepared a report on the Hispanic population of the United States (Bailey & Pauls, 1983), in which the authors reviewed data on the educational achievement of Hispanics and concluded that their low educational achievement could be accounted for by two factors—family income and parental education. The report notes the following:

> According to the *Condition of Education, 1980,* the higher the family income, the less likely that children will be behind in school. According to a NAEP study, families below the poverty line, which included approximately 21 percent of Hispanic families in 1977 (in contrast to 8 percent of non-Hispanic families) were more likely to have children enrolled below grade level than were families above the poverty line. (Bailey & Pauls, 1983, p. 26)

In addition, many Hispanic Americans show limited proficiency in English-language skills. Approximately 45% of the Hispanics in the United States speak only Spanish or consider Spanish to be their first language (USNCEP, 1982). Linguistic minorities, particularly those with limited education, will find it difficult to compete in a job market in which the skill requirements of fast-growing jobs are generally rising (Johnson & Packer, 1987). Hispanic subgroups and gender subgroups vary in the kinds of jobs they hold (USNCEP, 1982). When the occupations of Hispanic-American men are examined by subgroups, we find that Mexicans are most likely to hold blue-collar jobs, especially as craft workers or machine operators; Cubans are most likely to be professional and technical white-collar workers; and Puerto Ricans are most likely to be service workers. Hispanic women are most likely to be engaged in clerical or service work or be employed as machine operators (USNCEP, 1982).

A report prepared for the National Commission for Employment Policy examined the determinants of Hispanic occupational achievement for Hispanic subgroups using data from the 1976 Survey of Income and Education (SIE), a Census Bureau survey of members from 190,000 households, which included detailed questions on ethnicity and English-language ability (Stolzenberg, 1982). English-language capability was found to have a major effect on the potential occupational earnings of Hispanic men. The annual earnings of individuals were examined after controlling for the effects of schooling, number of potential years of labor-force experience, ratings of each person's ability to speak English, geographical location, and race. After statistically controlling for these variables, men's earnings did not show differences among major subgroups of Hispanics. The results of this type of regression analysis demonstrate the merits of controlling for background variables when studying the earning power of Hispanic subgroups.

Ramos's chapter in this volume presents data supporting the etic position on cultural diversity discussed in Anastasi's introductory chapter. Busch-Rossnagel's chapter describes behaviors that generalize across cultures and acknowledges the value of examining emic or culturally specific behaviors in order to understand human behavior. Camara's chapter presents an eclectic position on test-fairness research and public policy considerations.

Ramos reports on a large-scale operational application of the assessment center in which overall ratings of candidates—be they majority group members or Hispanics—were predictive of promotions to successively higher managerial jobs. The etic view is upheld because of the generalizability of the results across ethnic groups. Evaluations that are as comprehensive as those used by Ramos are likely to be fair (Primoff & Eyde, 1988) and are designed to avoid overreliance on test scores often found to be associated with test misuse (Eyde, Moreland, Robertson, Primoff, & Most, 1988).

Ramos's research, which shows that scholastic aptitude is an important predictor of managerial progress for one sample of Hispanic workers, serves to identify a common thread running through this book: the importance of identifying teaching strategies for increasing the academic achievement of Hispanics. The authors of the Congressional Research Report on Hispanics concluded that "no final best method of instruction" exists (Bailey & Pauls, 1983, p. 27). Durán's chapter on his dynamic assessment method offered a promising approach in which test results are used diagnostically to teach language-proficiency skills to Hispanics.

Busch-Rossnagel's chapter summarizes, for example, Laosa's significant research in which he studied maternal teaching strategies of bilingual Chicano mothers who taught their children to assemble Tinkertoy models. Laosa's research illustrated how the study of confounding variables, such as socioeconomic status, may contribute to our knowledge of psychological constructs. Camara's chapter points out the important association between years of schooling and performance on the Armed Services Vocational Aptitude Battery. Persons with high-test-score patterns, he notes, may have the opportunity to enter high tech military specialties, which in a later time could lead to good job opportunities in the civilian sector.

The applied and basic research reported in the next three chapters has implications not only for making employment decisions on the basis of test performance and for using test-score information in training, but also for using psychometric methods in cross-cultural research.

References

Bailey, D. J. & Pauls, F. H. (1983). Summary of report findings, Chapter I. In Congressional Research Service, *The Hispanic population of the United States: An overview.* Report prepared for the Subcommittee on Census and Population of the Committee on Post Office and Civil Service, U.S. House of Representatives. 98th Cong., 1st Sess. Committee Print 98-7. Washington, DC: U.S. Government Printing Office.

Bean, F. D., & Tienda, M. (1987). *The Hispanic population of the United States.* New York: Russell Sage Foundation.

Davis, C., Haub, C., & Willette, J. (1983). U.S. Hispanics: Changing the face of America. *Population Bulletin, 38,* 3.

Durán, R. P. (1983). *Hispanics' education and background: Prediction of college achievement.* New York: College Entrance Examination Board.

Eyde, L. D., Moreland, K. L., Robertson, G. J., Primoff, E. S., & Most, R. B. (1988). Test user qualifications: A data-based approach to promoting good test use. *Issues in Scientific Psychology.*

Report of the Test User Qualifications Working Group of the Joint Committee on Testing Practices. (Research Rep. No. 89-01). Washington, DC: American Psychological Association.

Johnson, W. B., & Packer, H. E. (1987). *Workforce 2000: Work and workers for twenty-first century.* Indianapolis, IN: Hudson Institute.

Primoff, E. S., & Eyde, L. D. (1988). The job element method of job analysis. In S. Gael (Ed.), *The job analysis handbook for business, industry, and government* (Vol. 2, pp. 807–824). New York: Wiley.

Stolzenberg, R. M. (1982). *Occupational differences between Hispanics and Non-Hispanics.* (N-1889-NCEP). Santa Monica, CA: Rand.

U.S. Bureau of the Census. (1989). The Hispanic population in the United States: March 1988. *Current Population Reports,* Series P-20, No. 444, p. 2.

U.S. National Commission for Employment Policy. (1982). *Hispanics and jobs: Barriers to Progress.* Washington, DC: Author.

Valdivieso, R., & Davis, C. (1988). U.S. Hispanics: Challenging issues for the 1990s. *Population Trends and Public Policy, 17,* 2.

Vobejda, B. (1991, March 11). Asian, Hispanic numbers in U. S. soared in 1980s, Census reveals. *The Washington Post,* p. A1.

CHAPTER 12

Testing and Assessment of Hispanics for Occupational and Management Positions: A Developmental Needs Analysis

Robert A. Ramos

The concepts of differential validity and test fairness as related to employment testing have been the subject of intensive debate since the passage of the Civil Rights Act of 1964 (American Psychological Association [APA] Task Force on Employment Testing of Minority Groups, 1969; Fincher, 1975; Glaser & Bond, 1981). The issues are complex, and the debate requires consideration of psychometric, psychological, professional, legal, and social ramifications. The effects of acculturation and bilingualism add to the complexity when discussing the psychological testing of Hispanics and other linguistic minorities (Olmedo, 1979, 1981).

Historically, the main purpose of psychological testing in industry has been to select from an available pool of candidates those individuals most likely to succeed on the job. Typically, a validity study identifies critical skills and abilities that are required for success in a position or occupational family. Individuals who demonstrate higher levels of these skills and abilities in their employment test performance are hired. Over the long term, an organization using valid selection methods will have more employees with the skills and abilities required for successful job performance than a company that does not use valid selection procedures. A competitive advantage will be established in the company that uses valid selection programs due to a higher general level of proficiency of its work force. Utility analyses have shown the large potential savings of expenses that would accrue from the use of valid selection programs leading to increases in worker productivity (Schmidt, Hunter, McKenzie, & Muldrow, 1979).

One of the issues to be explored in this volume is whether the historically positive results of psychological testing in industry generalize to the adult Hispanic labor population. In an attempt to contribute to the debate on this issue, I intend to summarize selected references from the empirical literature relevant to adult Hispanic employment testing. The unique contribution of this chapter is to provide data on the performance of Hispanics in an assessment center designed to predict success in management positions. Finally, the argument is made that information available on Hispanic test and assessment performance should be used to point to the educational and developmental needs of the Hispanic community.

Validity and Fairness

Key issues in discussions of employment testing of minorities are the concepts of validity and fairness. *Validity* has been defined by the profession as "the degree to which a certain inference from a test is appropriate or meaningful" (*Standards*, 1985) or "the degree to which inferences from scores are justified or supported by evidence" (Society for Industrial and Organizational Psychology, Inc., 1987). Cleary's (1968) regression model is the generally accepted statistical definition of fairness. In the regression model, bias is identified when the use of a predictor results in under- or overpredicted criterion performance for a particular group. Subgroup differences in mean predictor scores do not necessarily imply bias or unfairness. If low test scores are associated with low criterion performance for all applicants, the test is valid and statistically fair. Other, more socially driven definitions of fairness have been proposed, but none have achieved a high level of acceptance in the testing community (Cronbach, Yalow, & Schaeffer, 1980; Hunter, Schmidt, & Rauschenberger, 1977; Novick & Peterson, 1976).

Hispanic Employment Testing

Schmidt and Pearlman (1980) have shown that employment tests are neither differentially valid nor unfair for Hispanics relative to the majority group. They performed an analysis and review of all employment validity studies containing Hispanic participants available at the time of the study. These validity studies included 16 reports containing 21 independent samples of applicants for various occupational positions. Differences in validity coefficients between Hispanic and majority group members were found to be within less than .02 of each other. An analysis of Hispanic versus majority group differences in standard errors, slopes, and intercepts found significant differences in 6.32% of the comparisons. Results of the differences observed in differential validity and fairness comparisons are explained by chance and statistical artifacts.

The impact of language preference on employment test performance was investigated in a sample of Hispanic applicants for telephone operator and clerical positions (Ramos, 1979, 1981). Study participants were identified as Hispanics through an extensive interview procedure. As part of this procedure, Hispanic applicants were asked to express their preference on whether they wanted to be examined with Spanish or English test instructions. Applicants who expressed a preference for Spanish-language test instructions were identified as members of the Spanish-dominant group. Those applicants who expressed a preference for English-language test instructions were placed in the English-dominant group. Even though 94% of the sample described themselves as bilingual, only 29% indicated a preference for the Spanish-language instruction condition. Individuals who preferred the Spanish testing were generally immigrants to the United States, came from monolingual Spanish-speaking families, could read and write Spanish, and averaged about 10 years in a Spanish educational system outside the United States. About 98% of the sample born in the United States expressed a preference to be tested with English instructions and were thus identified as English dominant. Most members of the English-dominant group were educated in the United States.

The employment test battery administered to the applicants consisted of clerical-work sample tests and cognitive tests consisting of numerical computations and word meanings. Spanish-dominant applicants who received Spanish instructions scored an average of 1.3 stanines higher on the test battery composite than did a comparable group of Spanish-dominant applicants who received English instructions. Although this positive difference in test performance due to language-instruction condition is statistically significant ($t = 2.14$; $p < .05$; $df = 332$), the practical effect is small. The composite stanine obtained by the applicants under the Spanish-language instruction condition reached a level of about ½ of the score needed to achieve a passing score.

Test performance by the English-dominant group was significantly and substantially higher than by the Spanish-dominant group. On the composite, the English-dominant group scored 3.6 stanines higher than the Spanish-dominant group ($t = 7.75$; $p < .01$; $df = 653$). One of the implications of these results is the need to distinguish between immigrants and native borns when designing programs for Hispanics. Issues related to acculturation, bilingualism, and language preference appear to be heavily impacted by an individual's educational history. The correlation between the proportion of years in a U.S. curriculum (to their total educational history) and employment battery performance was $r = .29$ ($p < .01$; $df = 782$); whereas the correlation between proportion of years in a Spanish curriculum and battery performance was $r = -.25$ ($p < .01$; $df = 782$).

Assessment-Center Results

Most of the information available on test performance of Hispanics in industry has been obtained from applicants for occupational positions. In order to foster the advance of the Hispanic community in corporations, more information is required on the performance of Hispanics on predictors used to identify skills required for managerial positions. A competent Hispanic managerial labor pool may become a critical issue for those companies whose occupational candidate pools contain large numbers of Hispanics. One of the most widely used methods to identify managerial skills is the assessment-center method. Assessment centers generally consist of managerial work samples such as in baskets, leaderless group discussions, business games, objective tests, and writing samples. Good assessment-center design allows the candidate multiple opportunities to demonstrate ability on various techniques as evaluated by assessors. The first industrial application of assessment-center technology was the longitudinal research performed in the Management Progress Study at AT&T (Bray, Campbell, & Grant, 1974; Bray & Grant, 1966). Assessment centers have been shown to be valid predictors of managerial success across a broad spectrum of positions (Cohen, Moses, & Byham, 1974; Moses & Byham, 1977; Thornton & Byham, 1982).

The Personnel Assessment Program (PAP) was an operational program developed out of the original Management Progress Study simulations. Assessment exercises carried over from the Management Progress Study included the following:

1. Manufacturing Problem—This is a small business game wherein the participants, in a leaderless group, assumed the role of partners in an enterprise that manufactured toys for the Christmas trade. The participants were required to buy parts and sell finished products under varying market conditions, to maintain inventories, and to manufacture toys.

2. Interview—This is a discussion with each participant directed at obtaining insights into personal development, work objectives, attitudes toward the company, social values, scope of interests, interpersonal relationships, and idiosyncrasies.

3. In basket—This is a set of written materials such as mail, memos, and other papers that company managers might expect to find in their to-do trays. The 25 in-basket items ranged from telephone messages to detailed reports. In addition, the examinee was furnished with such necessary materials as a copy of the union contract, an organization chart, and stationery. The examinee was given 3 hours in which to review the materials and take appropriate action on each item by writing letters, memos, and notes. Following completion of the material in the basket, the examinee was interviewed concerning the approach taken to the task, the reasons for taking the actions indicated, and views on superiors, peers, and subordinates.

4. Group discussion—This is a leaderless group situation in which participants were instructed to assume the role of managers, each having a reporting foreman considered capable of promotion. Participants were required to discuss the merits and liabilities of their hypothetical foreman and to reach a group decision regarding the relative promotable status of each foreman.

5. Written or individual exercises—These included the SCAT, a cognitive test of verbal and quantitative ability; a Q sort with which individuals could de-

scribe themselves; a contemporary-affairs test, which measured knowledge of current events; a written exercise to evaluate writing skills; and a personal-history questionnaire.

Dimension names and definitions of variables evaluated in PAP are provided in Appendix A. Many of the PAP dimension ratings are substantially intercorrelated and may be summarized in terms of four factors: Interpersonal Effectiveness, Administrative Skills, Sensitivity, and Effective Intelligence (Huck & Bray, 1976). The Interpersonal Effectiveness factor includes energy, resistance to stress, forcefulness, behavior flexibility, and leadership. Administrative Skills include decision making, and organizing and planning. Sensitivity dimensions include self-objectivity, managerial identification, likability, and awareness of social environment. Effective Intelligence is defined by scholastic aptitude, written communications, and range of interests.

The behavior of assessment candidates over a 2½-day period was observed and recorded in reports written by the assessor team. All information obtained on each candidate, including reports and scores on individual exercises was reported at an evaluation session. Candidate performance on the various exercises was considered by a team of three assessors and a group leader who individually rated and then reached a consensus on their ratings for 18 managerial dimensions and an overall rating. The overall rating represented a judgment, based on all the information available, of the probability of successful performance in an entry-level management position if the individual was promoted immediately. Although individuals received feedback on their assessment performance on each of the dimensions, the overall rating was the single operational predictor used in promotional decisions. Each candidate was evaluated separately against a standard norm.

PAP was used to evaluate internal employees for selection to entry-level management positions from 1961 to 1979. Employees processed through this assessment center represent a heterogeneous population from a wide variety of nonmanagerial positions. In general, individuals who attended the assessment center were viewed by their supervisors as having some potential for success in a management position. Initial selection requirements associated with the various nonmanagerial positions from which the candidates were drawn differed substantially as a function of the complexity of associated task requirements. For example, the employment test battery (and typical education levels) associated with the selection of service representatives is more stringent than the battery used to identify telephone operators. As a consequence, there may be substantial differences in initial skill levels among the candidates. In addition, there is a relationship between date of assessment and promotion. Apparently, doing poorly in an assessment has the general effect of slowing rather than eliminating the possibility of a promotion. As a result, individuals assessed in the early years of the process have had a tendency to receive promotions eventually. Minorities and women are more recent participants in the assessment process. The net result is a lower number of working years in which to earn promotions. In addition, growth in a number of the Bell operating companies slowed considerably by the mid 1970s. Consequently, the number of promotional opportunities was reduced for assessment candidates evaluated during this time frame.

The PAP process is unique as an assessment program in that it has had several independently published evaluations of its validity and fairness. Campbell and Bray (1967) obtained measures of job performance and potential for further advancement for a group of craftworkers who had been promoted to entry level management positions through a highly structured interview with supervisors. A portion of the sample had been promoted prior to the introduction of the assessment program. The sample was split into two groups: above-average performers and below-average performers. A significantly higher level of job performance was obtained for individuals who received an *acceptable* or better overall rating than for those who had been promoted prior to the introduction of the assessment program. These data suggest that the assessment program was a definite aid in the selection of better performers at the first level of management. In addition, the acceptable group had substantially more individuals rated as having high potential for further progress in management than did the preassessment sample.

Moses (1972) examined assessment center performance and its relation to subsequent career progress. PAP data were obtained on 8,885 men from two companies who were evaluated from 1961 to 1970. All of the sample members were nonmanagement vocational employees at the time they were assessed. The management level attained as of the end of 1970 was used to construct the progress criterion. Progress in management, defined as the number of promotions to successively higher levels, was the criterion used to evaluate the effectiveness of the assessment ratings. Presumably, an individual who performs well at a particular level of management has a greater probability of receiving a promotion to the next level. A positive relation between assessment ratings and progress in management would provide evidence that assessment ratings are predictive of management performance. Assessment performance was one significant element considered in the initial decision to promote individuals to entry-level management. Consequently, one would expect a very high relationship between assessment ratings and initial movement into first-level positions. Subsequent promotion, however, would be heavily dependent on job performance in the first-level assignment, not on assessment results obtained when the individual was an occupational (nonmanagement) employee. The highest correlation with management level achieved was obtained with the overall assessment rating ($r = .44$; $p < .01$). All other assessment variables, including leadership, organizing and planning, decision making, perception, oral skills, and SCAT scores were significantly correlated with management progress.

Moses and Boehm (1975) replicated the Moses (1972) study with a sample of 4,846 women from seven companies who had been assessed between 1963 and 1971. The distribution of overall assessment ratings obtained by men and women were quite similar. About ⅓ of both groups received "more than acceptable" and "acceptable" ratings, a second ⅓ were "questionable," and the final ⅓ was "not acceptable." The median year of assessment for the female sample was 1969, and management level at the end of 1973 was the criterion measure. Four years is a very short time period for two or more promotions to occur. Consequently, the number of individuals promoted twice or more is relatively small in this sample. In spite of this, women receiving the highest overall rating were about 10 times more likely to have earned two or more promotions than those receiving the lowest rating. The highest dimension correlations with number of promotions for both men and women were obtained with overall rating, leadership, decision making, and organizing and planning. The rank-order correlation between men and women for all dimension ratings against the criterion was $r = .75$ ($p < .01$; $df = 10$).

Huck and Bray (1976) examined the fairness of the PAP process for White and African-American females. Behavioral rating scales, consisting of the major work-performance dimensions associated with effectiveness for each of two first-level jobs were developed. Supervisors then rated subordinates on job elements and rated and ranked sample members on overall effectiveness. In addition, supervisors rated each subordinate on potential for advancement. The overall assessment rating was significantly correlated with job-performance dimensions, overall job performance, and potential for advancement for both Whites and African Americans. Regression equations associated with the overall rating and performance for Whites and African Americans were compared. No differences were observed between slopes or intercepts. Consequently, a common regression line could be fairly applied to both White and African-American groups to predict performance.

Casio and Ramos (1986) demonstrated the utility of PAP and the assessment-center program that replaced it. The job performance of a sample of first-line supervisors was translated into an estimate of total dollar value. Individuals selected via an assessment program contributed about $1,500 more in job-performance value per year than did individuals identified by traditional panel discussions.

In short, the evidence clearly shows that PAP dimensions and overall ratings are predictive of entry-level management performance and potential for further management progress. PAP has been demonstrated to be fair for the prediction of performance of women and African Americans. In addition, the value of the assessment program to enhanced corporate profitability was shown by utility analyses. However, none of the previous PAP studies provided data on Hispanic candidates. Data on the validity of assessment performance in PAP for Hispanics are presented in this chapter as part of a 19-year follow-up. PAP was operational from 1961 to 1979 when it was replaced by a new assessment-center program. The analyses presented here essentially replicate the management-progress criterion model and logic provided by Moses (1972).

The 19-year PAP sample consists of 37,182 individuals from 17 companies that were part of the former Bell System. Demographics associated with this sample are as follows: The median assessment year was 1971, the median birth year was 1940, and the median hire year was 1963. About 66% of the sample were males, about 90% were White, about 1% were Hispanic, and about 8% were African Americans. The number of Asian Americans and other ethnic minorities was negligible. Management level attained as of the end of 1980 was used to construct the progress criterion. It should be noted that the management structure consisted of five levels. The majority of first-level positions were first-line supervisors (historically called foremen) or supervisors of various occupational groups; second levels were generally supervisors of a number of foremen; and third levels

TABLE 1

Number and Percentage in Overall Assessment-Rating Categories for Total, White, and Hispanic Samples

Assessment Rating	Total		White		Hispanic	
	N	%	n	%	n	%
More than acceptable	2,142	5.8	2,047	6.1	18	3.3
Acceptable	10,471	28.2	9,832	29.4	122	22.2
Questionable	11,298	30.4	10,257	30.6	155	28.2
Not acceptable	13,271	35.7	11,353	33.9	254	46.3
TOTAL	37,182	100.0	33,489	90.1	549	1.5

were middle-management personnel. The sixth level of management included the officers of the corporation. For an occupational (nonmanagerial) employee to attain a middle-management position via three promotions was relatively uncommon.

Overall assessment ratings obtained by total, White, and Hispanic samples over the 19-year time frame are shown in Table 1. About ⅓ of the total sample received a "more than acceptable" or "acceptable" rating, another ⅓ were evaluated as "questionable," and the final ⅓ obtained the lowest rating. These results follow the historical trend established in earlier analyses.

Overall assessment rating versus number of promotions achieved by the total sample is displayed in Table 2. The analysis of frequencies of overall ratings by number of promotions is significant ($X^2 = 6,655.05$; $p < .001$; $df = 12$). The correlation between overall assessment rating and number of promotions is $r =$

TABLE 2

Overall Assessment Rating Versus Number of Promotions for Total Sample

Assessment Rating	Total		At Least Once		At Least Twice		At Least Thrice	
	N	%	n	%	n	%	n	%
More than acceptable	2,142	5.8	1,919	89.4	721	33.7	100	4.7
Acceptable	10,471	28.2	8,594	82.1	2,161	20.6	151	1.4
Questionable	11,298	30.4	6,915	61.2	1,282	11.3	63	0.6
Not acceptable	13,271	35.7	4,905	37.0	683	5.1	24	0.2
TOTAL	37,182		22,330		4,847		338	

.345 ($p < .001$; $df = 37,180$). Due to the length of time covered in the present analysis, the relationship of overall rating to a third promotion is available for examination. Previous analyses were limited to the examination of two promotions. Individuals assessed as "more than acceptable" are six times more likely to obtain two or more promotions and over 22 times more likely to obtain three or more promotions as those candidates who received the lowest rating. These results differ somewhat with previous findings. Earlier studies (Moses, 1972; Moses & Boehm, 1975) found a 10 to 1 advantage on receiving two or more promotions for individuals with a "more than acceptable" rating versus those evaluated as "not acceptable." The data in the present analyses suggest that a substantial percentage of individuals with low assessment ratings tend to receive promotions over time. The correlation between date of assessment and promotion is $r = -.27$ ($p < .001$; $df = 37,180$). Individuals assessed during the first 10 years of the program, 1961 to 1970, accounted for 94% of the group receiving three or more promotions. The observed relationship of promotion with time becomes more evident in a long-term study such as the present one. This "time from assessment effect" attenuates the observed relationship between overall assessment rating and number of promotions. In spite of this, individuals receiving the highest assessment rating, about 6% of the candidates, accounted for about 30% of the individuals receiving three or more promotions. These results indicate a substantial relationship between performance in PAP and progress in management.

Overall assessment ratings and associated promotions for the majority sample are shown in Table 3. As one would expect, the results obtained for the White sample were very similar to the total-sample results. The relation between

TABLE 3

Overall Assessment Rating Versus Number of Promotions for White Sample

Assessment Rating	Total		At Least Once		At Least Twice		At Least Thrice	
	N	%	n	%	n	%	n	%
More than acceptable	2,047	6.1	1,832	89.5	703	34.3	97	4.7
Acceptable	9,832	29.4	8,078	82.2	2,081	21.2	147	1.5
Questionable	10,257	30.6	6,332	61.7	1,213	11.8	62	0.6
Not acceptable	11,353	33.9	4,372	38.5	661	5.8	24	0.2
TOTAL	33,489		20,614		4,650		330	

overall assessment rating and promotions is significant (X^2 = 5692.36; p < .01; df = 12; r = .336; p < .001; df = 33487).

Table 4 provides comparable data on overall rating and promotions for the Hispanic sample. These results also show a significant relationship between assessment ratings and promotions (X^2 = 127.66; p <.01; df = 9; r = .468; p < .001; df = 547). It should be noted that over 95% of the Hispanic sample attended PAP assessment during the years 1974 through 1979. As a consequence, Hispanics had a relatively short time in which to earn multiple promotions. Nevertheless, the same trends of higher overall ratings associated with higher levels of initial and subsequent promotions found for the majority group is evident in the Hispanic sample. A comparison of correlations between overall ratings and progress in the majority and Hispanic groups was performed using Fisher z transformations. A significantly higher correlation was obtained for the Hispanic group (z = -3.649, p <.01). This finding may be due to the fact that the time-from-assessment effect had less of a chance to impact the relationship between overall rating and progress in the Hispanic sample.

The PAP database contained data on six assessment dimensions and SCAT scores from 1961 to 1979. These six dimensions have historically been considered critical assessment dimensions. Means and standard deviations for this data set are shown in Table 5 for the total, White, and Hispanic sample groups.

Table 5 also contains the results of t tests performed on all variables comparing majority and Hispanic groups. The majority group obtained significantly higher scores on each of the variables. The large disparity in sample sizes between the majority and Hispanic groups created problems for interpreting results

TABLE 4
Overall Assessment Rating Versus Number of Promotions for Hispanic Sample

Assessment Rating	Total N	%	At Least Once n	%	At Least Twice n	%
More than acceptable	18	3.3	17	94.4	3	23.1
Acceptable	122	22.2	95	77.9	11	9.7
Questionable	255	28.2	76	61.7	8	5.8
Not acceptable	254	46.3	59	23.2	2	0.9
TOTAL	549		247		24	

TABLE 5

Means and Standard Deviations on Assessment Dimensions for Total, White, and Hispanic Samples (1961–1979)

	Total N = 36,613		White n = 32,948		Hispanics n = 546		
Variable	M	SD	M	SD	M	SD	t Value
Overall rating	2.04	0.93	2.08	0.93	1.83	0.89	6.48
SCAT verbal	35.92	9.75	36.57	9.57	32.28	9.55	10.39
SCAT quantitative	30.64	10.42	31.54	10.06	26.45	10.94	11.71
SCAT total	66.56	17.55	68.11	16.91	58.73	18.04	52.83
Oral communications	2.79	0.85	2.81	0.84	2.37	0.91	12.12
Written communications	2.75	0.92	2.77	0.91	2.51	1.04	6.61
Leadership	2.36	1.00	2.38	1.00	2.13	1.00	5.79
Awareness of social environment	2.80	0.79	2.81	0.79	2.73	0.82	2.35
Organizing and planning	2.39	0.95	2.42	0.94	1.97	0.97	11.09
Decision making	2.26	0.91	2.29	0.91	1.88	0.92	10.44
Progress	0.74	0.70	0.76	0.70	0.50	0.59	8.28

Note. All t values are significant at the $p < .05$ level.

when comparing the two samples. Small mean differences may result in statistically significant, but not necessarily substantial results. The largest differences were observed on SCAT scores, oral communications, organizing and planning, and decision making. On all these variables, mean differences between groups were approximately ½ a standard deviation or more.

Correlations of assessment ratings and SCAT scores with management progress and overall assessment rating is provided in Table 6. Also provided are the results of the analysis of differences in correlations between Hispanic and majority groups. These results show that all assessment dimensions predict the progress criterion and correlate with the overall rating. In addition, where a significant difference in correlations between the two groups was found for the prediction of the progress criterion, the correlation was higher for the Hispanic group. Results of the comparisons of correlations for the prediction of the overall rating are less clear. Assessment ratings on oral communications and leadership have a significantly greater relationship with the overall rating in the Hispanic sample. Organizing and planning and decision making have a significantly higher relationship with the overall rating in the majority group.

TABLE 6

Correlations of Assessment Dimensions With Progress and Overall Rating for Total, White, and Hispanic Samples

Variable	Total		White		Hispanics		z Progress	z Rating
	r Progress	r Rating	r Progress	r Rating	r Progress	r Rating		
SCAT total	.306	.451	.287	.433	.362	.525	−1.96	−2.28
Oral communications	.253	.494	.248	.493	.299	.510	−1.25	−0.55
Written communications	.180	.414	.172	.410	.230	.388	−1.40	0.61
Leadership	.248	.666	.241	.666	.337	.716	−2.42	−2.22
Awareness of social environment	.189	.571	.182	.575	.302	.569	−2.95	0.21
Organizing and planning	.293	.629	.282	.628	.310	.487	−0.71	4.79
Decision making	.266	.603	.254	.601	.283	.486	−0.70	3.75

Note. All z values are significant at the $p < .05$ level.

TABLE 7

Means and Standard Deviations on Assessment Variables for 1974–1979 Sample

Variable	Total n = 12,417		White n = 10,078		Hispanics n = 516		t-Values
	M	SD	M	SD	M	SD	
SCAT total	2.06	0.93	2.15	0.93	1.82	0.80	7.88*
SCAT verbal	35.56	9.94	36.91	9.56	32.14	9.48	9.39*
SCAT quantitative	29.61	10.35	31.23	9.73	26.45	10.90	10.82*
SCAT total	65.17	17.73	68.14	16.58	58.59	17.89	12.71*
Oral communications	2.76	0.97	2.80	0.95	2.35	0.91	10.52*
Written communications	2.91	1.02	2.98	1.00	2.49	1.04	10.83*
Leadership	2.55	1.07	2.63	1.06	2.12	0.99	10.63*
Forcefulness	3.02	1.01	3.07	0.99	2.93	0.95	3.14*
Energy	3.30	0.91	3.36	0.90	3.04	0.88	7.89*
Likability	3.31	0.61	3.30	0.61	3.25	0.60	1.19
Awareness of social environment	2.98	0.82	3.03	0.81	2.72	0.81	8.48*
Behavior flexibility							
Superiors	3.18	0.66	3.19	0.66	3.14	0.74	1.67
Need approval of peers	3.08	0.64	3.08	0.63	3.42	0.81	5.81*
Managerial identification	2.74	0.95	2.82	0.93	2.19	0.96	14.98*
Resistance to stress	3.48	0.97	3.51	0.97	3.23	0.91	6.01*
Range of interests	2.88	1.09	3.00	1.07	2.42	1.05	12.02*
Organizing and planning	2.42	1.05	2.52	1.04	1.96	0.97	6.20*
Decision making	2.23	0.99	2.31	1.00	1.86	0.92	10.01*
Scholastic aptitude	2.46	1.15	2.61	1.13	2.09	1.09	10.85*
Progress	0.52	0.56	0.55	0.56	0.47	0.56	3.17*

*$p < .05$

From 1974 to 1979, the PAP database was expanded to include ratings on all 18 dimensions evaluated in the program. Means and standard deviations for these data are shown in Table 7. Also shown are t test comparisons on all variables between majority and Hispanic groups. No differences between groups were found for likability and need supervisor's approval. The Hispanic group, however, was significantly higher on need for peer approval. Significantly higher scores on all other dimensions were obtained by the majority group. The largest differences were observed on SCAT scores, oral communications, written communications, leadership, behavioral flexibility, self-objectivity, management identification, range of interests, organizing and planning, decision making, and scholastic aptitude.

Correlations between the 18 assessment dimensions and management level achieved and overall rating are presented in Table 8. With the exception of need approval of supervisors, all dimensions are significantly correlated with progress and overall rating in both majority and Hispanic samples. Written communica-

TABLE 8

Correlations of Assessment Variables With Progress and Overall Rating for 1974–1979 Sample

Variable	Total N = 12,417		White n = 10,078		Hispanics n = 516		z Progress	z Rating
	r Progress	r Rating	r Progress	r Rating	r Progress	r Rating		
Oral communications	.256	.524	.256	.524	.269	.501	−.285	.711
Written communications	.217	.441	.217	.441	NA	.396	NA	3.727*
Leadership	.291	.689	.291	.689	.322	.712	−.780	−1.030
Forcefulness	.269	.597	.269	.597	.167	.565	2.366*	1.065
Energy	.289	.619	.289	.619	.196	.585	2.161*	1.178
Likability	.146	.339	.146	.339	.182	.362	−.817	−.608
Awareness of social environment	.242	.587	.242	.587	.284	.558	−.996	.923
Behavior flexibility	.265	.652	.265	.652	.286	.642	−.526	.380
Need approval of superiors	−.030	−.084	−.030	−.084	NA	.060	NA	−.533
Need approval of peers	−.100	−.195	−.100	−.195	−.093	.189	−.685	−.137
Self-objectivity	.253	.566	.253	.566	.349	.563	−2.335*	.239
Inner work standards	.230	.476	.230	.476	.210	.454	.464	.621
Managerial identification	.231	.433	.231	.433	.293	.469	−1.472	−.996
Resistance to stress	.244	.521	.244	.521	.214	.554	.698	−1.056
Range of interests	.202	.420	.202	.420	.194	.410	.183	.267
Organizing and planning	.266	.589	.266	.589	.327	.501	−1.372	2.768*
Decision making	.236	.545	.236	.545	.281	.492	−1.043	1.571
Scholastic aptitude	.272	.430	.272	.430	.375	.517	−2.521*	−2.452*

*Denotes that the z value is statistically significant at the $p < .05$ level.

tions, forcefulness, and energy had a significantly higher degree of relationship with the progress criterion in the majority group. Self-objectivity and scholastic aptitude had a significantly higher correlation with progress in the Hispanic group. No significant differences in correlations between groups were observed on any of the remaining dimensions for the progress criterion. For the prediction of the overall rating, organizing and planning had a significantly higher correlation for the majority group, and scholastic aptitude had a higher correlation in the Hispanic group.

Discussion

Results showed that assessment-center performance predicted progress for His panics as well as for the majority group. Data from the present and previous analyses demonstrated that tests and assessment results are both fair and valid for the prediction of Hispanic performance. Previous PAP investigations identified the overall rating, SCAT, leadership, decision making, and organizing and planning as variables most highly related to promotions. The highest correlations with the progress criterion in the Hispanic group were obtained for the overall rating, scholastic aptitude, leadership, self-objectivity, organizing and planning, and leadership. Other dimensions with substantial relationships to progress in the Hispanic group included decision making, managerial identification, awareness of social environment, and behavior flexibility. In general, the same variables predicted progress for both Hispanics and the majority group. The evidence does not suggest that a different set of predictors is required for the prediction of Hispanic progress in management.

In order to increase the rate of progress of the Hispanic community in industry, developmental programs focused on the improvement of skills and abilities that are known to be valid predictors of successful job performance are necessary. Besides the overall rating, the assessment variable with the highest degree of relationship to progress in the Hispanic sample was scholastic aptitude. Scholastic aptitude ratings are largely determined by SCAT scores. Improvements in basic verbal and math skills would appear to be a prerequisite to management progress for the Hispanic community. Assessment variables defining the four assessment factors, that is, Interpersonal Effectiveness, Administrative Skills, Sensitivity, and Effective Intelligence, are also all significantly correlated with progress and have substantially lower mean scores in the Hispanic sample relative to the majority group. Improvements in the four basic-skill areas will require extensive time and effort in education and training. However, remedial efforts focused on variables shown to be valid predictors of managerial progress offer the promise of significant payoffs. Howard (1986) indicated some potential positive relationships between college experiences obtained after initial employment and their possible effects on assessment dimensions and managerial performance. Moses and Ritchie (1976) demonstrated the value of behavior-modeling training for the development of supervisory problem-solving skills.

The selection model assumes a labor-force condition where a relatively small number of positions are to be filled from a large number of qualified candidates. As the year 2000 approaches, characteristics of the labor force may severely impact the basic premise of the selection model. Present predictions of the work force in the year 2000 are characterized by lower absolute numbers of recruits with less developed skills. The great majority of the available labor force will consist of women, minorities, and immigrants (Greller & Nee, 1989). Given these circumstances, corporations may be required to apply a placement rather than a selection model for hiring. Using the placement model, employment testing would provide information concerning a number of jobs at which an individual is most likely to be successful and what training might be required for a specific position. It is likely that the work force in the year 2000 will provide a major opportunity for the advancement of minorities.

The debate on bias in testing may have reached an impasse. The statistical and psychometric evidence demonstrating that valid tests accurately reflect developed abilities and predict criterion performance is clear (Wigdor & Garner, 1982). Opponents of testing argue that a lack of equal opportunity precludes the accurate measurement of ability (e.g., Gordon & Terrell, 1981). Most members of the testing community question this argument in light of the substantial empirical evidence supporting the use of tests for the fair prediction of job performance in all groups. For example, Pearlman, Schmidt, and Hunter (1980) summarized 698 studies on the prediction of clerical performance showing the generalized relationship between particular ability traits and performance. Research on the use of tests and assessment centers for management selection has pointed to a number of skills and abilities required for successful performance in management positions. Some testing critics call for eliminating the use of tests and recommend their replacement by more subjective measures. The irony is that subjective measures are generally less reliable, less valid, and more prone to bias and discrimination than objective tests. Reilly and Chao (1982) analyzed the validity and fairness of alternative employee-selection procedures and found that only biographical data and peer evaluations had validities equal to ability tests. Tenopyr (1981) argued that there are no alternatives better than tests when validity, degree of adverse impact, and feasibility of use are taken into account.

Assuming that poor test performance generally reflects less developed levels of ability, which in turn mirror educational achievement, our society faces serious social problems associated with the average level of development in many minority communities. Gordon and Terrell (1981) suggested that the testing community should become more concerned with facilitating equal opportunity. I would echo this sentiment by proposing a joint effort supported by government agencies, industry, and self help organizations directed at the development of critical skills identified as necesary for successful job performance. Valid employment test batteries could be used to identify specific weaknesses in these skills, and identification of skill deficiencies would assist in assigning individuals to developmental programs to help improve in these areas. Data on test-performance deficiencies would be an invaluable source of planning information for agencies concerned with providing programs designed to aid underemployed groups. Using valid tests as a placement vehicle would help to ensure that scarce training resources would be spent on relevant work-related skills and abilities. Focused developmental programs would be a very expensive effort and certainly less efficient than hiring only the presently qualified. However, as the work force of 2000 approaches, focused developmental programs may become one of a limited number of choices available to provide industry with a qualified work force. At the same time, the societal need to address work-related problems in minority communities would begin to be met.

References

American Psychological Association Task Force on Employment Testing of Minority Groups. (1969). Job testing and the disadvantaged. *American Psychologist, 24,* 637–650.

Bray, D. W., Campbell, R. J., & Grant, D. L. (1974). *Formative years in business: A long-term AT&T study of managerial lives.* New York: Wiley Interscience.

Bray, D. W., & Grant, D. L. (1966). The assessment center in the measurement of potential for business management. *Psychological Monographs, 80* (17, Whole No. 625).

Campbell, R. J., & Bray, D. W. (1967). Assessment center: An aid in management selection. *Personnel Administration, 30,* 6–13.

Casio, W., & Ramos, R. A. (1986). Development and application of a new method for assessing job performance in behavioral/economic terms. *Journal of Applied Psychology, 71,* 20–28.

Cleary, T. A. (1968). Test bias: Prediction of grades of Negro and White students in integrated colleges. *Journal of Educational Measurement, 5,* 115–124.

Cohen, B. M., Moses, J. L., & Byham, W. C. (1974). *The validity of assessment centers: A literature review.* [Monograph II]. Pittsburgh Development Dimensions Press.

Cronbach, L. J., Yalow, E., & Schaeffer, G. (1980). A mathematical structure for analyzing fairness in selection. *Personnel Psychology, 33,* 693–704.

Fincher, C. (1975). Differential validity and test bias. (1975). *Personnel Psychology, 28,* 481–500.

Glaser, G., & Bond, L. (1981). Testing: Concepts, policy, practice, and research. *American Psychologist, 36,* 997–1189.

Gordon, E. W., & Terrell, M. D. (1981). The changed social context of testing. *American Psychologist, 36,* 1167–1171.

Greller, M. M., & Nee, D. M. (1989). *From baby boom to baby bust: How can business meet the demographic challenge?* Reading, MA: Addison-Wesley.

Howard, A. (1986). College experiences and managerial performance. *Journal of Applied Psychology, 71,* 530–552.

Huck, J. R. & Bray, D. W. (1976). Management assessment center evaluations and subsequent job performance of White and Black females. *Personnel Psychology, 2,* 13–30.

Hunter, J. E., Schmidt, F. L., & Rauschenberger, J. M. (1977). Fairness of psychological tests: Implications of four definitions for selection, utility, and minority hiring. *Journal of Applied Psychology, 62,* 245–260.

Moses, J. L. (1972). Assessment center performance and management progress. *Studies in Personnel Psychology, 4,* 7–12.

Moses, J. L., & Boehm, V. R. (1975). Relationship of assessment center performance to management progress of women. *Journal of Applied Psychology, 60,* 527–529.

Moses, J. L., & Byham, W. C. (1977). *Applying the assessment center method.* New York: Pergamon Press.

Moses, J. L., & Ritchie, R. J. (1976). Supervisory relationships training: A behavioral evaluation of a behavior modeling program. *Personnel Psychology, 29,* 337–343.

Novick, M. R., & Peterson, N. W. (1976). Towards equalizing educational and employment opportunity. *Journal of Educational Measurement, 13,* 77–88.

Olmedo, E. L. (1979). Acculturation: A psychometric perspective. *American Psychologist, 11,* 1061–1070.

Olmedo, E. L. (1981). Testing linguistic minorities. *American Psychologist, 36,* 1078–1085.

Pearlman, K., Schmidt, F. L., & Hunter, J. E. (1980). Validity generalization results for tests used to predict job proficiency and training success in clerical occupations. *Journal of Applied Psychology, 65,* 373–406.

Ramos, R. A. (1979, June). *Language preference and associated employment test performance of Hispanic applicants.* Paper presented at the meeting of the International Personnel Management Association Assessment Council, San Diego, CA.

Ramos, R. A. (1981). Employment battery performance of Hispanic applicants as a function of English or Spanish test instructions. *Journal of Applied Psychology, 66,* 291–295.

Reilly, R. R., & Chao, G. T. (1982). Validity and fairness of some alternative employee selection procedures. *Personnel Psychology, 35,* 1–62.

Schmidt, F. L., Hunter, J. E., McKenzie, R. C., & Muldrow, T. W. (1979). Impact of valid selection procedures on work-force productivity. *Journal of Applied Psychology, 64,* 609–626.

Schmidt, F. L., & Pearlman, K. (1980). The validity and fairness of employment and educational tests for Hispanic Americans: A review and analysis. *Personnel Psychology, 33,* 705–724.

Society for Industrial and Organizational Psychology, Inc. (1987). *Principles for the validation and use of personnel selection procedures.* (3rd ed.). College Park, MD. Author.

Standards for educational and psychological testing. (1985). Washington, DC: American Psychological Association.

Tenopyr, M. L. (1981). The realities of employment testing. *American Psychologist, 36,* 1120–1127.

Thornton, G. C., & Byham, W. C. (1982). *Assessment centers and managerial performance.* New York: Academic Press.

Wigdor, A. K., & Garner, W. R. (Eds.). (1982). *Ability testing: Uses, consequences, and controversies* (Vol. 1). Washington, DC: National Academy Press.

Appendix A: Personnel Assessment Program Variables and Definitions

1. *Oral Communication Skills*: To what extent can this individual effectively present an oral report to a small conference group?

2. *Written Communication Skills*: To what extent can this individual effectively express his or her ideas in writing?

3. *Leadership Skills*: To what extent can this individual get people to perform a task effectively without arousing hostility?

4. *Forcefulness*: To what extent does this individual make an early impact on others?

5. *Energy*: To what extent can this individual maintain a continuous high level of work activity?

6. *Likability*: To what extent is this individual likable to others?

7. *Awareness of Social Environment*: To what extent can this individual perceive subtle cues in the behavior of others toward him or her?

8. *Behavioral Flexibility*: To what extent can this individual, when motivated, modify his or her behavior to reach a goal?

9. *Need Approval of Superiors*: To what extent does this individual need to have his or her behavior approved of by those he or she views as superiors?

10. *Need Approval of Peers*: To what extent does this individual need to have his or her behavior approved of by those he or she views as peers?

11. *Self-Objectivity*: To what extent does this individual realize his or her own assets and liabilities?

12. *Inner Work Standards*: To what extent does this individual want to do a good job— even if he or she could get by with doing a less adequate job?

13. *Managerial Identification*: To what extent does this individual relate to management's views and problems?

14. *Resistance to Stress*: To what extent can this individual's work performance stand up in the face of unusual pressures?

15. *Range of Interests*: To what extent is this individual interested in a variety of fields of activity, such as science, politics, sports, music, or art?

16. *Organizing and Planning*: To what extent can this individual effectively organize and plan his or her work?

17. *Decision Making*: To what extent can this individual make decisions of high quality, and how likely is he or she to make decisions when required?

18. *Scholastic Aptitude*: To what extent does this individual compare with other individuals in his or her ability to learn new things?

CHAPTER 13

Commonalities Between Test Validity and External Validity in Basic Research on Hispanics

Nancy A. Busch-Rossnagel

The purpose of this chapter is to examine the contributions of the psychological testing of Hispanics to basic psychological science. Whereas other chapters in this volume focus on the risks and benefits of psychological testing for Hispanics themselves, the focus here is on the potential risks and benefits to psychological theory associated with the inclusion of psychological testing of Hispanics in our basic research studies. If the ultimate goal of psychology is to understand behavior, then basic research should focus on both the explanation (the why) and the interpretation (the how) of behavior (Washington & McLoyd, 1982). As Anastasi suggested in the introductory remarks of this volume, test users should interpret test results within both the antecedent and the anticipated context. Hispanics vary greatly in their antecedent and anticipated contexts, so the basic premise to be developed here is that research with Hispanics can contribute significantly to our understanding of the how of behavior, not just of Hispanics, but of all humans.

To support this position, this chapter incorporates the perspectives of cross-cultural psychology and life-span developmental psychology. The choice of cross-cultural psychology is fairly obvious given that we are focusing on a group with different cultural origins than the majority group in our country. Cross-cultural psychology attempts to understand behavior as a function of the individual's interactions with the cultural environment (Eckensberger, 1972). Cultures, then, are the independent variables with which the dependent variables of behavior covary. However, culture is usually an assigned or status variable, which cannot be manipulated easily. Therefore, research involving culture is limited in its ability to enhance our explanation of behavior, especially when compared with the rigor obtained in traditional experimental psychology.

Because cross-cultural research holds limited promise for establishing the why of behavior, much cross-cultural work or subcultural work on different ethnic groups is conducted to examine the population generalizability of the tests or results. Such research on population generalizability can yield two results: significant differences between the groups or no significant group differences. The finding of no significant group differences is essentially meaningless because it is a test of the null hypothesis. The finding of group differences can also be problematic because ethnicity or culture is often confounded with other variables, such as socioeconomic status or education (Laosa, 1978), rendering interpretation of results impossible.

Such potential confounding variables suggest an appropriate use for cross-cultural or ethnic-group research: Identification of the confounding variables and other dimensions of the context of research enhances the interpretation of the research findings. However, much cross-cultural research falls short because the context, that is, the culture, is not adequately defined. Culture is a concept from anthropology that includes shared norms, values, and beliefs along with structural aspects, such as material entities (e.g., paintings, music, and dress), organizations, and institutions (Diaz-Guerrero, 1991); defined as such, it is not a psychological process. Specifying culture as a psychological context means that the psychological processes that are assumed to be the mediating variables between culture and behavior must be explicitly defined in research hypotheses (Eckensberger, 1972).

Once the psychological constructs underlying culture are defined, the effective use of cross-cultural studies becomes clear. Cross-cultural research is useful to basic psychological science when the environments explored are maximally different along the psychological dimension of interest. For example, middle-class American mothers show little variability in their attitudes toward child rearing. If we are interested in the effect of maternal child-rearing attitudes on children's socioemotional development, then we need to find environments that show variability in child-rearing attitudes. Such environments may very well be from different cultures. Inclusion of a sample in a study that is different in national origin will not automatically increase the heterogeneity of the independent variable, particularly when the groups being compared are subcultural in nature (as is true with many groups of Hispanics). Indeed, attempting to increase variability through the inclusion of ethnic groups alone may lead to confounding variables as mentioned earlier. In this example, there would likely be a confounded relationship between level of maternal education and child rearing attitudes. However, when one specifies the psychological concept underlying the relationship between culture and behavior, then the assumption of variability can be tested, along with the possible confounding effects of other variables.

There are many links between the approaches of cross-cultural research and those of life-span developmental psychology, which focuses on the possibility of age-related changes in behavior. Traditionally, behavioral changes were described by references to maturation as indexed by chronological age. In this framework, age is an independent variable that, like culture, is not under the control of the researchers. However, similar to the paradigm for cross-cultural research, advocates of life-span developmental psychology highlight the importance of specifying the psychological concepts mediating the relationship between age and behavior (Baltes, Reese, & Nesselroade, 1977). In this way, age-related changes are portrayed as a function of heredity, past environmental events, and present environmental events (Baltes & Goulet, 1970). Studying the effect of past and present environments—the antecedents and correlates of individual behavior—enhances our interpretation of test results consistent with the valid use of tests (Anastasi, this volume; Geisinger, this volume). Because of this concern for the context of behavior in interpreting results, much of what follows in this chapter focuses on the validity, not just of tests, but of the research design itself—what generations of psychology students know as internal and external validity.

To maximize the variability in the past and present environmental events, developmental psychology may turn to other cultures or ethnic groups. Both socialization strategies and schooling vary in different cultural environments, and these two constructs are among the most popular independent variables for developmental psychology. Variables such as these will be used to examine both the validity of research designs and the validity of measures as used in developmental research involving Hispanics.

The framework developed by Lloyd Rogler and his colleagues (Rogler, Malgady, Costantino, & Blumenthal, 1987) classifies the level of cultural sensitivity shown by professionals in mental health services with specific reference to Hispanics. To illustrate such design and construct validity, Rogler's approach is extremely helpful. Using Rogler's classifications as the backdrop, I developed four questions to explore systematically the population sensitivity of research on a particular cultural group. Phrased for Hispanics and developmental psychology, the questions are as follows: (a) How well represented are Hispanics in the developmental literature? (b) What are the characteristics of Hispanics represented in the developmental literature? (c) How has developmental research been adapted to include Hispanics among the populations studied? (d) What developmental research questions have arisen from the study of Hispanics, and have the answers to such questions been integrated into mainstream developmental studies? In order to explore the status of research on the psychological development of Hispanics, this chapter addresses each of these questions, with a particular emphasis on the last two.

The Representation of Hispanics in the Literature

When I began work at Fordham University's Hispanic Research Center in 1984, I was struck by the paucity of developmental research on Hispanic socialization. This intuition was supported by a computerized literature search, which located only six articles in this area. Computerized literature searching is problematic when there are multiple descriptors for the same group, but even searching for Hispanic, Latino, Spanish-speaking, as well as descriptions of national origin (Mexican, Chicano, Puerto Rican), does not change the picture much 7 years later. A recent search of PsychLit did not reveal any citations with psychological, development, and the various Hispanic descriptors coupled. In the PsychLit database, less than 1% of the references to development also included any Hispanic descriptor. Other sources document the underrepresentation of Hispanics in the psychological literature as well. In the entries of a bibliography on Hispanic women, less than 20% were published in psychology-related journals (Amaro, Russo, & Pares-Avila, 1987).

The picture is equally bleak in the two leading journals in developmental psychology: *Developmental Psychology* and *Child Development*. In the years 1988, 1989, and 1990, only 6% of the empirical articles in *Developmental Psychology* and 8% of the *Child Development* articles included any Hispanics as subjects. Interestingly, the vast majority of the articles did not report the ethnicity of their subjects (a finding supported by other reviews of *Developmental Psychology* and *Child Development*, see Fisher & Brennan, in press). Selecting the one issue of *Developmental Psychology*, for example, which contained the greatest percentage of articles including any Hispanics, the percentage of Hispanics in all the samples combined was 0.004%! These figures suggest that Hispanics are underrepresented in the developmental literature. (For the representation of Hispanics in our entire population, see the chapters by Eyde and Costantino earlier in this volume.)

In April of 1990, *Child Development* published a special edition on ethnic minority children, which included seven empirical studies with Hispanics. An analysis of these seven articles on Hispanics provides some answers to the second question, "What are the characteristics of the Hispanics represented in the literature?"

No study in the *Child Development* special issue reported the percentage of subjects tested in English versus Spanish or tested for a language-of-testing effect in spite of the fact that Hispanics are often portrayed as a linguistic minority (Geisinger, this volume; Marín, this volume). Three studies, all using school children, included measures available only in English. Of the four studies with Spanish measures, two reported using the method of back-translation, and two did not report how the Spanish versions were developed. Only one of the studies took the necessary step of pretesting measures with the non-Anglo population to look at their validity, and one study simultaneously developed English and Spanish versions of the measures.

It is not surprising that six of the studies in the special issue used lower or lower middle-class subjects given the socioeconomic status of Hispanics in American society (Eyde, this volume; Rodriguez, this volume). However, only three of the studies recognized the possible confounded relationship between ethnicity and social class. One study controlled the confounding by comparing middle-class Mexican Americans and middle-class Anglo Americans, whereas the other two statistically partialled out the effects of education and income.

Padilla and Lindholm (1984) characterized acculturation as a major dimension for future research on Hispanics, but only three studies in the special issue of *Child Development* included some aspect of acculturation. However, five of the articles acknowledged the diversity of Hispanics by specifying the national origin of the sample; three studied Mexican Americans, whereas two compared Puerto Ricans and Dominicans.

The computerized search of the literature, coupled with a brief survey of articles in the two leading journals of developmental psychology and an in-depth look at the articles in one special issue devoted to ethnic minority children, suggests that the representation of Hispanics in basic developmental research lacks the diversity that characterizes the Hispanic population (Laosa, 1978; Padilla & Lindholm, 1984). What is most distressing about the articles is the focus on demographic variables (e.g., ethnicity, education, and income) as opposed to a definition of culture based on psychological constructs. Thus, the subcultural work in the developmental literature falls short in terms of defining the psychological processes underlying ethnic differences.

Characteristics of Research on Hispanics

Answers to questions 3 (how research has been adapted for Hispanics) and 4 (what research has focused directly on Hispanics and its influence on non-Hispanic studies) require an examination of the specific content and approaches of basic research studies. In the special issue of *Child Development,* the most popular dependent variables were parent–child relations (including family socialization) and attachment or mother–infant interaction (McLoyd, 1990). These areas do not use measures usually subsumed under the heading of testing, but as representatives of the state of the art in developmental science, attachment and maternal teaching strategies are used in this chapter to examine the nature of research involving Hispanics. In addition, the classic cross-cultural study of Holtzman, Diaz-Guerrero, and Swartz (1975) and the subsequent work of Diaz-Guerrero (cf. 1986, 1991; Diaz-Guerrero & Diaz-Loving, 1990) are explored to illustrate developmental studies using traditional testing approaches.

Attachment Research

Attachment is an affectional bond, "a relatively long-enduring tie in which the partner is . . . interchangeable with none other" (Ainsworth, 1989, p. 711). The primary attachment is seen as occurring between mother and infant. Much of the work on attachment in infancy has been guided by the ethological perspective of Bowlby (1982, 1988). Ethologists view attachment as unique among affectional bonds because close proximity to the mother in times of danger and stress provides security to the infant, yet a secure attachment allows the infant to explore away from the secure base of the mother. This balance of security resulting from contact versus exploration is seen as contributing to species survival.

Although all infants become attached to their caregivers, individual differences in the quality of attachment have been researched primarily through observations of infants' behavior in a laboratory procedure known as the *strange situation*. This measurement technique places infants in an unfamiliar environment with both their caregiver and an unfamiliar person and involves brief separations from their caregivers (Ainsworth & Wittig, 1969). The qualitative differences in behavior in the strange situation have been categorized as *A*—avoidant–insecure, *B*—secure, and *C*—ambivalent–insecure (Ainsworth, Blehar, Waters, & Wall 1978); a *D*—disorganized category was proposed by Main and Solomon (1986), but few instances have been found except with abused children (Carlson, Cicchetti, Barnett, & Braunwald, 1989). In Anglo-American samples, the typical distribution of the categories is ⅔ avoidant (A), ⅔ secure (B), and ⅑ ambivalent (C) (van IJzendoorn & Kroonenberg, 1988).

The findings of qualitative differences in attachment have been replicated in cross-cultural studies, with the result that cultural differences in the distribution of attachment classifications have been observed. A meta-analysis of these studies showed that Japanese studies classified significantly more infants as ambivalent; a similar increase in ambivalent classifications was found in Israeli studies. Studies in Western Europe, particularly in Germany, categorized more infants as avoidant and significantly fewer infants as ambivalent. The meta-analysis showed that the secure pattern of attachment was the modal pattern in all cultures, but that there was considerable intracultural variability (van IJzendoorn & Kroonenberg, 1988).

In a longitudinal study of Anglo-American families (Ainsworth et al., 1978), the antecedents of qualitative differences in attachment were traced to the quality of the caregiving provided by the mother. Mothers who were sensitive and responsive in the first year of the infant's life were more likely to have infants who were securely attached.

Differences in caregiving have been the post hoc explanation for cultural differences in attachment patterns as well. Child-rearing practices were seen as culturally determined and, therefore, as leading to culturally unique distributions of avoidant, secure, and ambivalent infants. The German style of parenting was characterized as didactic and was likely to be associated with an avoidant style of attachment (Grossmann, Grossmann, Huber, & Wartner, 1981), whereas cultural practices in Japan encouraged considerable proximal interaction, which is likely to encourage ambivalent attachment in infants (Miyake, Chen, & Campos, 1985; Takahashi, 1986).

In contrast to this post hoc work, Fracasso's (1987) research provided an a priori test of this explanation of cultural differences in a sample of infants from Puerto Rico and the Dominican Republic. Descriptive studies of child-rearing practices and cultural values showed that Hispanics engaged in authoritarian and restrictive, yet nurturing and overprotective child-rearing. Authoritarian, restrictive behaviors have been shown to be associated with avoidant attachment, whereas smothering behaviors to ambivalent attachment, so Fracasso hypothesized that her sample should show a distribution of attachment categories with a higher proportion of the two insecure attachment patterns. More important, because the parenting practices associated with the distribution of attachment categories were presumed to be based on cultural values and practices, maternal behaviors were also hypothesized to vary as a result of acculturation.

Fracasso did indeed find a pattern in which more Hispanic infants were classified as insecurely attached than were found in samples of Anglo infants. However, her most striking finding was the sex differences in patterns of attachment. In the developmental literature, the distribution of attachment classifications has not been significantly different for boys and girls (with the exception of one study by Carlson et al., 1989, on abused infants). In the Fracasso study, the Puerto Rican and Dominican boys showed a pattern very similar to that found with Anglo-American infants. However, ⅔ of the Hispanic girls were classified as insecurely attached.

Fracasso's findings can be interpreted in two ways. If we take the perspective that patterns of attachment behaviors have the same meanings across cultures (the universal perspective), then the cultural differences indicate true differences in security of attachment. Because the long-term implications of insecure attachment are psychosocial problems, the universal perspective posits that the increased number of insecurely attached girls that Fracasso observed means that Puerto Rican and Dominican females are at risk for later psychosocial problems and implies the need for intervention into the parenting practices of Hispanics. Two assumptions underlie this intervention suggestion: that the same mothering behaviors lead to the same attachment categories across cultures (and across sexes) and that the consequences of attachment are the same across cultures. In effect, these assumptions require an assessment of the validity of the strange situation measure across cultures.

The validity of the measure (or lack thereof) as used in different cultures lies at the heart of the second interpretation of Fracasso's findings. Fracasso examined the maternal behaviors correlated with attachment categories and found that maternal behavior observed during a home visit was related significantly to the security of the infant attachment, but the specific behaviors were not the same as found by Ainsworth et al. (1978). In one case, the relationship between maternal behavior and security of attachment was reversed; Ainsworth et al. found that physical interventions were significantly related to *insecure* attachment, whereas Fracasso found that such interventions were related to *secure* attachments in Hispanic girls. Physical interventions have been seen as integral aspects of caregiving in Hispanic populations (Minturn & Lambert, 1964), so the mothers in the Fracasso study may have been following cultural prescriptions. However, support for this cultural specific view of attachment was undermined because Fracasso did not find a relationship between maternal behavior and acculturation. In sum, Fracasso's findings support the idea that maternal behaviors are related to the quality of attachment, an idea that we might hold as a psychological principle because it is culturally generalizable. However, the specific behaviors related to the quality of attachment, which would be the psychological facts, may differ among cultures.

The implications of Fracasso's research for a better understanding of the development of Hispanics are not clear because of these questions about the validity of the strange situation measure for this population. Unfortunately, the attachment literature used value-laden terms, such as *securely* and *insecurely* attached, which lead the unsuspecting reader to the assumption that the validity of the attachment classifications has been established across cultures. This assumption has been questioned by critics of the strange situation (Lamb, Thompson, Gardner, Charnov, & Estes, 1984), who noted that the research has implicitly valued only one pattern of behavior—that of the securely attached infant—rather than defining adaptability within an environment. An example can be seen in the physical interventions of the Hispanic mothers in the Fracasso study; in the inner city environments of these Puerto Rican and Dominican mothers, such interventions may indicate appropriate concern for the child's safety, rather than inappropriate caregiving.

This research on attachment illustrates how basic research has been adapted to include Hispanics (question [c]). Because the strange situation is an observational measure, language issues that might contaminate other tests have been minimized. However, this reliance on observation has lead to inadequate concern with the interpretation of the categories, that is, with the validity of the measure as used. To improve research on attachment in Hispanics, we need not only studies of the antecedents of attachment, such as that by Fracasso, but we also need to have follow-up studies on the consequences of attachment. Furthermore, we need to define the context of the attachment behaviors carefully so that the psychological construct of caregiving is not confounded with other processes (e.g., the stresses associated with low-income environments), which may also be present in the environments of Hispanics.

Child Development in Two Cultures

The cross-national study of Holtzman et al. (1975) provided a different picture of how research has been adapted to include Hispanics (question [c]). This ambitious examination of personality development from 6 to 18 years of age compared 450 Anglo-American children from Austin, Texas, with 450 Mexican children from Mexico City. Begun in 1963 before life-span developmental psychology had proposed the longitudinal sequential design (Schaie & Baltes, 1975), Holtzman et al. used overlapping cross-sectional and longitudinal sequences to examine age-related functions. Although the samples were representative of school populations and two social classes, the authors also acknowledged the possible confounding of culture with socioeconomic status (SES) and opted for examining this confounded relationship in a subsample that was carefully matched for parental education and occupation. Thus, the influences of age, SES, and sex were analyzed along with culture.

The dependent measures for the children in the study included mental abilities, perceptual–cognitive style, and an array of personality traits. Children were also rated by their teachers and mothers, and mothers were interviewed to measure maternal attitudes and values and to assess family life-style and home environment (e.g., intellectual stimulation and parental aspirations for child achievement). Although the research used measures primarily developed in the United States, there was considerable pretesting and training of examiners to maximize comparability of measures.

The stabilities of the measures across the 6 years of the study were also examined. These stabilities were relatively high and similar across the two cultures. When cultural differences existed, the stabilities were lower for Mexican children. These lower stabilities can be attributed to the use of measures initially developed for American rather than Mexican children. However, this explanation is too simplistic—the meaning of the lower stabilities still needs to be explained. Holtzman et al. suggested that the lower stabilities may have been due "in part to a greater sensitivity to situational factors at the time of testing" (1975, p. 296).

Examination of the influence of culture, SES, age, and sex showed some cultural similarities and many cultural differences. The authors used the findings to draw a picture of normal cultural behavior for each sample, which requires a simple review here. From the viewpoint of developmental research, two findings are worth considering in more detail: the interactions of culture with age and with SES. There were numerous age-by-culture interactions. In the mental abilities and cognitive style variables, such as WISC block design and a measure of perceptual maturity, the interactions originally favored Mexicans, (i.e., younger Mexicans earned higher scores than Americans). The reverse was true for personality variables, such as the Understanding factor on the *Jackson Personality Research Form*. For personality, the interactions had the effect of limiting cultural differences with increasing age, suggesting a strong general socialization influence: "It is almost as though socialization in the two cultures and the influences of society, peer groups, and the school, as contrasted to the family, brought the two populations of children closer together on certain psychological characteristics" (Holtzman et al., 1975, p. 357).

However, as for mental abilities, the effect of the interactions was to reverse the early superiority of the Mexicans, so that American adolescents were performing better than their Mexican counterparts. This developmental trend was often qualified by SES effects, which augment our understanding of cultural differences. In particular, Holtzman et al. examined the relationship of mental abilities to home environment. Although there were initial cultural differences (favoring Americans) in intellectual stimulation in the home, there were also subsequent cultural and SES differences in schooling. In the American sample, the public schooling was relatively well funded and homogeneous. In contrast, the Mexican schooling was highly heterogeneous, ranging from overcrowded public schools for the lower class to enriched private schools for the upper class. Thus, it is not surprising that the culture-by-SES-by-age interactions, in general, showed an age-related increase in social class differentiation for the Mexican sample. When sex was also a significant influence, the effect was to place lower class Mexican girls at a disadvantage compared with upper class Mexican girls or Mexican boys of either class.

The interpretation of the interactions of culture, age, and SES is enhanced considerably by the later work of Diaz-Guerrero on historic–sociocultural premises (HSCPs). An HSCP is a "deep-seated belief or assumption about life . . . held by a majority of individuals belonging to a given culture, subculture, or group" (Holtzman et al., 1975, p. 330). HSCPs govern the thinking, feeling, and situation-permitting behavior of individuals within that culture and, thus, are intervening variables between culture and behavior. HSCPs are the focus of Diaz-Guerrero's culture–counterculture dialectic, which hypothesizes that "the older an individual in a given culture is, and in particular the more liberal education he or she has received, the less the individual's thinking, feeling, and behavior will be governed by the HSCPs of his or her culture" (Diaz-Guerrero & Diaz-Loving, 1990, p. 518.). HSCPs have been the springboard for the discipline of ethnopsychology, which argues for understanding a culture on its own terms and with full awareness of the power of the subjective ecosystem that is exemplified by the HSCPs.

The ultimate result from research, which has been adapted to include Hispanics, is that we are starting to identify what is meant by culture in psychological terms. At the very least, the implications of the cross-national study are remarkably clear from a methodological viewpoint. Given the preponderance of interactions between culture and age, SES, or sex, studies that do not systemically explore the effects of these variables along with culture or ethnicity would have hopelessly confounded results. In addition, many of the findings of Fracasso, Holtzman et al., and Diaz-Guerrero have relevance for the validity of test use with Hispanics and adaptations that might be appropriate when interpreting test results. At its best, the adaptation of research to include Hispanics has suggested one avenue—the HSCPs—that may help us to discover the psychological processes mediating the relation between culture and behavior. Unfortunately, some of Diaz-Guerrero's work is available only in Spanish, so the challenge of his ideas has not excited many American researchers.

Maternal Teaching

The area of parent–child relations also contains an example of research that has focused on Hispanics with results that have transcended subcultural boundaries and have been integrated into the mainstream literature (question 4). The work of Luis Laosa on maternal teaching strategies is exemplary in terms of test development, the systematic exploration of questions for Hispanics, and the implications for understanding the behavior of all families. Laosa's studies of maternal teaching strategies began with the development of the Maternal Teaching Observation Technique (MTOT). The materials for the MTOT consist of an assembled Tinkertoy model and the pieces necessary to create that model. The mother is asked to teach her child how to make a toy like the assembled model. During the ensuing interaction, the frequencies of nine maternal behaviors are scored (Laosa, 1980a).

The development of the MTOT was carried out with concern for validity, reliability, and language equivalence—in short, qualities on which test development and use should focus, but which are often lacking in measures in the developmental literature (as with the construct of attachment). The categories selected for inclusion are empirically based, yet theory guided, so that the MTOT is representative of the major approaches to the psychology of teaching (Laosa, 1980a). For example, cognitive–developmental perspectives highlighted the importance of inquiry, whereas information processing suggested the inclusion of attentional devices such as visual cues. The work of Bandura (1977) and other social learning theorists emphasized modeling, whereas the operant learning perspective mandated the inclusion of positive and negative reinforcement. By including each major theoretical approach, Laosa demonstrated a concern for content validity from the beginning. Laosa was also careful to draw on the extensive body of work on social class and ethnic diversity in child rearing (cf. Hess & Shipman, 1965), which allowed MTOT results to be compared with, yet extend, the previous work done with Anglo and Black families.

Laosa also demonstrated a concern for possible confounding variables of his measure. For example, he found no evidence to support the possible effect of prior exposure to Tinkertoys. More important, Laosa developed the English and Spanish versions of the MTOT simultaneously. Using bilingual Chicano mothers, his pilot testing showed that the English and Spanish directions elicited different behaviors. Apparently, the Spanish verb *enseñar* was interpreted as meaning *to show* because the Spanish version showed modeling as a strategy more frequently than the English version. The Spanish version was subsequently changed to "Hoy quiero que usted haga que _____ (niño) aprenda como hacer ..." [Today I want you to make _____ (child's name) learn how to do ...] (Laosa, 1980a).

In his initial use of the MTOT with Chicano families, Laosa (1978) used Chicanos as a means to increase the variability of two aspects of SES (i.e., parental occupation and schooling), which he hypothesized to be related to maternal teaching behavior. He found a significant relationship between MTOT behaviors and parental schooling, but not with parental occupation. In further research with Hispanics, SES needs to be defined as a set of psychological constructs (not just occupation and schooling) in order to enhance our understanding of both social class and ethnic differences in behavior.

Laosa's use of the MTOT in comparisons of Anglos and Hispanics illustrates the proper use of different cultural (or subcultural) groups in developmental research. Maternal teaching strategy was hypothesized to be the psychological construct linking culture and behavior, and the two ethnic groups provided more variability than would be expected in one alone. However, the use of both Chicanos and Anglos also confounds the relationship between ethnicity and SES. Laosa explored this confounded relationship to explicate the nature of maternal teaching behaviors. Significant main effects for ethnicity were found on six of the nine MTOT behaviors (inquiry, directive, praise, visual cue, modeling, and negative physical control). Using one indication of social class—parental occupation—as a covariate, did not change this pattern substantially. When either mother or father's education was included as a covariate, the pattern changed dramatically; no ethnic differences remained (Laosa, 1980b). Thus, for maternal teaching behaviors, schooling and culture correlate highly and, hence, confound proper interpretation of the results.

Laosa's programmatic research efforts have included the use of the MTOT to develop models of the antecedents and consequences of maternal teaching behaviors in both Chicano and Anglo families. In one study of Anglos, Laosa (1982) elaborated on the meaning of the relationship between schooling and maternal teaching behaviors in a structural model of familial influences on preschool children's intellectual development. Schooling of the mother was seen as one indication of the psychological construct of "mother's socioeducational values." This construct had both a direct and an indirect influence on the child's intellectual performance; the indirect effect was through the maternal teaching behavior of modeling.

Laosa's work shows the promise of basic cross-cultural research, both in its meaning for Hispanics and for its wider applications. Laosa interpreted his work as providing considerable optimism for the improvement of the lot of Hispanics. Other research (cf. LeVine, 1980) suggested that the maternal teaching behaviors shown by the Anglo mothers and the Chicano mothers with higher levels of education are similar to the teaching strategies used in most American elementary school classrooms. The mismatch between maternal teaching style at home and what the Chicano child receives at school might be one cause of poor educational achievement on the part of Hispanics. If this is the case, then as the education levels of Hispanic mothers improve—as is happening—their maternal teaching behaviors will change to correspond more closely to the strategies used in schools. This match should facilitate the learning and achievement of Hispanic children.

The larger implications of Laosa's work are illustrated by its integration into the mainstream developmental literature. When reviewing citations of his work, the most referenced idea is the confounding of ethnicity with education. His findings also question the accepted superiority of verbal inquiry as a teaching technique when compared with modeling. Because inquiry lies at the heart of many of the cognitive approaches to development, and the cognitive approach has gained acceptance over social learning approaches emphasizing modeling, his findings challenge our understanding of psychological processes in all ethnic groups. Many questions remain about maternal teaching behaviors, such as the possibility of developmental differences in the appropriateness of teaching strate-gies (e.g., modeling vs. inquiry) and whether the match with the teaching style of the school system is a critical influence on its effectiveness (LeVine, 1980). Nevertheless, this programmatic effort, which began with Hispanics, represents a contribution to all of psychology, not just to Hispanic studies.

Conclusion

We have seen that the representation of Hispanics in basic developmental re-search is limited, both in terms of subjects and in terms of the homogeneity of the samples used. The restricted representation curtails the generalizability that is often the purpose of cross-cultural research; such was the case for cross-cul-tural research in attachment. However, simple comparisons of different cultural groups provide only limited evidence of external validity; although findings of no significant differences cannot confirm the null hypothesis, findings of differences among groups disconfirm population generalizability. Even the findings of signifi-cant differences may be problematic because they are often confounded by other variables (as was the case with ethnicity and education in Laosa's studies). These confounded relationships are seen as threats to external validity in the traditional approach to validity of research design (Cook & Campbell, 1979), which seeks to ascertain general laws that hold regardless of other variables. In the language familiar to most psychologists, that of ANOVA, the focus is on main effects, with interactions seen as impeding clear interpretations of research findings.

However, many developments in psychology suggest that interactions, not main effects, may be the key to human behavior. For example, the use of theory based on laboratory research findings has been criticized because of poor predic-tion of events outside the laboratory; that is, main effects are overshadowed by interactions that are apparent outside the control of the lab. When interactions are the focus of research, a new approach to external validity becomes necessary (Hultsch & Hickey, 1978). This approach, which predominates in life-span devel-opmental psychology, assumes that people are organized complexities—systems—that cannot be broken down in order to ascertain general laws. The relations involved in understanding human behavior are infinite because behavior includes interactions among biological, psychological, historical–social–cultural, and other levels. Riegel (1975) proposed a dialectic among these levels to account for development. Thus, each of the levels and their interactions become possible independent variables, so an assessment of the external validity of the research requires an answer to the question, "Have we adequately considered all dimensions in order to characterize the complexity of the possible influences on the behavior we are studying?" This approach to external validity is similar to a definition of content validity for a test: We need to specify the universe of the possible relations among independent variables and then take a fair sample of those relations (Pepper, 1942).

Just as life-span approaches have replaced traditional experimental approaches to child and developmental psychology, ethnopsychology (Diaz-Guerrero, 1986, 1991) is the logical extension of cross-cultural psychology. With its focus on the culture–counterculture dialectic and awareness of the complexities of the ecosystem of human behavior, ethnopsychology in many ways parallels the assumptions of life-span developmental psychology. A merging of the two approaches appears to be a fruitful avenue for future research on Hispanics.

Hispanics are a growing minority in our society, and our society is rapidly changing from mono- to multicultural. This multicultural background can be translated into improved basic research in several ways. Research with Hispanics can show the many ways in which environments may vary, and by using the environments of Hispanics, the variability of the psychological constructs can be maximized. When possible interactions are explored at the stage of research design, the assumption of the increase in environmental variance is confronted directly, as is the possibility of confounded relationships with variables other than the psychological construct under study. Designed in this way, research with different cultural or ethnic groups will contribute to our understanding of psychological processes across cultures as well as enhance our knowledge of behavior that may be culture specific.

References

Ainsworth, M. D. S. (1989). Attachments beyond infancy. *American Psychologist, 44*, 709–716.

Ainsworth, M. D. S., Blehar, M. C., Waters, E., & Wall, S. (1978). *Patterns of attachment.* Hillsdale, NJ: Erlbaum.

Ainsworth, M. D. S., & Wittig, B. A. (1969). Attachment and exploratory behavior of one-year-olds in a strange situation. In B. M. Foss (Ed.), *Determinants of infant behavior* (Vol. 4). New York: Wiley.

Amaro, H., Russo, N. F., & Pares-Avila, J. A. (1987). Contemporary research on Hispanic women. *Psychology of Women Quarterly, 11,* 523–532.

Baltes, P. B., & Goulet, L. R. (1970). Status and issues of a life-span developmental psychology. In L. R. Goulet & P. B. Baltes (Eds.), *Lifespan developmental psychology: Research and theory* (pp. 3–21). New York: Academic Press.

Baltes, P. B., Reese, H. W., & Nesselroade, J. R. (1977). *Life-span developmental: Introduction to research methods.* Monterrey, CA: Brooks-Cole.

Bandura, A. (1977). *Social learning theory.* Englewood Cliffs, NJ: Prentice-Hall.

Bowlby, J. (1982). *Attachment and loss* (2nd ed.). New York: Basic Books.

Bowlby, J. (1988). Developmental psychiatry comes to age. *American Journal of Psychiatry, 145,* 1–10.

Carlson, V., Cicchetti, D., Barnett, D., & Braunwald, K. (1989). Disorganized/disoriented attachment relationships in maltreated infants. *Developmental Psychology, 25,* 525–531.

Cook, T. D., & Campbell, D. T. (1979). *Quasi-experimentation: Design and analysis issues for field settings.* Chicago: Rand McNally.

Diaz-Guerrero, R. (1986, July). A Mexican ethnopsychology. In J. W. Berry & U. Kim (Chairs), *Indigenous psychology.* Paper presented at the 8th congress of the International Society of Cross-Cultural Psychology, Istanbul, Turkey.

Diaz-Guerrero, R. (1991, February). *Mexican ethnopsychology: Pictures in an exhibition.* Paper presented at the 20th annual meeting of the Society for Crosscultural Research, Isla Verde, Puerto Rico.

Diaz-Guerrero, R., & Diaz-Loving, R. (1990). Interpretation in cross-cultural personality assessment. In C. R. Reynolds & R. W. Kamphaus (Eds.), *Handbook of psychological and educational assessment of children: Personality, behavior, and context* (pp. 491–523). New York: Guilford Press.

Eckensberger, L. H. (1972). Methodological issues of cross-cultural research in developmental psychology. In J. R. Nesselroade & H. W. Reese (Eds.), *Lifespan developmental psychology: Methodological issues* (pp. 43–64). New York: Academic Press.

Fisher, C. B., & Brennan, M. (in press). Applications and ethics in developmental psychology. In D. Featherman, R. M. Lerner, & M. Perlmetter (Eds.), *Life-span development and behavior* (Vol. 11) Hillsdale, NJ: Erlbaum.

Fracasso, M. P. (1987). Quality of infant attachment as a consequence of parenting behavior and acculturation in Hispanic mothers. *Unpublished doctoral dissertation, Fordham University, Bronx, NY.*

Grossmann, K. E., Grossmann, K., Huber, F., & Wartner, U. (1981). German children's behavior towards their mother at 12 months and their fathers at 18 months in Ainsworth's strange situation. *International Journal of Behavioral Development, 4,* 157–181.

Hess, R. D., & Shipman, V. (1965). Early experience and the socialization of cognitive modes in children. *Child Development, 34,* 869–887.

Holtzman, W. H., Diaz-Guerrero, R., & Swartz, J. D. (1975). *Personality development in two cultures.* Austin: University of Texas Press.

Hultsch, D. F., & Hickey, T. (1978). External validity in the study of human development: Theoretical and methodological issues. *Human Development, 21,* 76–91.

Lamb, M. E., Thompson, R. A., Gardner, W., Charnov, E. L., & Estes, C. (1984). Security of attachment as assessed in the strange situation: Its study and biological interpretation. *The Behavioral and Brain Sciences, 7,* 127–147.

Laosa, L. M. (1978). Maternal teaching strategies in Chicano families of varied educational and socioeconomic levels. *Child Development, 49,* 1129–1135.

Laosa, L. M. (1980a). Measures for the study of maternal teaching strategies. *Applied Psychological Measurement, 4,* 355–366.

Laosa, L. M. (1980b). Maternal teaching strategies in Chicano and Anglo American families: The influence of culture and education on maternal behavior. *Child Development, 51,* 759–765.

Laosa, L. M. (1982). Families as facilitators of children's intellectual development at 3 years of age. In L. M. Laosa & I. E. Siegel (Eds.), *Families as learning environments for children* (pp. 1–45). New York: Plenum Press.

LeVine, R. A. (1980). Influences of women's schooling on maternal behavior in the third world. *Comparative Education Review, 24,* S78–S105.

Main, M., & Solomon, J. (1986). Discovery of a disorganized/disoriented attachment pattern. In T. B. Brazelton & M. W. Yogman (Eds.), *Affective development in infancy* (pp. 95–124). Norwood, NJ: Ablex.

Minturn, L., & Lambert, W. (1964). *Mothers of six cultures: Antecedents of child rearing.* New York: John Wiley.

Miyake, K., Chen, S., & Campos, J. (1985). Infant temperament, mother's mode of interaction and attachment in Japan: An interim report. *Monographs of the Society for Research in Child Development, 50.* (Serial No. 209).

McLoyd, V. C. (1990). Minority children: Introduction to the special issue. *Child Development, 61,* 263–266.

Padilla. A. M., & Lindholm, K. J. (1984). Hispanic behavioral science: Recommendations for future research. *Hispanic Journal of Behavioral Sciences, 6,* 13–32.

Pepper, S. C. (1942). *World hypotheses.* Berkeley: University of California Press.

Riegel, K. F. (1975). Toward a dialectical theory of development. *Human Development, 18,* 50–64.

Rogler, L. H., Malgady, R. G., Costantino, G., & Blumenthal, R. (1987). What do culturally sensitive mental health services mean? The case of Hispanics. *American Psychologist, 42,* 565–570.

Schaie, K. W., & Baltes, P. B. (1975). On sequential strategies in developmental research and the Schaie-Baltes controversy: Description or explanation? *Human Development, 18,* 384–390.

Takahashi, K. (1986). Examining the strange situation procedure with Japanese mothers and 12-month infants. *Developmental Psychology, 22,* 265–270.

van IJzendoorn, M. H., & Kroonenberg, P. M. (1988). Cross-cultural patterns of attachment: A meta-analysis of the strange situation. *Child Development, 59,* 147–156.

Washington, E., & McLoyd, V. C. (1982). The external validity of research involving American minorities. *Human Development, 25,* 324–339.

CHAPTER 14

Fairness and Fair Use in Employment Testing: A Matter of Perspective

Wayne J. Camara

This chapter seeks to contrast fairness in employment testing, based on the evidence that has accumulated concerning differential prediction and validity, with the continued public policy debate on the fair use of tests with minority groups, specifically Hispanics.

In this volume, Ramos framed the major issue in the industrial testing of Hispanics: "whether the historically positive results of psychological testing in industry generalize to the adult Hispanic labor population." Psychometricians, lawyers, employers, civil rights groups, and policymakers all believe that their own perspective best balances concerns of both the employing organizations and the minority applicants seeking equitable jobs.

About Predictors

Differences in the performances of members of minority and nonminority groups have been well documented with most common forms of cognitive tests (e.g., em-

I would like to thank Dianne Lane and Lynn T. Doty for their assistance in the preparation of this manuscript.

ployment, achievement, certification, and intelligence), often with minorities scoring up to a standard deviation below nonminorities. In such cases, lower score distributions or lower passing rates for members of minority groups occur. These differences in test scores have been cited as indicators of test bias resulting in adverse impact on minority groups. However, such differences in test performance are of little use in addressing the utility and validity of employment tests with minorities. The extent to which a test displays the same properties and patterns of relationships within different groups becomes the pervasive and perennial empirical question (Messick, 1989).

A substantial body of research indicates that differences in the test performance of minorities and nonminorities are reflected in differences in actual performance on the job (Pearlman, Schmidt, & Hunter, 1980; Ramos, this volume; Schmidt, 1988). That is, differential prediction studies indicate the comparability of validity coefficients (as reflected in correlations between test scores and job performance) between minority and nonminority groups.

Certainly the use of a test observed to have significantly lower validity for minorities than for nonminorities would be considered an unfair use of the test by many. Schmidt, Pearlman, and Hunter (1980) cautioned that such conclusions about differential validity can rarely be confirmed in a single study because minority sample sizes are often inadequate. Furthermore, differences between groups, found when combining data across studies to increase statistical power, are usually within the range expected by chance plus the operation of various statistical artifacts.

On the other hand, identical validity coefficients may be observed between groups, yet substantially different prediction equations may exist. When employers then apply a single solution to selection, one group may to be favored over another. Therefore, a differential validity approach is only partially helpful in determining whether employment tests have positive or penalizing effects for Hispanics.

The fact that there is no consensus definition for the terms *fairness* and *test bias* confuses science-based policy and even technical discussions further. Depending on the context in which the terms are used, the definitions may be broad or mechanistic, emotional or technical, or abstract or concrete (Gregory & Lee, 1986).

Ramos cited in this volume several varying definitions of fairness in the psychological literature, and even more disparate definitions are found in legislation and in the popular press. Cleary (1968) proposed a model of fairness based on regression that remains accepted by many today. The model defines a test as fair to a group if it does not underpredict job performance for that group.[1] The *Uniform Guidelines on Employment Selection Procedures* (Equal Employment Opportunity Commission [EEOC], U.S. Civil Service Commission, U.S. Department of Labor, & U.S. Department of Justice, 1978) provides an operational definition of "unfairness" of selection procedures:

> When members of one race, sex, or ethnic group characteristically obtain lower scores on a selection procedure than members of another group, and the differences in scores are not reflected in differences in a measure of job performance. (p. 38,308)

They state that under such conditions the use of the selection procedure may unfairly deny opportunities to members of the group that obtains the lower scores. When the EEOC guidelines were originally developed, suspicion prevailed that a single regression line would underpredict job performance of minorities. Today these EEOC guidelines still require studies of differential validity despite their narrow focus and the absence of confirmatory research on this point (Linn, 1978). Regardless of findings in studies of differential validity, differential prediction studies are required to determine if the benefits of tests as determined on nonminority populations generalize to groups such as Hispanics. Such studies determine if different prediction equations result from different groups. Differences in prediction equations are more relevant to discussions of fairness than are comparisons of validity coefficients alone.

The *Standards for Educational and Psychological Testing* (1985) stated the following:

> The accepted technical definition of predictive bias implies that no bias exists if the predictive relationship of two groups being compared can be adequately described by a common algorithm (e.g., regression line)...If different regression slopes, intercepts, or standard errors of estimate are found among different groups, selection decisions will be biased when the same interpretation is made of a given score without regard to the group from which a person comes. Differing regression slopes

---

[1] *For a more detailed discussion and critique of alternative definitions of fairness and test bias, see Hunter and Schmidt (1976).*

> or intercepts are taken to indicate that a test is differentially predictive for the groups at hand. (pp. 12–13)

Such differences in standard errors, slopes, or intercepts can indeed occur when validity coefficients are equal. In conclusion, differences in average test performance do not confirm (or disconfirm) test bias. Differences in test performance, job performance, and predictive equations must all be considered within the context of methodological issues (e.g., criterion relevance and sample size) in studies in order to evaluate differential prediction. As Ramos noted in his chapter, there is no consistent evidence supporting differential prediction or differential validity for Hispanics in employment selection or promotion.

The National Commission on Testing and Public Policy (1990) was optimistic that alternative assessment techniques will have less adverse impact on minorities without sacrificing validity in employment settings. There is some evidence that biographical data provide equal levels of validity with somewhat lessened adverse impact, yet the stability of initial validity in these instances may not be established. Reilly and Chao (1982) found that no alternatives to the cognitive, paper-and-pencil tests demonstrated equal levels of validity with less adverse impact. Tenopyr (1981) stated that when the practicality of more subjective methods is considered in addition to test validity and degree of adverse impact, no alternatives fare better than cognitive, paper-and-pencil tests.

About Criteria

With the convergence of evidence that neither differential validity nor differential prediction (specifically, underprediction for members of minority groups) hold up (Wigdor & Garner, 1982), researchers have attempted to locate the causes for the disparity in employment and educational opportunities for minority-group members that result from test performance.

The quality of criterion data used to measure job performance has been of growing interest. Recognizing that most job performance data used to test theories of differential validity and differential prediction were based on supervisory ratings and that some research has shown that raters tend to give higher ratings to members of their own race (Landy & Farr, 1980), meta-analyses have sought to contrast group differences on these and other types of criteria (Bernardin & Beaty, 1984; Ford, Kraiger, & Schectman, 1986; Kraiger & Ford, 1985). These studies demonstrated differences in performance when supervisory ratings were contrasted with other types of performance data. These studies confirmed that race effects on supervisory ratings account for some of the differences in job performance across criteria, but such race-related differences cannot be attributed solely to rater bias.[2] Although researchers have disagreed about the importance of these preliminary findings (see Hartigan & Wigdor, 1989; and Schmidt, 1988, for differing interpretations), more research is clearly needed in the area of objective performance measures.

Researchers have also discussed the quality of criterion data used as indicators of job performance. The statistical arguments concerning differential prediction and differential validity depend on assumptions that the criterion score is job relevant, reliable, and unbiased (Thorndike, 1971). The concern that criterion measures of job performance are inadvertently culture bound appears more plausible than similar concerns with predictors because of reliance on more subjective measures of job performance (e.g., supervisor ratings) and the potential for moderating effects. There have been few empirical studies conducted with Hispanics that examine this hypothesis.

Other researchers and policymakers have pointed to the rather low correlations between test performance and job performance criteria as indicators of the unfair use of tests (Hartigan & Wigdor, 1989). The multiple selection of cut-off points has continued to be suggested for employment selection. This approach would have tests regarded as measures of performance relative only to the subgroup of which one is a member (Mercer, 1977). In such situations, different passing scores are used for each group relative to the performance of that group on the test. Additional discussion of the unfair use of tests appears later in this chapter.

Research Findings: Performance of Hispanics on Employment Tests

As Busch-Rossnagel's chapter reported, literature on Hispanics' performance on employment tests is scarce. And much of the discussion is based on all compari-

---

[2] *It is also possible, of course, that non-Spanish-speaking supervisors may systematically undervalue the importance of bilingualism in the workplace in many settings.*

sons of nonminorities and minorities (which are dominated by studies comparing Whites and African Americans). Schmidt, Pearlman, and Hunter (1980) found only 19 published and unpublished studies reporting Hispanics as a separate ethnic group and having sample sizes of 50 or more in each group. They found it impossible to differentiate studies by ethnic subgroup (e.g., Mexican American or Puerto Rican) and reported several studies that identified Hispanics as "Spanish-surnamed Americans." Nevertheless, mean validities were within .02 for majority and Hispanic groups across studies. Differences in fairness analyses (using the Cleary model) were within limits of chance and statistical artifacts. In a study of assessment-center performance, Huck and Bray (1976) indicated that a common regression line could be applied fairly to both African Americans and Whites in predicting management progression (number of promotions). Ramos, in this volume, reinforced this finding, comparing Hispanic and White groups on management progression over a 19-year period. These results were obtained despite significantly lower progression rates for the minority group in both studies.

Unfortunately, much of the remaining research concerning differential prediction contrasts minorities and nonminorities, without reporting separate results for Hispanics. One major exception involves the Armed Services Vocational Aptitude Battery (ASVAB), the most widely used employment test in the United States. Data from the ASVAB, which contrasted the performance of Hispanics with Whites and other minority groups, are also applicable to nonmilitary screening because prediction estimates based on aptitude tests used with civilians, such as the ASVAB and the General Aptitude Test Battery (GATB), show considerable overlap in skills assessed and predictions made and show high subtest intercorrelations (Moore, 1989).

Several conclusions are apparent from analyses of ASVAB data. First, performance of individuals in all groups (Whites, African Americans, and Hispanics) is enhanced with increased education (with high school graduates and above scoring higher than those holding GED high school equivalency certificates, and GED holders, in turn, scoring higher than those with less than a high school education). Second, substantial gaps exist between these groups at each educational level. Third, Hispanics generally score slightly higher than African Americans at each educational level.[3] Finally, differences between subgroups decrease slightly

---

[3]*Eitelberg and Doering (1982) reported that average performance of the total Hispanic subgroup is significantly higher than the total African American subgroup only for high school graduates and above (p < .05) on the Armed Forces Qualifications Test, which comprises four subtests from the ASVAB.*

as educational level increases. There has been no substantial evidence of differential validity or differential prediction for Hispanics or African Americans on the ASVAB (Department of Defense, 1982). Differential prediction analyses found that the ASVAB slightly overpredicted performance in the military for Hispanic men (Eitelberg, Laurence, Waters, & Perelman, 1984), despite significantly lower high school completion rates for Hispanics than for any other group.

Fair Use of Employment Tests

Policymakers and the public appear to have been more persuaded by social-policy arguments of fair test use than by the statistical arguments of test fairness that this chapter has focused on up to now. The primary contribution of psychological researchers must be to present and demystify important scientific issues. Several scientific issues have been identified that could benefit from additional research.

The decision of how best to weight the scientific data on test fairness with the social-policy implications based on fair test use relies on value judgments, which researchers need to study empirically. Yet, such value-based judgments should not be portrayed as empirically optimal solutions.

Psychometrically optimal solutions for test use may be contrasted with socially optimal solutions that are based on empirical evidence. Ledvinka (1979) contrasted the psychometric arguments, which have tended to minimize damage to the employer at the expense of minority groups, with the fair use arguments, which require equal opportunities for members of all groups at the likely expense of productivity to the employer. He recommended a decision-theoretical formulation to force these value judgments into the open, that is, to be made explicitly. This model would consider several scientific-policy questions. For example, how much should the economic interests of employers in using merit selecton be valued as opposed to socio-economic interests of adversely affected groups? How should the applicant's views of utility be weighted against those of the employer? Research overwhelmingly supports the validity of employment tests for minorities and nonminorities. However, significant differences in test scores between groups, which result in relatively fewer opportunities for minorities, remain. These two findings are not incompatible as many policymakers imply.

The National Commission on Testing and Public Policy (1990) notes that because of the fallibility and imprecision of tests (and criterion measures) and the fact that such fallibility disproportionately affects certain lower scoring groups, fewer minorities who could perform successfully on the job are selected. The general limitations of test scores in predicting real-life performance have been recognized by testing specialists for decades and are reinforced in professional standards (*Standards*, 1985).

Basing selection decisions exclusively on test performance will often result in selecting a nonminority candidate whose score is marginally, but not statistically, higher than that of a minority candidate. In such an instance, the practical impact (utility in psychometric terms) of that specific selection decision may hurt the minority-group member who may have been repeatedly passed over for jobs. Certainly, adhering to such rigid and repeated decision rules could result in a work force composed primarily of nonminorities if an adequate applicant pool exists. Alternatively, the proponents of the fair test use argument call for relatively equal representation of different ethnic groups following the use of a test (O'Conner, 1989). Several empirically based and socially conscious strategies for selection have been advanced. Strategies such as race-(or ethnic-group-) conscious cut-off scores, score adjustments, or the use of test-score bands rather than individual test scores increase minority representation, with what many consider insignificant losses in test utility and validity for employers.

The political consequences of such actions are also worth noting. The following example is illustrative of many similar statistical adjustments made to test scores. In 1976, the Chicago Police Department was ordered by a federal court to increase the percentage of minorities promoted to the position of sergeant. The department then standardized test results by raising the mean score for African Americans and Hispanics to equal the mean score for nonminorities. As a result, the actual percentage of minorities promoted nearly doubled (Edsall, 1991). Originally, the police department successfully argued that as little as one point in test performance resulted in a moving up or down on the promotion ladder by as many as 200 places in the rank-ordered system. However, the court, noting the insignificance of a few points on a test, found that the utility afforded to the employer was outweighed by the opportunities denied to minority-group members with a top-down scoring approach. Although many may agree with this decision, it was necessarily a value-based decision because the test was found to be a valid predictor of job performance for all groups. This ruling no doubt has caused additional criticism from nonminorities who have been denied promotions but have scored above minorities who have been promoted. As Jenne Britell, a historian with Educational Testing Service stated in an interview, "The argument really boils down to a debate over the proper division of goods in our society. That's what it's really about and that's why it remains so difficult to resolve" (Ringle, 1978, C4).

The National Research Council's report entitled *Fairness in Employment Testing* (Hartigan & Wigdor, 1989) made a similar recommendation justifying score adjustments for minority group test takers on the General Aptitude Test Battery (GATB). Citing the modest validities of the GATB and possible criterion contamination (but admittedly no differential prediction), the National Research Council (NRC) recognized that this race-conscious decision would result in some loss in test validity and utility.

The high school drop-out rate for Hispanics is 33%, the highest of any minority group because educational level has such a dramatic effect on increasing performance on cognitive ability tests (Department of Defense, 1982), Hispanics seem to be at the greatest disadvantage on tests like the ASVAB and GATB. Such educational disadvantages on tests will also follow Hispanics even after entrance into the military. Higher scores on cognitively-based subtests are used for classification and placement in high-tech jobs, which often translate into increased civilian opportunities (Moore, 1989). The Department of Defense's Project A is a comprehensive effort to establish reliable and valid predictors and criteria of job performance that can increase the fair use of tests without implementing practices based solely on social values.[4] Ramos, in this volume, provided additional recommendations on how assessment data may be of value in identifying Hispanic adults who would benefit from developmental and educational programs aimed at providing the required job skills.

Personality Assessment of Hispanic Adults

Because Hispanic populations include people from Mexico, Cuba, Puerto Rico, the Caribbean, and other South and Latin American countries, with each group having varying degrees of familiarity and proficiency with written and spoken English, it is very difficult for statements about Hispanics' test performance to be

---

[4]*For more information on Project A, see a special issue of* Personnel Psychology, 43(2), *Summer 1990, edited by John Campbell.*

conclusive. Several examples of these limitations are evident with personality tests. Dahlstrom, Lachar, and Dahlstrom (1986) confirmed that several studies illustrate that Hispanics score above non-Hispanics on the Minnesota Multiphasic Personality Inventory's (MMPI's) *L* scale. Such performance is consistent with striving to make a good impression and tendencies toward conventionality. Yet studies of Hispanic performance on the MMPI rely heavily on Mexican Americans in the Southwest United States. In a study of assessment-center performance, Ramos noted in his chapter that Hispanic managers were found to score significantly higher on only 1 of the 18 job dimensions, need for peer approval, which adds some credence to this hypothesis.

Nonlinguistic differences may also impact personality test responses. O'Bannon (cited in Martin, 1990) observed that ethnic minority groups that are more religious because of cultural and social values would appear to be more pathological on questions of religious belief that are included in some personality tests. Martin (1990) discussed how response to an item on an integrity test, such as "I have never been tempted to cheat on my tax returns" or "I would not buy a bargain item if I suspected that it might be stolen," may be biased. Conceivably, these items might be empirically keyed in opposite directions for two groups; for example, the same item might be scored as true for nonminorities and false for minorities.[5] Yet, justifying this to the employer using the test, the applicants taking the test, or the judge deciding a trial would be complex and difficult because of common sense alone. Additional concerns about the moderating effects of education, socioeconomic status, culture, and employment experiences are also relevant.

With personality inventories, which often comprise true–false items, separate scoring keys translate into different acceptable responses to the same item for members of different ethnic groups. Certainly the face validity for a test can suffer when an objective item can be scored differently based on one's race or ethnicity.

Indeed two integrity tests, the Phase II and the TrueTest, have developed separate norms and scoring keys for Whites and minority-group members. Although the use of separate scoring keys and norms undoubtedly reduces the op-

---

[5]*These examples were cited by Martin (1990) as test items #53 and #71 contained on the TrueTest, which uses separate scoring keys for White men, White women, Black men, and Black women. However, because the scoring keys are not released for proprietary reasons, this description is only illustrative.*

portunity for adverse impact of selection procedures, it may also reduce the efficiency of norm-based comparisons of minorities and nonminorities.

Assessment Instruments for Hispanics

Many have documented the enormous disadvantages of Hispanic adults in social, political, and economic terms. It is clear that these disadvantages are not only related to the large test score differences, but also to the equally large differences observed in actual job performance. The National Commission on Testing and Public Policy (1990) asserted that no matter how carefully a test is designed, it typically includes a degree of cultural bias that artificially lowers test scores for Hispanics. Yet, if cultural bias is responsible for lowering test performance for minorities, one would expect that culture-specific tests would result in increased test performance. Although this chapter does not review the numerous studies conducted in the 1960s and 1970s on culturally fair tests, little data were found to suggest that minorities perform better on culturally fair tests (Arvey, 1972).

Nevertheless, assessment of Hispanics may require some additional considerations beyond those required for testing other ethnic minorities. First, language ability becomes a primary concern as Hispanics are the largest linguistic minority in the United States. The term *linguistic minority* means many things to many people. Olmedo (1981) noted that it is a convenient way to refer to Hispanics, Asian and Pacific Islanders, American Indians, Eskimos, and other groups whose members vary in their proficiency in English, which is their second language. O'Connor (1989) noted that Hispanics comprise both nonnative English speakers (NNESs) and native speakers of English who have been exposed from birth to Spanish in their home. Further differences exist among Hispanics in terms of their English proficiency and dialectic variation in both vocabulary and grammar (Acevedo, 1986). According to Olmedo (1981), individuals testing Hispanics must (a) understand the kind and degree of bilingualism of the test taker and (b) separate out any deficits with respect to standard English-language usage from acculturation and basic knowledge, skills, abilities, and traits required on the job. (Marín's chapter in this volume discusses some of these points in greater detail.)

Thus, language proficiency should be a more important consideration in assessment than membership in a particular ethnic group (Scheuneman & Briel, 1988). Research on Hispanics should define the degree of bilingualism and preference or proficiency for English of a given sample. An individual may understand Spanish, but express him- or herself best in English, or the reverse. Proficiency in a spoken language is not a perfect indicator of one's written language ability (Durán, this volume).

Translations

The last issue to be discussed in this chapter is the availability and proper use of translations of tests. Questions such as when to use translations or how best to combine such data with other assessment procedures have been examined, primarily in regard to educational tests, for decades. The testing of NNES minorities may present the greater difficulties for test users. When validated translations are available, the user is still faced with at least two problems: (a) determining when to use the English or Spanish version, and (b) determining to what extent performance on either version is impaired by linguistic deficiencies.

As stated earlier, a prime consideration in testing linguistic minorities is the degree of language proficiency of the test taker. Thus, accurate assessment of language proficiency may become part of the assessment. In this chapter, Durán provided a pessimistic appraisal of current measures used to determine language proficiency, noting that existing instruments lack a theoretical consensus about what language proficiency is and fail to assess the full range of competencies associated with being a proficient speaker of English (no matter which approach or theory defines *proficient*). Finally, such tests often lack normative studies and evidence of their reliability and validity. Lacking comprehensive and objective techniques, decisions of language proficiency typically rely on a substantial degree of subjective judgment.

In situations where language deficiencies of Hispanic test takers require the use of translated tests, the choice of assessment instrument may present a greater obstacle for the test user than it would for many other ethnic minority groups. Perhaps the greatest problem with nearly all published Spanish versions of tests is the generalizing of test norms to populations other than those for which they were developed and standardized. Even when Hispanic norms are available, they may not solve this problem. The NNES Hispanic population in the United States exhibits diversity in language structure, dialect, and cultural assimilation. Subcultural differences account for the substantial variation within the Hispanic population.

In employment settings, Spanish versions of tests are much less likely to be available, particularly for measures of general cognitive ability and specific skills.

A substantial number of personality tests are available in Spanish and a growing number of integrity tests are becoming available in Spanish translations. However, test users should question their applicability for employment screening when the existence of appropriate norms and the equivalency of translations are not documented. For example, integrity tests that have been translated into Spanish lack research demonstrating their equivalency to English forms and provide little other advice to test users (American Psychological Association, 1991). This problem is particularly troublesome because integrity tests are primarily for entry-level positions in retail and fast-food industries, and these applicants are increasingly members of ethnic and language minorities. When Spanish versions of tests are available, they typically report using back-translations or provide no documentation on how the tests were developed (Busch-Rossnagel, this volume). When translated tests are developed for NNES groups, test developers should provide data on the equivalence of reliability and validity between test versions.

Tests developed and marketed for use with linguistically diverse groups (e.g., Hispanics with limited English proficiency) should similarly provide explicit data on the applicability of test results and norms for test takers with limited writing and reading abilities in English (*Standards*, 1985). In essence, when assessing NNES (or limited-English-speaking) Hispanics, the first assessment must be to determine the limitations of the instrument intended for use.

There is recognition in educational and clinical settings of the unique concerns presented in assessing Hispanics and other linguistic minorities. Suggested modifications in test administration and inclusion of relevant interpretative cautions are found in many of such settings. However, there appears to be little evidence that consideration of linguistic differences is widely applied in employment testing. Even when linguistic abilities are not of prime concern on an instrument, cultural factors can be associated with response patterns, especially on noncognitive tests and interest inventories. Those studying industrial testing programs have performed little work other than comparative validations using Hispanics in contrast to nonminority populations.

Summary

This chapter has focused on some of the statistical consideratons of fairness and some of the social policy consideratons for the fair use of tests. It has also described the unique considerations in testing Hispanics in employment settings and the inadequacies of translations and measures of language proficiency.

Although research has confirmed significant test score differences between Hispanics and non-Hispanics, these have been comparable with performance differences observed on the job in industrial settings. The remaining statistical questions tend to center on the adequacy and objectivity of the criteria used in evaluating test validity and job performance. The fair-use argument entails an assumption of equality for all groups despite performance differences on tests. If this argument is accepted in its most extreme form, the rationale for any scientifically based assessment would be dismissed, and utility would become severely compromised.

Despite the lack of empirical support for differential validity or differential prediction in employment testing, it is evident that linguistic minorities may not perform as well on tests, both because of social realities and also because of limited English proficiency (especially on assessments that do not incorporate a measure of language proficiency). Extreme caution must be exerted in assessing linguistic minorities in all phases of selection—choice of instruments, evaluation of responses, interpretation, and decisions based on test results. Standardized, objective, and valid indicators of language proficiency and acculturation are needed to improve the efficiency of selection decisions with adult Hispanics.

Finally, there is little agreement in the literature concerning the proper role of tests with Hispanics or other ethnic minorities. What appears most elusive is any common agreement on definitions of terms such as *bias, fairness,* and *fair use* of tests. Ringle (1978) provided an illustration of how individuals with such disparate perspectives continue to define the terms differently:

Cultural bias these days . . . is a sort of butterfly net for a lot of loose flying concepts. To linguists it is the communication problem that exists between two people to whom the same words may mean different things. To anthropologists it is the tendency to interpret and evaluate other cultures in terms of one's own. To psychologists it is a potential impediment to fair and accurate psychological testing. To educators it is a reason standardized test scores aren't rising. To a job-hunter it's an employment test which asks non-job-related questions. To many civil rights leaders it is the successor to legal and institutional bias as the major impediment preventing minority groups from sharing fully in the American dream. (p. C4)

Perhaps this quote is most useful in understanding why employers, educators, test takers, lawyers, and the general public continue to approach these issues from their own very different perspective.

References

Acevedo, M. A. (1986). Assessment instruments for minorities. *ASHA Reports, 16,* 46–51.

American Psychological Association. (1991). *Questionnaires used in the prediction of trustworthiness in pre-employment selection decisions: An APA Task Force report.* Washington, DC: Author.

Arvey, R. D. (1972). Some comments on culturally fair tests. *Personnel Psychology, 25,* 433–448.

Bernardin, J., & Beaty, R. (1984). *Performance appraisal: Assessing human behavior at work.* Boston: Kent.

Cleary, T. A. (1968). Test bias: Prediction of grades of Negro and White students in integrated colleges. *Journal of Educational Measurement, 5,* 115–124.

Dahlstrom, W. G., Lachar, D., & Dahlstrom, L. E. (1986). *MMPI patterns of American minorities.* Minneapolis: University of Minnesota Press.

Department of Defense. (1982). *Profile of American youth: 1980 nationwide administration of the Armed Services Vocational Aptitude Battery.* Washington, DC: Office of the Assistant Secretary of Defense (Manpower, Reserve Affairs, and Logistics).

Edsall, T. B. (1991, January 15). Racial preferences produce change, controversy—Effect on police and fire departments in many U.S. communities has been dramatic. *The Washington Post,* p. A4.

Eitelberg, M. J., & Doering, Z. (1982). *Uniforms and jeans.* Paper presented at the annual convention of the American Educational Research Association, Chicago, IL.

Eitelberg, M. J., Laurence, J. H., Waters, B. K., & Perelman, L. S. (1984). *Screening for service: Aptitude and education criteria for military entry.* Alexandria, VA: Human Resources Research Organization.

Equal Employment Opportunity Commission, U.S. Civil Service Commission, U.S. Department of Labor, & U.S. Department of Justice. (1978, August 25). Uniform guidelines on employee selection procedures. *Federal Register, 43(166),* 38290–38309.

Ford, J. K., Kraiger, K., & Schectman, S. L. (1986). Study of race effects in objective indices and subjective evaluations of performance: A meta-analysis of performance criteria. *Psychological Bulletin, 99,* 330–337.

Gregory, S., & Lee, S. (1986). Psychoeducational assessment of racial and ethnic minority groups: Professional implications. *Journal of Counseling and Development, 64,* 635–637.

Hartigan, J. A., & Wigdor, A. K. (1989). *Fairness in employment testing—Validity generalization, minority issues, and the general aptitude test battery.* Washington, DC: National Academy Press.

Huck, J. R., & Bray, D. W. (1976). Management assessment center evaluations and subsequent job performance of White and Black females. *Personnel Psychology, 2,* 13–30.

Hunter, J. E., & Schmidt, F. L. (1976). A critical analysis of statistical and ethical implications of various definitions of "test bias." *Psychological Bulletin, 83*, 1053–1071.

Kraiger, K., & Ford, J. K. (1985). A meta-analysis of ratee race effects in performance ratings. *Journal of Applied Psychology, 70*, 56–65.

Landy, F. J., & Farr, J. L. (1980). A process model of performance rating. *Psychological Bulletin, 87*, 72–107.

Ledvinka, J. (1979). The statistical definition of fairness in the federal selection guidelines and its implications for minority employment. *Personnel Psychology, 32*, 551–562.

Linn, R. L. (1978). Single-group validity, differential validity, and differential prediction. *Journal of Applied Psychology, 63*, 507–512.

Martin, J. (1990, December). Workplace testing—Why can't we get it right? *Across the Board*, pp. 32–39.

Mercer, J. (1977). Identifying the gifted Chicano child. In J. Martinez (Ed.), *Chicano Psychology* (pp. 153–173). New York: Academic Press.

Messick, S. (1989). Validity. In R. L. Linn (Ed.), *Educational Measurement* (3rd ed., pp. 13–103). New York: American Council on Education and MacMillan.

Moore, E. G. J. (1989). Ethnic group differences in the armed services vocational aptitude battery (ASVAB) performance of American youth: Implications for career prospects. In B. R. Gifford (Ed.), *Test policy and test performance: Education, language, and culture* (pp. 183–206). Boston: Kluwer Academic.

National Commission on Testing and Public Policy. (1990). *From gatekeeper to gateway: Transforming testing in America*. Chestnut Hill, MA: Author.

O'Connor, M. C. (1989). Aspects of differential performance by minorities on standardized tests: Linguistic and sociocultural factors. In B. R. Gifford (Ed.), *Test policy and test performance: Education, language, and culture* (pp. 129–181). Boston: Kluwer Academic.

Olmedo, E. L. (1981). Testing linguistic minorities. *American Psychologist, 36*, 1078–1085.

Pearlman, K., Schmidt, F. L., & Hunter, J. E. (1980). Validity generalization results for tests used to predict job proficiency and training success in clerical occupations. *Journal of Applied Psychology, 65*, 373–406.

Reilly, R. R., & Chao, G. T. (1982). Validity and fairness of some alternative employee selection procedures. *Personnel Psychology, 35*, 11–62.

Ringle, K. (1978, March 19). Overcoming cultural bias. *The Washington Post*, pp. C1, C4.

Scheuneman, J. D., Briel, J. B. (1988, April). *Differential effects of selected item features on the performance of Hispanic and White examinees*. Paper presented at the 1988 meeting of the American Educational Research Association, New Orleans, LA.

Schmidt, F. L. (1988). The problem of group differences in ability test scores in employment selection. *Journal of Vocational Behavior, 33*, 272–292.

Schmidt, F. L., Pearlman, K., & Hunter, J. E. (1980). The validity and fairness of employment and educational tests for Hispanic Americans: A review and analysis. *Personnel Psychology, 33*, 705–724.

Standards for educational and psychological testing. (1985). Washington, DC: American Psychological Association.

Tenopyr, M. L. (1981). The realities of employment testing. *American Psychologist, 36,* 1120–1127.

Thorndike, R. L. (1971). Concepts of culture-fairness. *Journal of Educational Measurement, 8,* 63–70.

Wigdor, A. K., & Garner, W. R. (1982). *Ability testing: Use, consequences, and controversies, part I: Report of the committee.* Washington, DC: National Academy Press.

PART FOUR

Cultural and Clinical Issues in the Testing of Hispanics

CHAPTER 15

Issues in the Measurement of Acculturation Among Hispanics

Gerardo Marín

In a recent analysis of the literature on drug use among ethnic and racial minority groups, Trimble (1990–1991) lamented the lack of attention paid by researchers in defining their samples. Specifically, Trimble criticized the use of "ethnic glosses" or overly general labels (e.g., *Hispanics*), without acknowledging heuristically important differences among the respondents. Among these characteristics that define members of a group are generational history, national background, and those demographic characteristics that may be of relevance for a given study such as poverty level, educational attainment, and migration history. Trimble also suggested that a proper measure of people's ethnicity becomes essential in order to understand properly the psychological makeup and behavior of the members of ethnic groups.

Preparation of this chapter was partially funded by grants AA08545 from the National Institute of Alcohol Abuse and Alcoholism (Gerardo Marín, principal investigator) and CA39260 from the National Cancer Institute (Eliseo Pérez-Stable, Barbara Marín, and Gerardo Marín, coprincipal investigators).

As a process variable that must be measured on a continuum (Smith, 1980), ethnic identification has been defined as including at least three basic components: (a) birth and generational history; (b) culture-specific behaviors and practices (e.g., language use, peer preferences, and media use); and (c) culture-specific attitudes that include adherence to a culture's values and norms as well as in-group and out-group attitudes, and, of course, self-identification (Smith, 1980). Changes in these components of ethnicity have usually been considered in the psychological literature as part of the acculturative process of cultural groups or of ethnic–racial minorities (Gordon, 1964).

This chapter examines problems in the definition and measurement of acculturation among Hispanics as found in the physical and mental health literature and also examines some findings related to the usefulness of the construct in understanding the characteristics of the fastest growing ethnic group in the United States. The following arguments support Trimble's original notion that research with ethnic groups must go beyond the ethnic gloss of identifying respondents at a macrogroup level and suggest that at a minimum, research with Hispanics must address behavioral and attitudinal differences that may be due to the acculturative process.

The Nature of Acculturation

Most psychological research defines the construct of acculturation as the product of culture learning due to contacts between the members of two or more groups (Berry, 1980). Acculturation, as such, is a process of attitudinal and behavioral change undergone by individuals who reside in multicultural societies (e.g, the United State, Israel, Canada, and Spain) or who come in contact with a new culture due to colonization, invasions, or other important political changes. The psychological and social changes that are part of the acculturation process are usually perceived to be dependent on the characteristics of the individual (e.g., level of initial identification with the values of the culture of origin) as well as on the intensity and importance of the contact between the various cultural groups. Of utmost importance to the psychological understanding of acculturation is the fact that it is perceived as a fluid, never-ending process (Berry, Trimble, & Olmedo, 1986).

The study of acculturation has a long history. Berry (1980) suggested that acculturation as a construct was being used in the social sciences as early as 1880. However, the lack of consensus on the conceptualization of acculturation is easily recognized when the works of various social scientists are reviewed. For example, the psychological changes that take place in an individual owing to his or her interaction with a new culture were usually not considered part of the definition of acculturation until the publication of the work of Redfield, Linton, and Herskovitz (1936). In addition, many of the early definitions of acculturation suggested that other processes were either related to or part of the acculturation of an individual. Because of this, macrosocial concepts such as value diffusion and cultural change have often been associated with or equated to acculturation. By the same token, assimilation has been used interchangeably with acculturation, or else one of these concepts has been made part of the other. Nevertheless, the initial definition of acculturation proposed by Redfield et al. (1936) differentiated the individual process of culture learning (acculturation) from culture change (when cultures modify norms and values) and from assimilation or culture diffusion.

Among psychologists, the concept of acculturation usually denotes those changes in individuals that are produced by contact with one or more cultural groups. These changes may be the product of violent events such as wars, invasions, the conquest of certain lands, or of more peaceful events such as the federation of states, the creation of common markets, missionary activities, or tourism. Furthermore, acculturative changes are probably more commonly produced by the migration of an individual to a new culture.

The culture learning taking place as part of the acculturation process can be perceived as occurring at three levels. First, and probably at the most superficial level, is the learning (and forgetting) of the facts that are part of one's cultural history or tradition. An acculturating individual could, for example, forget the names of important historical figures from his or her country of origin, significant dates in the country's history, or parts of the national anthem of his or her country of origin, while learning the same aspects of the new culture. Immigrants from Latin America, for example, may forget (or if they are children, never learn) the names of historical figures such as San Martín, Bolívar, Juárez, and Nariño, but remember important facts about Washington, Jefferson, and Lincoln.

Also part of the superficial level of acculturation are changes in the consumption of foods and in the uses of media. An acculturating Hispanic would probably consume fewer Latin American foods (e.g., tamales, white rice, and corn products such as arepas or tortillas) and increase the consumption of more "American" foods (e.g., hamburgers, french fries, and stews). At this same superficial level, one would probably find a decrease in the significance of holidays such as "El Día de Reyes" (January 6), whereas Thanksgiving would take on a new meaning for an acculturating family.

A question could be raised here as to whether significant changes are really taking place in the individual who is acculturating, as is implied in the definition of acculturation, or rather if most of the changes reflect curiosity, adaptation to the new environment, and the availability of food and ethnic media. For example, high levels of exposure to English-language media may indeed reflect a significant change in the individual as a function of acculturation, but it may also reflect the lack of Spanish-language media in the place of residence, the programming quality and preferences, the transmission schedules, as well as the technical quality and frequency of the media.

A second and intermediate level at which culture learning can be expected to take place as a function of acculturation involves the more central behaviors of the acculturating individual, behaviors perceived to be at the core of a person's social life. Language preference and use are but two of these central behaviors that may reflect a more significant change in an acculturating individual. These two aspects of a person's linguistic behavior can, of course, be perceived as merely utilitarian in cultural exchanges, because people need to speak at least rudiments of the language of the host country in order to obtain a job or shop. Nevertheless, changes in linguistic-preference patterns signal more profound acculturation than do changes in knowledge of historical facts or food-consumption patterns. Other possible indicators of this level of acculturation are ethnicity of friends, neighbors, and coworkers, ethnicity of spouse, names given to children, and preference for ethnic media in multicultural environments.

A third, more significant level at which changes can take place in individuals as a function of acculturation is in terms of their values and norms, those constructs that prescribe people's worldviews and interaction patterns. Changes at this level can be expected to be more permanent and to reflect actual culture learning (or adoption). For example, a number of studies have suggested that Hispanic cultural values encourage positive interpersonal relationships and discourage negative, competitive, and assertive interactions—what we have called the "simpatia" script (Triandis, Marín, Lisansky & Betancourt, 1984). Acculturative pressures on Hispanics could be expected to change this social script so that it either becomes less central to the individual or it becomes a behavioral standard only when interacting with other Hispanics who have not been acculturated. Other group-specific values and norms of Hispanics that could be changed as a function of acculturation are the significance of familialism (Sabogal, Marín, Otero-Sabogal, Marín, & Pérez-Stable, 1987) and collectivism (Marín & Triandis, 1985; Triandis, 1990). As a matter of fact, it has been shown (Sabogal et al., 1987) that some aspects of familialism (e.g., sense of obligation and the power of the family as a behavioral referent) change as a function of acculturation, but others (e.g., support received and expected from relatives) remain important for highly acculturated Hispanics as well as for the less acculturated.

This differentiation of levels at which acculturation can take place is useful because it helps researchers to define the type of instrumentation that can be used to measure acculturation at each level. Superficial changes brought about by contact with different cultures can be measured by diffusion of information (e.g., learning about a culture's heroes) or experience with cultural objects (e.g., changes in diet to include food from the host culture). Measuring more significant changes in an individual's behavior as a function of acculturation may imply evaluating changes in values and norms, something that is not as easy as measuring language preference or patterns in food consumption.

One can argue that, ideally, acculturation should be measured at the more significant level of changes in values and norms. At the same time, and as mentioned later, measurements at an intermediate level (e.g., of language use and preference) seem to have produced reliable and valid instruments to evaluate a person's level of acculturation. Researchers must nevertheless bear in mind that these instruments are tapping a less central aspect of the acculturation process and, therefore, are not the most valid possible measurements of a person's values and norms and his or her acculturation. A nagging question left for researchers is whether, by concentrating on the more superficial changes (e.g., media use and language preferences) produced by acculturation, we are dealing with highly unreliable estimates of an important personal process. Unfortunately, the literature of Hispanic acculturation has seldom addressed this issue, and future studies must deal with the personal relevance of the behaviors being studied.

As mentioned earlier, central to the psychological understanding of acculturation has been the assumption that contact has taken place between the individual and members of the host culture as well as with the latter's institutions (e.g., mass media, education, literature, civic and voluntary organizations, local and federal governments, and armed forces). Some immigrants who arrived in the United States at the beginning of the 20th century were able to remain relatively isolated from the host culture of the United States by virtue of the fact that they resided in ethnic enclaves where all or most of society reflected the country of origin. Nevertheless, the advent of mass media and of a mobile service-oriented society has made it more difficult for more recent Hispanic immigrants to remain isolated from the influences of the host culture. Contemporary Hispanic immigrants may find it impossible to avoid contact with the host culture even if they reside in heavily Hispanic enclaves such as East Los Angeles, Hialeah, San Antonio, or the Bronx. Although contact with the host culture can be considered inescapable for contemporary immigrants, the intensity and quality of the contact can vary from one individual to another due to their employment and education as well as to their level of exposure to the mass media and to the nation's institutions (e.g., hospitals, schools, social service agencies, and churches).

Operationalization of Acculturation

Although most researchers agree with the perception of acculturation as a culture learning process that individuals undergo when coming in contact with different cultures, there are differences in the ways in which acculturation has been operationalized. One common perspective considers acculturation as a unidimensional process that moves individuals away from their original culture toward the host culture. The end result of this process would be to make the acculturating individuals as similar as possible to those of the host culture and, thus, to be able to "pass" as members of the new culture, nation, or group. This definition of acculturation is probably best described as assimilation (Berry, 1980), because individuals are expected to become part of the new group, to "fold in" with the members of the host culture.

An alternative possibility, labeled *integration* by Berry (1980) or *biculturality* by most other researchers, suggests that individuals undergoing acculturative presses will learn the characteristics of the new culture while retaining some or all of the cultural components of the original group. In this sense, bicultural or "integrated" individuals will feel equally comfortable with both cultures, will hold the values and respect the norms of both cultures, and will retain a dual cultural identity. This construct of biculturality does not imply a schizophrenic perception of the world or a forced inaction of the individual owing to dual demands, but rather proposes that individuals learn to react to cultural cues in a culturally appropriate (group-specific) fashion. A bicultural Hispanic, for example, would act, think, and feel as a Hispanic when dealing with other Hispanics, but would switch with equal ease to a non-Hispanic perspective when interacting with non-Hispanics.

Berry (1980) and others also suggested that the process of contact between cultures can also produce a rejection of either culture or the "deculturation" of the individual. Rejection is assumed to take place when individuals choose to or are forced to stay separated from the host culture, a phenomenon that can take place when segregationist rules or laws are promulgated or when a territory is invaded or annexed by another country. Deculturation is defined by Berry (1980) as a process by which individuals are forced to lose contact with their original culture, but are prevented from learning or joining the new one.

The rest of this chapter deals primarily with assimilation and biculturalism as possible results of acculturation because they seem to be the most applicable options for Hispanics in the United States. It should be remembered though, that historically, Hispanics have suffered the societal circumstances (prejudice and institutional racism) that could have led to deculturation among some individuals.

Berry (1980) suggested that there are six areas of psychological functioning where acculturation has a direct effect: language, cognitive styles, personality, identity, attitudes, and acculturative stress. Berry posited that as the individual moves through the process of acculturation, there are changes in each of these areas in reaction to the acculturation process. In terms of language use, for example, an individual undergoing acculturation may learn the new language (English in the case of Hispanics) while maintaining his or her ability to speak Spanish; may remain primarily monolingual in Spanish; or may lose significant ability in Spanish, thus becoming primarily monolingual in English. Additional options are the development of language mixes or of creole languages. Among Hispanics, it is easy to find people who are primarily English or Spanish speaking, regardless of either their place of birth or their length of residence in the United States, as well as individuals who are fully bilingual.

Berry's (1980) suggestions of possible outcomes for acculturation are particularly relevant because they point to the need for conceptualizing acculturation as a multidimensional process where individuals move at different speeds across different cultural planes. It is possible, for example, to think of acculturation among Hispanics as influencing language use and preference so that we can consider two intercepting lines in a two-dimensional space where one line refers to the individual's ability in Spanish and the other to the individual's ability in English. Each of these lines would have a gradient of *poor* to *excellent* in ability, or at least from *less preferred* to *most preferred* in terms of use. One particular Hispanic, for example, may be at the point of excellent ability for Spanish, but at the poor gradient for English. This primarily monolingual Spanish speaker may acquire additional abilities in English and move along the English-language continuum toward greater ability while remaining at the excellent gradient for his or her Spanish ability. Likewise, this same individual may acquire fluency in English, but lose vocabulary or fluidity in Spanish, moving from the excellent gradient to a less-than-excellent point along the Spanish-language continuum. The point is that the result of acculturation is not an all-or-none situation (which is implied by assimilation), but rather a fluid process that implies movement at different speeds across various dimensions and planes.

From this discussion, it is easy to see that the definition and operationalization of acculturation has changed throughout the years. Currently, it has moved away from a simplistic unidimensional process and now emphasizes a comprehensive, multidimensional perspective. Central to this new understanding of acculturation is the fact that the acculturating individual is now perceived as a person who may indeed be comfortable in both cultures and who, by acculturating, is gaining new cultural knowledge and information rather than sacrificing previously held abilities or values. It seems essential, then, that researchers consider acculturation as a fluid process (probably a lifelong event) that involves many dimensions of an individual's life (e.g., behaviors, attitudes, norms, and values) and that does not typically follow a deficit model, but rather implies growth across a variety of continua.

The Measurement of Acculturation

Given the heuristic value of acculturation as an explanation for behavior and attitudinal changes among Hispanics, a number of researchers have developed and published various acculturation scales and indices. Unfortunately, most of them have dealt with only two Hispanic subgroups: Mexican Americans (Burnam, Telles, Karno, Hough, & Escobar, 1987; Cuellar, Harris, & Jasso, 1980; Deyo, Diehl, Hazuda, & Stern, 1985; Olmedo, Martinez, & Martinez, 1978; Padilla, 1980) and Cubans (Szapocznik & Kurtines, 1980; Szapocznik, Scopetta, Kurtines, & Aranalde, 1978). The fact that these researchers have concentrated on only two Hispanic subgroups leaves open the question of the possible usefulness of those acculturation scales and indices with other Hispanic subgroups (e.g., Puerto Ricans, Central and South Americans). A detailed review of each of the published instruments that measure acculturation among Hispanics is beyond the scope of this chapter, but some common limitations of the various published acculturation scales are mentioned later because they need to be taken into account when considering studies that have used these scales or when planning future research.

A primary problem with a large number of the studies that have measured acculturation or that have looked at the effect of acculturation on certain behaviors is that little effort has been given to studying the psychometric qualities of the items used to measure acculturation. It is common in a study, for example, for researchers to ask participants two or three or more questions related to be haviors usually considered part of the acculturation process (e.g., language use and preference, patterns of contact with ethnic media, and ethnicity of peers, friends, and relatives) and to score these items as if they together formed an acculturation scale. Usually these researchers fail to conduct even the most minimal analysis of internal consistency of the items before treating them as a psychometric scale. Validity analyses are also frequently missing from reports on the construction of new ad hoc acculturation scales. In many cases, it is indeed difficult to identify criterion variables to use in the validation of an acculturation scale. Nevertheless, researchers have used indices, such as age at arrival, generational history, and length of residence in the United States, when validating their acculturation scales. New indices and scales should be validated against these criteria before the assumption is made that acculturation is indeed being measured. One additional significant problem of many of the acculturation scales published to date is the fact that they have used socio-demographic characteristics (e.g., generation of respondents) as measures rather than as correlates of acculturation. This problem is especially serious when the validation criteria (e.g., generation, self-identification, place of birth, and age at arrival) are included as part of the scale that is being validated. This decision on the part of researchers produces spuriously high correlations between the criteria and the scale. The acculturation measure included in the very large and important study known as the Hispanic Health and Nutrition Examination Survey (H-HANES) included this mixture of criterion and measurement variables in trying to identify the acculturation level of the individuals sampled.

A second important concern when analyzing the currently published research on acculturation is the assumption made by some researchers that a simple measure of language use, dominance, or preference is a valid measure of acculturation or at least a reliable proxy measure for acculturation. Many of these researchers suggest that knowledge of the language in which respondents answered an instrument is enough to obtain a measurement of their acculturation level. Similar arguments have been made for respondents' educational level, where acculturation is expected to correlate positively with level of formal education. Undoubtedly, one of the most easily measured changes produced by acculturation is language use and, hence, it has become a common shorthand measure for evaluating acculturation. As a matter of fact, most of the recently published acculturation scales have relied heavily on changes in and preferences for language use. Nevertheless, our data show that when language used in answering a survey is used alone as a proxy variable for acculturation, well over 12% of the respondents are misclassified when compared with their scores on a valid and reliable acculturation scale. The same is probably true when researchers argue for using level of education as a proxy measure of acculturation. Recent Hispanic immigrants have high levels of education although their level of acculturation is relatively low.

A third problem with the measurement of acculturation is the fact that most scales have operationalized acculturation as a unidimensional phenomenon despite the large literature on the need to consider acculturation as a multidimensional process. Most instruments ask respondents to rate a behavior, value or attitude using a unidimensional answer scale, such as a rating of their language proficiency on a scale that goes from *only English* to *only Spanish,* with inbetween ratings labeled something like *mostly Spanish, mostly English,* and *both equally well.* This unidimensionality assumes that individuals move from one end of the scale toward the other and that as this process continues, the respondents lose some of their original ability as they gain a different cultural perspective. For example, as Hispanics acculturate, the unidimensional perspective on acculturation assumes that the ability to speak Spanish decreases as they become more proficient in English. Furthermore, this type of scaling assumes that biculturalism (or bilingualism in the case of this example) is logically someplace between being totally monocultural in both cultures (or languages). This assumption, of course, disagrees with the operationalizations of acculturation that have already been mentioned. A simpler method for making these measurements would be to perform a separate assessment for both languages or cultures.

Despite the fact that the mentioned assumptions are untenable, acculturation scales continue to be constructed and used although they are unidimensional operationalizations of the construct. The fact that scales constructed in this fashion produce heuristically important findings and that the scales show good psychometric characteristics may reflect the importance of the construct of acculturation. For example, our acculturation scale (Marín, Sabogal, Marín, Otero-Sabogal, & Pérez-Stable, 1987) can be shortened up to four times (all items dealing with language) and has still shown good psychometric characteristics. The scale has correlated highly with the usual validity criteria, such as respondents' generation ($r = .69$), length of residence in the United States for foreign-born respondents ($r = .76$), and age at arrival in the United States ($r = -.72$). There have been some efforts to develop two-dimensional acculturation scales for Hispanics (e.g., Szapocznik & Kurtines, 1980), but unfortunately, those scales have not received appropriate attention on the part of researchers.

A fourth central issue in the measurement of acculturation concerns the type of phenomena that must be studied or measured in order to establish a valid measurement of an individual's acculturation level. As mentioned earlier, most acculturation scales tend to emphasize language ability and preference as measures of acculturation. This tendency probably is based on the results of factor analyses of acculturation-scale items, where items dealing with language preference and ability tend to account for the majority of the variance. In the development of our acculturation scale (Marín et al., 1987), we found that a first factor made up of five language-related items accounted for 54.5% of the total variance. Nevertheless, it can be argued that language preference and ability do not cover all the changes that take place with acculturation and that other behaviors, attitudes, and values should be measured in order to obtain a better, more complete indicator of a person's acculturation level. Berry's (1980) seminal chapter on the topic would certainly argue for this more complete measure of acculturation level, which goes beyond language to study cognitive styles, personality, attitudes, and levels of stress. Unfortunately, researchers have not been able to identify appropriate measuring instruments for these additional phenomena that are sufficiently strong to account for appreciable variance in the statistical analyses of the scales.

An opposing argument could be presented that would support the idea of measuring acculturation in the most economical way, that is, with the fewest items and constructs. This position defends the use of items dealing with language use and preference in acculturation scales as long as they continue to show the high predictive value that has been found by most researchers. The point, of course, is how much information is being gained by adding items and constructs and how much is being lost or left unaccounted for when only language-related items are used. Unfortunately, we have no research that addresses this issue among Hispanics.

One final issue to consider when studying the measurement of acculturation of Hispanics is the practice common among some researchers of changing the wording of items or deleting or adding items because of personal preferences. These researchers then assume that the modified scale continues to have the same psychometric characteristics as the original one. These faulty assumptions lead to the use of an instrument that may have lost reliability and validity in the process of modification. Furthermore, the modifications render the data noncomparable with those previously collected with the original instrument. Despite the fact that these psychometric principles are well-known, the literature continues to accrue studies that have introduced these manipulations, and the authors of the studies seem to discount the fact that their results may be due to the manipulations and modifications of the instruments.

Significance of Acculturation

Despite the limitations of theories, operationalizations, and instrumentation of acculturation of Hispanics that have been already mentioned, researchers continue to include acculturation level as an important intragroup characteristic of Hispanics. In this sense, acculturation is a way of eliminating the ethnic glosses that Trimble (1990–1991) considered as a limitation of current research with ethnic groups in the United States. The importance of considering acculturation as a variable that differentiates among subgroups of Hispanics can be seen in the large number of studies that have shown acculturation as a significant modifier (or correlate) of a number of variables. For example, acculturation levels have been shown to affect, among other things, Hispanics' mental health status (Szapocznik & Kurtines, 1980), levels of social support (Griffith & Villavicencio, 1985), social deviancy, alcoholism, and drug use (Graves, 1967; Padilla, Padilla, Ramirez, Morales, & Olmedo, 1979), political and social attitudes (Alva, 1985), and health behaviors such as the consumption of cigarettes (Marín, Pérez-Stable, & Marín, 1989) and the practice of preventive cancer screening (Marks, Solis, Richardson, Collins, Birba, & Hisserich, 1987).

Despite the psychometric limitations that plague most acculturation scales, research findings continue to show important behavioral and attitudinal differences among Hispanics that can be attributed to their acculturation level. A recent study showed that as acculturation levels increased, psychological distress also increased among young adults, but not among older individuals (Kaplan & Marks, 1990). That study analyzed the responses of Mexican Americans to the Center for Epidemiological Studies—Depression Scale (CES-D) in the H-HANES. It found for both men and women that the total score on the CES-D increased as their acculturation score increased among young adults (20–30 years of age), but tended to decrease for older individuals. Interestingly, these results were found to be independent of education and income. The results may reflect the stress Hispanic young adults undergo as they learn to deal with the culture of the United States, and they are forced to learn new culture-specific behavioral patterns and attitudes. Another study (Burnam, Hough, Karno, Escobar, & Telles, 1987) found similar relationships between acculturation and psychological distress when utilizing a different measure of acculturation and a different measure of psychological distress (the Diagnostic Interview Schedule). In this study, high levels of acculturation were related to depression, alcohol abuse, and antisocial personalities. Other studies have reported similar findings (Golding & Karno, 1988; Moscicki, Locke, Rae, & Boyd, 1989).

Although the studies mentioned earlier support the idea that the effects of acculturation on behavior are pervasive enough to appear despite differences in the validity of the instruments used to measure the acculturation construct, data from studies of other behaviors are not as consistent. For example, a number of studies have analyzed the possible role of acculturation in patterns of consumption of alcoholic beverages by Hispanics. These studies have usually involved large national samples of Hispanics (e.g., Caetano, 1987) or representative samples of Hispanic subgroups (e.g., Markides, Ray, Stroup-Benham, & Treviño, 1990). The assumption that alcohol consumption is correlated with acculturation has been supported by studies with other ethnic communities such as Italian Americans (Blane, 1977) and Canadian Indians (Drew, 1988). Nevertheless, research with Hispanics has failed to produce consistent results. One study (Caetano, 1987) found that acculturation was related to decreased abstention among older men and that highly acculturated younger men and women tended to drink alcoholic beverages frequently. The study by Markides et al. used the Mexican-American samples of the H-HANES and found that acculturation was not related to alcohol consumption among men, but was positively related to intake among younger women. The measures of acculturation used in each of these studies were different, so comparisons across studies are difficult to make, and the lack of consistent findings could be explained in terms of differential instrumentation (both of acculturation and of drinking patterns). Another possible explanation for these different results is that there may be cultural norms and values that current acculturation measures do not tap, but are closely related to alcohol consumption among various Hispanic subgroups. Unpublished analyses of our data on alcohol consumption among Mexicans and Central Americans in California indicate that although acculturation level is an important predictor of alcohol consumption among Mexican Americans, the same is not true among Central Americans.

As mentioned earlier, acculturational presses have been used in a number of studies to explain the behavior of Hispanics. The last few paragraphs briefly reviewed the possible effect of acculturation on mental health (depression) and on public health (alcohol consumption) behaviors of Hispanics. Most studies have found that acculturation is an important predictor of behavior despite the limitations in its conceptualization, operationalization, and measurement. Future studies will probably produce more appropriate measures of acculturation that will help us to resolve some of the inconsistencies currently found in the literature. Irrespective of those future developments, it seems essential that research with

Hispanics addresses and properly identifies behavioral differences that could be attributed to the acculturation level of the respondents. Research using methods permitting causal inferences must take place whether we are dealing with descriptions of the social behavior of Hispanics, their mental health status, or their physical health. Irrespective of the behavioral domain (e.g., depression, consumption of cigarettes, use of contraceptives, or preferences for friendship networks), acculturation seems to play an important role in defining the behavior of Hispanics. Ignoring this variable may obscure important intragroup differences and produce inconsistent and irrelevant findings that will only impede our proper understanding of Hispanics.

References

Alva, S. A. (1985). Political acculturation of Mexican American adolescents. *Hispanics Journal of Behavioral Sciences, 7*, 345–364.

Berry, J. (1980). Acculturation as varieties of adaptation. In A. M. Padilla (Ed.), *Acculturation: Theory, models, and some new findings* (pp. 9–25). Boulder, CO: Westview Press.

Berry, J. W., Trimble, J., & Olmedo, E. L. (1986). Assessment of acculturation. In W. J. Loner & J. W. Berry (Eds.), *Field methods in cross-cultural research.* (pp. 291–324). Beverly Hills, CA: Sage Publications.

Blane, H. T. (1977). Acculturation and drinking in an Italian American community. *Journal of Studies of Alcohol, 38*, 1324–1346.

Burnam, M. A., Telles, C. A., Karno, M., Hough, R. L., & Escobar, J. I. (1987). Measurement of acculturation in a community population of Mexican Americans. *Hispanic Journal of Behavioral Sciences, 9*, 105–130.

Burnam, M. A., Hough, R. L., Karno, M., Escobar, J. I., & Telles, C. A. (1987). Acculturation and lifetime prevalence of psychiatric disorders among Mexican Americans in Los Angeles. *Journal of Health and Social Behavior, 28*, 89–102.

Caetano, R. (1987). Acculturation and drinking patterns among U.S. Hispanics. *British Journal of Addiction, 82*, 789–799.

Cuellar, I., Harris, L.C., & Jasso, R. (1980). An acculturation scale for Mexican American normal and clinical populations. *Hispanics Journal of Behavioral Sciences, 2*, 199–217.

Deyo, R. A., Diehl, A. K., Hazuda, H., & Stern, M. P. (1985). A simple language-based acculturation scale for Mexican Americans: Validation and application to health care research. *American Journal of Public Health, 75*, 51–55.

Drew, L. L. (1988). Acculturation stress and alcohol usage among Canadian Indians in Toronto. *Canadian Journal of Public Health, 79*, 115–118.

Golding, J. M., & Karno, M. (1988). Gender differences in depressive symptoms among Mexican Americans and non-Hispanic Whites. *Hispanic Journal of Behavioral Sciences, 10*, 1–19.

Gordon, M. M. (1964). *Assimilation in American Life.* New York: Oxford University Press.

Graves, D. T. (1967). Acculturation, access, and alcohol in a tri-ethnic community. *American Anthropologist, 69,* 306–321.

Griffith, J., & Villavicencio, S. (1985). Relationships among acculturation, sociodemographic characteristics and social support in Mexican American adults. *Hispanic Journal of Behavioral Sciences, 7,* 75–92.

Kaplan, M. S., & Marks, G. (1990). Adverse effects of acculturation: Psychological distress among Mexican American young adults. *Social Science and Medicine, 31,* 1313–1319.

Marín, G., Pérez-Stable, E. J., & Marín, B. V. (1989). Cigarette smoking among San Francisco Hispanics: The role of acculturation and gender. *American Journal of Public Health, 79,* 196–198.

Marín, G., Sabogal, F., Marín, B. V., Otero-Sabogal, R., & Pérez-Stable, E. J. (1987). Development of a short acculturation scale for Hispanics. *Hispanic Journal of Behavioral Sciences, 9,* 183–205.

Marín, G., & Triandis, H. C. (1985). Allocentrism as an important characteristic of the behavior of Latin Americans and Hispanics. In R. Diaz-Guerrero (Ed.), *Cross-cultural and national studies in social psychology* (pp. 85–104). Amsterdam: Elsevier Science Publishers.

Marks, G., Solis, J., Richardson, J. L., Collins, L. M., Birba, L., & Hisserich, J. C. (1987). Health behavior of elderly Hispanic women: Does cultural assimilation make a difference? *American Journal of Public Health, 77,* 1315–1319.

Markides, K. S., Ray, L. A., Stroup-Benham, C. A., & Treviño, F. (1990). Acculturation and alcohol consumption in the Mexican American population of the Southwestern United States: Findings from H-HANES 1982–84. *American Journal of Public Health, 80* (Supp.), 42–46.

Moscicki, E. K., Locke, B. Z., Rae, D. S., & Boyd, J. H. (1989). Depressive symptoms among Mexican Americans: The Hispanic Health and Nutrition Examination Survey. *American Journal of Epidemiology, 130,* 348–360.

Olmedo, E. L., Martinez, J. L., & Martinez, S. R. (1978). Measure of acculturation of Chicano adolescents. *Psychological Reports, 42,* 159–170.

Padilla, A. M. (1980). The role of cultural awareness and ethnic loyalty in acculturation. In A. M. Padilla (Ed.), *Acculturation: Theory, models and some new findings* (pp. 47–84). Boulder, CO: Westview Press.

Padilla, E. R., Padilla, A. M., Ramirez, R., Morales, A., & Olmedo, E. L. (1979). Inhalent, marihuana, and alcohol abuse among barrio children and adolescents. *International Journal of the Addictions, 14,* 943–964.

Redfield, R., Linton, R., & Herskovitz, M. J. (1936). Memorandum on the study of acculturation. *American Anthropologist, 38,* 149–152.

Sabogal, R., Marín, G., Otero-Sabogal, R., Marín, B. V., & Pérez-Stable, E. J. (1987). Hispanic familism and acculturation: What changes and what doesn't? *Hispanic Journal of Behavioral Sciences, 9,* 397–412.

Smith, T. W. (1980). Ethnic measurement and identification. *Ethnicity, 7,* 78–95.

Szapocznik, J., & Kurtines, W. (1980). Acculturation, biculturalism, and adjustment among Cuban Americans. In A. M. Padilla (Ed.), *Acculturation: Theory, models, and some new findings* (pp.139–159). Boulder, CO: Westview Press.

Szapocznik, J., Scopetta, M. A., Kurtines, W., & Aranalde, M. A. (1978). Theory and measurement of acculturation. *Interamerican Journal of Psychology/Revista Interamericana de Psicología, 12,* 113–130.

Triandis, H. C. (1990). Toward cross-cultural studies of individualism and collectivism in Latin America. *Interamerican Journal of Psychology/Revista Interamericana de Psicología, 24,* 199–210.

Triandis, H. C., Marín, G., Lisansky, J., & Betancourt, H. (1984). Simpatia as a cultural script of Hispanics. *Journal of Personality and Social Psychology, 47,* 1363–1375.

Trimble, J. (1990–1991). Ethnic specification, validation prospects, and the future of drug use research. *International Journal of the Addictions, 25(2A),* 149–170.

CHAPTER 16

Psychological Testing of Hispanic Americans in Clinical Settings: Overview and Issues

Roberto J. Velásquez and Wendell J. Callahan

I t is now almost 20 years since Padilla and Ruiz (1973, 1975) published their landmark reviews on the psychological testing and assessment of Hispanic Americans in clinical, psychiatric, and mental health settings. In their reviews, Padilla and Ruiz emphasized the paucity of research on Hispanics, the need for validation studies on such instruments as the Minnesota Multiphasic Personality Inventory (MMPI) and Rorschach, and the need to reexamine unwarranted assumptions regarding the clinical interpretation of Hispanics' test performance. For example, with respect to test interpretation, Padilla and Ruiz came to the following conclusion:

> It appears that the interpretation of personality test responses from [Hispanic] American subjects are based on the implicit assumption that this group is somehow "no different" from the majority group [i.e., White Americans]. Another way of presenting this assumption is to assert that cultural differences exert minimal influence upon personality test responses; and therefore, "unique," "unusual," or "atypical"

response patterns obtained from these subjects have the same meaning as they would among subjects who are not of [Hispanic] origin. (1975, p. 103).

Since the publication of Padilla and Ruiz's (1973, 1975) reviews, there has been an explosion of interest concerning the psychological testing of Hispanics in clinical settings, as evidenced by the large number of published and unpublished studies (e.g., theses and dissertations) that have documented the performance of Hispanics on a variety of psychological tests. This increase is also evidenced by the number of review or position papers that have examined various aspects (e.g., validity) of testing Hispanics (e.g., Butcher & Clark, 1979; Butcher & Garcia, 1978; Cervantes & Castro, 1985; Fabrega, 1990; Malgady, Rogler, & Costantino, 1987; Rogler, Cortes, & Malgady, 1991; Rogler, Malgady, & Rodriguez, 1989; Ziskin, 1981). There have also been a number of focused reviews on instruments such as the MMPI (e.g., Campos, 1989; Dahlstrom, 1986; Greene, 1987, 1991; Velásquez, 1984b, in press).

The purpose of this chapter is to present an overview of psychological testing research on Hispanics in clinical settings. We attempt to answer the following four questions concerning this body of literature: (a) Why is it necessary to test and assess Hispanics in clinical or mental health settings? (b) What are the instruments that are most frequently used in research on Hispanics? (c) What are the strategies most frequently used by researchers who study Hispanics? (d) What are the problems that continue to plague this body of research?

Consistent with the structure implied by these questions, this chapter is organized into four major sections. The first section offers a rationale for testing and assessing Hispanics in clinical settings. It is our belief that the use of tests has a legitimate role in the delivery of mental health services to Hispanics. The results of tests, when used appropriately, can aid the clinician in generating diagnostic hypotheses and formulating treatment plans. The second section describes the breadth of research on Hispanics from 1949 to 1992. For example, there is an overrepresentation of research with the MMPI (see Velásquez, in press) and a marked underrepresentation of research with other instruments such as the Rorschach or Thematic Apperception Test (TAT). Reasons for this phenomenon include psychologists' preference for objective tests over projective instruments in the assessment of Hispanics.

The third section critically examines the methods that are most frequently used in research on testing Hispanics. For example, the most popular approach involves the comparison of Hispanics' test performance with that of other ethnic groups, most notably White, non-Hispanic Americans. Furthermore, it is frequently assumed that White, non-Hispanic Americans constitute an appropriate control group in such research. The final section examines the problems that continue to plague this body of research. For example, a major problem relates to the testing of Hispanics who vary with respect to degrees of bilingualism and acculturation. It is important to note that although it is beyond the scope of this chapter to review specific studies, we do cite seminal research where appropriate.

A Rationale for Testing Hispanics in Clinical Settings

Hispanics, like non Hispanics, are frequently seen in clinical settings for a variety of mental health problems, including depression, alcoholism, anxiety, psychoses, and personality disorders (Cuellar, 1982; Cuellar & Roberts, 1984; Ruiz, 1982; Rosenstein, 1980; Snowden & Cheung, 1990). These settings include inpatient psychiatric facilities, drug and alcohol treatment programs, community mental health centers, rehabilitation clinics, university counseling centers, correctional institutions, and medical facilities (Velásquez, 1984a). Also, like non-Hispanics, Hispanics are routinely administered psychological tests to assess their mental health status.

Typically, these tests are used by psychologists to identify and describe psychopathologies (i.e., specific symptoms and disorders), assist in diagnostic decision making (i.e., clarify specific psychiatric diagnoses or distinguish between disorders), aid in treatment selection (i.e., inpatient vs. outpatient treatment, individual vs. group therapy, brief vs. long-term therapy), and determine treatment prognoses for Hispanic clients.

Malgady, Rogler, and Costantino (1987), in discussing the importance of psychological testing in the treatment of Hispanics, noted that "at the root of effective mental health care [for Hispanics] is valid diagnosis, premised upon accurate psychometric technology and sound clinical judgement" (p. 228). They also noted that "...the diagnosis rendered [by psychologists] should clarify the nature and extent of psychological distress that initially gives rise to help-seeking behavior and should structure the path of...treatment and subsequent follow-up efforts to facilitate readjustment [for Hispanics] within the community..." (p. 228).

Padilla and Ruiz (1975) argued that "...in many psychiatric and community mental health clinics, the initial...evaluation of a new [Hispanic] client begins with the administration of...psychological tests" (p. 107) and that "...a [Hispanic] client's [test] performance...is extremely important since it is used to determine whether treatment will be offered; and if so, what type" (p. 107). Finally, Malgady et al. (1987) noted that Hispanics' "...early contacts with a mental health agency are likely to be diagnostic in nature whether the assessment performed is formal or informal, brief or intensive" (p. 228).

Overview of Clinical Testing Research on Hispanics

Table 1 describes the number of studies that have been conducted with Hispanics between 1949 and 1992. The most compelling finding relates to the use of the MMPI and the near absence of research with other instruments including the Rorschach and TAT. Of the 103 investigations noted in Table 1, 86 (83%) have used the MMPI.

Table 2 describes the pronounced growth of Hispanic MMPI research when compared with Rorschach research over the past 4 decades. For example, 75% of all MMPI research on Hispanics has been conducted within the last decade. Table 3 describes the number of MMPI studies conducted within specific clinical settings (e.g., psychiatric, correctional, and rehabilitation settings).

TABLE 1

Number of Studies on Hispanics by Test and Setting (Clinical vs. Nonclinical)

Instrument	Clinical	Nonclinical
MMPI	61	25
Rorschach	3	6
TAT	1	2
CPI	0	2
16PF	0	1
BDI	0	1
CPS	0	1
Total	65	38

Note. MMPI = Minnesota Multiphasic Personality Inventory; TAT = Thematic Apperception Test; CPI = California Personality Inventory; BDI = Beck Depression Inventory; CPS = Comrey Personality Scales.

TABLE 2

Evolution of Hispanic Testing Research: MMPI Versus Rorschach

Test	1949–1959	1960–1969	1970–1979	1980–1992
MMPI	1 (1%)	6 (7%)	15 (17%)	64 (75%)
(n = 86)				
Rorschach	3 (33%)	2 (23%)	0	4 (44%)
(n = 9)				

Note. MMPI = Minnesota Multiphasic Personality Inventory.

There are several reasons for the overrepresentation of the MMPI and the underrepresentation of other tests in the literature. First, and irrespective of ethnicity or race, the MMPI is the most widely used test instrument in research in clinical settings (Greene, 1991). Hispanics, like African Americans, have been frequently studied with this measure in a variety of clinical settings (Greene, 1987, 1991). In fact, Hispanic MMPI research mimics or parallels African-American MMPI research in terms of methodology (see next section). Second, because of its psychometric features (e.g., validity and clinical scales, special indices, and supplemental scales), the MMPI has become the most convenient instrument for researchers to use in the investigation of Hispanics. Also, when compared with projective measures, the MMPI is easy to administer, score, and interpret. This

TABLE 3

Hispanic MMPI Research by Type of Clinical Setting and Source

Source Setting	Published	Unpublished	Dissertation	Thesis
Drug/Alcohol	11	1	3	0
(n = 15)				
Correctional	9	1	0	2
(n = 12)				
Psychiatric	8	7	9	1
(n = 25)				
Rehabilitation	2	2	5	0
(n = 9)				
Nonclinical	11	4	7	3
(n = 25)				
Total	41	15	24	6
(N = 86)				

Note. Nonclinical settings include school and employment settings. MMPI = Minnesota Multiphasic Personality Inventory.

ease of use can often give the misleading impression of clean, objective, or quantifiable comparisons between Hispanics and non-Hispanics, especially when contrasted with the subjective results obtained with the Rorschach or TAT.

Third, the MMPI has been translated into a variety of languages (Williams, 1987) including Spanish and has been used extensively throughout Latin America (Butcher & Garcia, 1978; Butcher & Pancheri, 1976). Finally, the recent restandardization of the MMPI (the MMPI-2) has, for the first time, included Hispanics in its test norm development (Butcher, Dahlstrom, Graham, Tellegen, & Kaemmer, 1989). To date, other than tests of intelligence, the MMPI-2 is the only major psychological test of a clinical nature that has included Hispanics as a subgroup in the normative sample.

Research Designs Most Frequently Used in Hispanic Clinical Testing Research

A methodological review of all psychological testing research indicates that there are essentially two approaches to the study of Hispanics in clinical settings. The approaches are distinguished by the following questions: (a) Are there differences between Hispanics and non-Hispanics on a particular test instrument? (b) Are there differences among Hispanic subgroups on a particular test instrument?

The first and most popular approach involves the comparison of Hispanics with other ethnic groups, most notably non-Hispanic Whites, on a psychological test such as the MMPI (e.g., Dolan, Roberts, Robinowitz, & Atkins, 1983; Hibbs, Kobos, & Gonzalez, 1979; Holland, 1979; Lawson, Kahn, & Heiman, 1982; McCreary & Padilla, 1977; Penk, Robinowitz, Roberts, Dolan, & Atkins, 1981; Plemons, 1977; Velásquez & Callahan, 1990). This prototypic approach includes the following steps: (a) gathering test data in a clinical setting, (b) sorting the data by ethnicity to create comparison groups (e.g., Hispanic vs. White non-Hispanic), (c) comparing the groups' test performances (e.g., MMPI scales), and (d) determining whether the groups' test performances differ significantly.

Pritchard and Rosenblatt (1980) illustrated this approach in their discussion of cross-cultural MMPI research. They noted the following:

> The most popular research strategy...has been to compare racial [ethnic] subgroups in convenient samples of respondents on their respective test score means. If racial [ethnic] subgroups significantly differ in univariate means (on MMPI scales), in

multivariate means (on the MMPI profile), in endorsement rates (of MMPI items), or in selection ratios (e.g., based on MMPI code type), the results are offered as...evidence of test bias [or ethnic differences]. (p. 263)

Greene (1987) echoed Pritchard and Rosenblatt's comments by stating, "If differences occur between the two groups on any scale, the typical conclusion is that either the...MMPI or a subtest is affected by membership in that ethnic group" (p. 497).

The second approach involves the comparison of Hispanics with other Hispanics on a given psychological test (e.g., Pando, 1974; Quiroga, 1972; Velásquez, 1987; Velásquez, Callahan, & Carrillo, 1989, 1991; Velásquez & Gimenez, 1987). The advantage of this approach is that it takes into account Hispanic's intracultural variation. For example, there is a growing body of research that indicates that level of acculturation impacts Hispanic's psychological test performance (Fuller, 1984; Kaplan, 1955; Leung, 1986; Montgomery & Orozco, 1985; Padilla, Olmedo, & Loya, 1982; Plemons, 1980). (See also Marín's chapter in this volume.) There is also evidence that Hispanics vary on psychological tests as a function of psychiatric diagnoses (e.g., Velásquez, Callahan, & Carrillo, 1989, 1991). This approach, although less popular in the literature, appears to be more appropriate for future research.

Problems in the Testing of Hispanics in Clinical Settings

There are at least four significant problems that continue to plague the psychological testing of Hispanics in clinical settings. First, there is an absence of research linking the results of epidemiological studies (Koegel, Burnam, & Farr, 1988; Roberts, 1980, 1981; Vega, Kolody, & Warheit, 1985; Vernon & Roberts, 1982) with testing studies. For example, knowing the base rates or prevalence of certain psychiatric disorders improves the accuracy of the assessment process with Hispanics.

Second, although numerous studies have investigated Hispanics' performance on Spanish versions of the MMPI (Azán, 1989; Bohn & Traub, 1986; Fuller & Malony, 1984; Ledwin, 1983; Pando, 1974; Prewitt-Diaz, Norcross, & Draguns, 1984; Traub & Bohn, 1985; Whitworth, 1988), there remains an absence of research on the validity of these translations. This lack of validity data has obvious implications for clinical practice.

Third, this literature has failed to consider the relationship between bilingualism and the expression of psychopathology. For example, there is evidence to suggest that individuals who are interviewed by clinicians in both English and Spanish report different features of their mental illness as a function of the interview language (e.g., Gomez, Ruiz, & Rumbaut, 1985; Marcos, Alpert, Urcuyo, & Kesselman, 1973; Price & Cuellar, 1981; Vasquez, 1982). Malgady et al. (1987) posed the questions, "In which language, English or Spanish, do bilinguals express greater psychopathology? ...Which language conveys the true nature and extent of pathology?" (p. 231).

Finally, there is an absence of research that examines the performance of Hispanics on multiple clinical measures. This approach would more realistically approximate the test procedures of a clinical evaluation (i.e., test batteries). A review of this body of literature indicates that no study has included more than one psychological test in examining Hispanic test performance in clinical settings.

Summary and Recommendations

In summary, based on historical trends, it appears that the volume of Hispanic psychological-testing research will (along with the Hispanic population of the United States) continue to grow well into the 21st century. In keeping with this trend, research will undoubtedly increase in methodological sophistication and relevance to clinical practice. The following recommendations are offered to both researchers and clinicians.

1. Researchers should be cognizant of the role of various moderator variables that impact Hispanics' test performance (e.g., age, gender, socioeconomic status, education, acculturation, and psychiatric diagnosis).
2. The level of acculturation of Hispanics should always be assessed as an integral part of a clinical evaluation. We recommend the use of acculturation rating scales [e.g., Acculturation Rating Scale for Mexican Americans (ARSMA); Cueller, Harris, & Jasso, 1980].
3. Prior to assessing Hispanic clients in English or Spanish, it is important to determine their language proficiency or language dominance. (Marín's chapter earlier in this volume provided some guidance in solving this problem.)

4. Although there is a relative abundance of MMPI research in the literature, there remains a need for research on projective instruments and psychiatric rating scales.

5. Because there is empirical evidence indicating that Hispanics may respond on the MMPI in a manner that may be interpreted as being indicative of greater psychopathology, we strongly recommend that clinicians integrate scale elevations with behavioral and observational correlates.

6. There is a need for research that examines the predictive and concurrent validity of such measures as the MMPI and Rorschach for Hispanics.

In closing, we cite the reflections of Malgady et al. (1987) concerning the psychological testing of Hispanics in clinical settings:

> Clearly, it is pretentious to believe that non-minority clinicians can achieve valid psychodiagnoses of Hispanic patients, even if armed with statistically "validated" psychometric technology, as long as they remain ignorant of Hispanic culture. Because it is equally unreasonable to pretend that Hispanic patients must become assimilated to majority culture, and articulate in English as a second language, the onus of acculturation rests on the diagnostician. (p. 232)

References

Azán, A. A. (1989). The MMPI Version Hispana: A standardization and cross-cultural personality study with a population of Cuban refugees (Doctoral dissertation, University of Minnesota, 1989). *Dissertation Abstracts International, 50,* 2144–2145B.

Bohn, M. J., & Traub, G. S. (1986). Alienation of monolingual Hispanics in a federal correctional institution. *Psychological Reports, 59,* 560–562.

Butcher, J. N., & Clark, L. A. (1979). Recent trends in cross-cultural MMPI research and application. In J. N. Butcher (Ed.), *Recent developments in the use of the MMPI* (pp. 205–257). Minneapolis: University of Minnesota Press.

Butcher, J. N., Dahlstrom, W. G., Graham, J. R., Tellegen, A., & Kaemmer, B. (1989). *Manual for the restandardized Minnesota Multiphasic Personality Inventory: MMPI-2. An administrative and interpretative guide.* Minneapolis: University of Minnesota Press.

Butcher, J. N., & Garcia, R. E. (1978). Cross-national application of psychological tests. *Personnel and Guidance Journal, 4,* 472–475.

Butcher, J. N., & Pancheri, P. (1976). Developments in the use of the MMPI in several countries. In J. N. Butcher & P. Pancheri (Eds.), *Cross-national MMPI research.* Minneapolis: University of Minnesota Press.

Campos, L. P. (1989). Adverse impact, unfairness, and bias in the psychological screening of His-panic peace officers. Hispanic Journal of Behavioral Sciences, 11, 127–135.

Cervantes, R. C., & Castro, F. G. (1985). Stress, coping, and Mexican American mental health: A systematic review. Hispanic Journal of Behavioral Sciences, 7, 1–73.

Cuellar, I. (1982). The diagnosis and evaluation of schizophrenic disorders among Mexican Ameri-cans. In R. M. Becerra, M. Karno, & J. I. Escobar (Eds.), Mental health and Hispanic Ameri-cans: Clinical services (pp. 61–81). New York: Grune & Stratton.

Cuellar, I., Harris, L. C., & Jasso, R. (1980). An acculturation rating scale for Mexican American normal and clinical populations. Hispanic Journal of Behavioral Sciences, 2, 199–217.

Cuellar, I., & Roberts, R. E. (1984). Psychological disorders among Chicanos. In J. L. Martinez & R. H. Mendoza (Eds.), Chicano psychology (2nd ed., pp. 133–161). San Diego: Academic Press.

Dahlstrom, L. E. (1986). MMPI findings on other American minority groups. In W. G. Dahlstrom, D. Lachar, & L. E. Dahlstrom (Eds.), MMPI patterns of American minorities (pp. 50–86). Minne-apolis: University of Minnesota Press.

Dolan, M. P., Roberts, W. R., Robinowitz, R., & Atkins, H. G. (1983). Personality differences among Black, White, and Hispanic-American male heroin addicts on MMPI content scales. Journal of Clinical Psychology, 39, 807–813.

Fabrega, H. (1990). Hispanic mental health research: A case for cultural psychiatry. Hispanic Jour-nal of Behavioral Sciences, 12, 339–365.

Fuller, C. G. (1984). Comparisons of unacculturated and acculturated Hispanics with Blacks and Whites on the Minnesota Multiphasic Personality Inventory (Doctoral dissertation, Fuller The-ological Seminary, 1984). Dissertation Abstracts International, 45, 1283B.

Fuller, C. G., & Malony, H. N. (1984). A comparison of English and Spanish (Nunez) translations of the MMPI. Journal of Personality Assessment, 48, 130–131.

Gomez, R., Ruiz, P., & Rumbaut, R. D. (1985). Hispanic patients: A linguocultural minority. Hispanic Journal of Behavioral Sciences, 7, 177–186.

Greene, R. L. (1987). Ethnicity and MMPI performance: A review. Journal of Consulting and Clini-cal Psychology, 55, 497–512.

Greene, R. L. (1991). Specific groups: Adolescents, the aged, Blacks, and other ethnic groups. In R. L. Greene (Ed.), The MMPI-2/MMPI: An interpretive manual (pp. 331–354). Needham Heights, MA: Allyn & Bacon.

Hibbs, B. J., Kobos, J. C., & Gonzalez, J. (1979). Effects of ethnicity, sex, and age on MMPI profiles. Psychological Reports, 45, 591–597.

Holland, T. R. (1979). Ethnic group differences in MMPI profile patterns and factorial structure among adult offenders. Journal of Personality Assessemnt, 43, 72–77.

Kaplan, B. (1955). Reflections of the acculturation process in the Rorschach test. Journal of Projec-tive Techniques, 19, 30–35.

Koegel, P., Burnam, A., & Farr, R. K. (1988). The prevalence of specific psychiatric disorders among homeless individuals in the inner city of Los Angeles. Archives of General Psychiatry, 45, 1085–1092.

Lawson, H. H., Kahn, M. W., & Heiman, E. M. (1982). Psychopathology, treatment outcomes and attitudes toward mental illness in Mexican American and European patients. *International Journal of Psychiatry, 28*, 20–26.

Ledwin, A. G. (1983). A comparative study of the MMPI Español and a cultural-sensitive linguistic version (Doctoral dissertation, U. S. International University, 1982). *Dissertation Abstracts International, 43*, 3884A.

Leung, R. (1986). MMPI scoring as a function of ethnicity and acculturation: A comparison of Asian, Hispanic, and Caucasian gifted high school students (Doctoral dissertation, Biola University, 1986). *Dissertation Abstracts International, 47*, 2622B.

Malgady, R. G., Rogler L. H., & Costantino, G. (1987). Ethnocultural and linguistic bias in mental health evaluation of Hispanics. *American Psychologist, 42*, 228–234.

Marcos, L. R., Alpert, M., Urcuyo, L., & Kesselman, M. (1973). The effect of interview language on the evaluation of psychopathology in Spanish-American schizophrenic patients. *American Journal of Psychiatry, 130*, 549–553.

McCreary, C., & Padilla, E. (1977). MMPI differences among Black, Mexican-American, and White male offenders. *Journal of Clinical Psychology, 33*, 171–177.

Montgomery, G. T., & Orozco, S. (1985). Mexican Americans' performance on the MMPI as a function of level of acculturation. *Journal of Clinical Psychology, 44*, 203–212.

Padilla, E. R., Olmedo, E. L., & Loya, F. (1982). Acculturation and the MMPI performance of Chicano and Anglo college students. *Hispanic Journal of Behavioral Sciences, 4*, 451–466.

Padilla, A. M., & Ruiz, R. A. (1973). *Latino mental health: A review of literature* (DHEW Publication No. ADM 74-113). Washington, DC: U.S. Government Printing Office.

Padilla, A. M., & Ruiz, R. A. (1975). Personality assessment and test interpretation of Mexican Americans: A critique. *Journal of Personality Assessment, 39*, 103–109.

Pando, J. R. (1974). Appraisal of various clinical scales of the Spanish version of the Mini-Mult with Spanish Americans (Doctoral dissertation, Adelphi University, 1974). *Dissertation Abstracts International, 34*, 5688B.

Penk, W. E., Robinowitz, R., Roberts, W. R., Dolan, M. P., & Atkins, H. G. (1981). MMPI differences of male Hispanic-American, Black, and White heroin addicts. *Journal of Consulting and Clinical Psychology, 49*, 488–490.

Plemons, G. (1977). A comparison of Anglo- and Mexican-American psychiatric patients. *Journal of Consulting and Clinical Psychology, 45*, 149–150.

Plemons, G. (1980). *The relationship of acculturation to MMPI scores of Mexican American psychiatric outpatients.* Unpublished doctoral dissertation, Palo Alto School of Professional Psychology, CA.

Prewitt-Diaz, J. O., Norcross, J. A., & Draguns, J. (1984). MMPI (Spanish translation) in Puerto Rican adolescents: Preliminary data on reliability and validity. *Hispanic Journal of Behavioral Sciences, 6*, 179–190.

Price, C. S., & Cuellar, I. (1981). Effects of language and related variables on the expression of psychopathology in Mexican American psychiatric patients. *Hispanic Journal of Behavioral Sciences, 3,* 145–160.

Pritchard, D. A., & Rosenblatt, A. (1980). Racial bias in the MMPI: A methodological review. *Journal of Consulting and Clinical Psychology, 48,* 263–267.

Quiroga, I. R. (1972). The use of a linear discriminant function on Minnesota Multiphasic Personality Inventory scores in the classification of psychotic and non-psychotic Mexican American psychiatric patients (Doctoral dissertation, University of Oklahoma, 1972). *Dissertation Abstracts International, 33,* 448–449B.

Roberts, R. E. (1980). Prevalence of psychological distress among Mexican Americans. *Journal of Health and Social Behavior, 21,* 134–145.

Roberts, R. E. (1981). Prevalence of depressive symptoms among Mexican Americans. *Journal of Nervous and Mental Disease, 169,* 213–219.

Rogler, L. H., Cortes, D. E., & Malgady, R. G. (1991). Acculturation and mental health status among Hispanics: Convergence and new directions for research. *American Psychologist, 46,* 585–597.

Rogler, L. H., Malgady, R. G., & Rodriguez, O. (1989). *Hispanics and mental health: A framework for research.* Malabar, FL: Robert E. Krieger.

Rosenstein, M. J. (1980). *Hispanic Americans and mental health services: A comparison of Hispanic, Black, and White admissions to selected mental health facilities, 1975.* (Series CN No. 3, National Institute of Mental Health). Washington, DC: U. S. Government Printing Office.

Ruiz, P. (1982). The Hispanic patient: Sociocultural perspectives. In R. M. Becerra, M. Karno, & J. I. Escobar (Eds.), *Mental health and Hispanic Americans: Clinical perspectives* (pp. 17–27). New York: Grune & Stratton.

Snowden, L. R., & Cheung, F. K. (1990). Use of inpatient mental health services by members of ethnic minority groups. *American Psychologist, 45,* 347–355.

Traub, G. S., & Bohn, M. J. (1985). Note on the reliability of the MMPI with Spanish speaking inmates in the federal prison system. *Psychological Reports, 56,* 373–374.

Vasquez, C. A. (1982). Research on the psychiatric evaluaton of the bilingual patient: A methodological review. *Hispanic Journal of Behavioral Sciences, 4,* 75–80.

Vega, W. A., Kolody, B., & Warheit, G. (1985). Psychoneuroses among Mexican Americans and other Whites: Prevalence and caseness. *American Journal of Public Health, 75,* 523–527.

Velásquez, R. J. (1984a). *Use of psychological tests in the assessment of Hispanic Americans in clinical or mental health settings.* Unpublished manuscript.

Velásquez, R. J. (1984b). *An atlas of MMPI group profiles on Mexican Americans* (Occasional paper No. 19). Los Angeles: Spanish Speaking Mental Health Research Center.

Velásquez, R. J. (1987). Minnesota Multiphasic Personality Inventory differences among Chicano state hospital patients (Doctoral dissertation, Arizona State University, 1986). *Dissertation Abstracts International, 47,* 4668B.

Velásquez, R. J. (in press). Hispanic American MMPI research (1949–1992): A comprehensive bibliography. *Psychological Reports.*

Velásquez, R. J. & Callahan, W. J. (1990). MMPIs of Hispanic, Black, and White schizophrenics. *Psychological Reports, 66,* 819–822.

Velásquez, R. J., Callahan, W. J., & Carrillo, R. (1989). MMPI profiles of Hispanic-American inpatient and outpatient sex offenders. *Psychological Reports, 65,* 1055–1058.

Velásquez, R. J., Callahan, W. J. & Carrillo, R. (1991). MMPI differences among Mexican-American male and female psychiatric inpatients. *Psychological Reports, 48,* 123–127.

Velásquez, R. J., & Gimenez, L. (1987). MMPI differences among three groups of Mexican-American state hospital patients. *Psychological Reports, 60,* 1071–1074.

Vernon, S. W., & Roberts, R. E. (1982). Use of the SADSRDC in a tri-ethnic community survey. *Archivos of General Psychiatry, 39,* 47–52.

Whitworth, R. H. (1988). Anglo- and Mexican-American performance on the MMPI administered in Spanish or English. *Journal of Clinical Psychology, 44,* 891–899.

Williams, C. L. (1987). Issues surrounding psychological testing of minority patients. *Hospital and Community Psychiatry, 38,* 184–189.

Ziskin, J. (1981). Challenging assessment of ethnic minority group members. In J. Ziskin, *Coping with psychiatric and psychological testimony* (pp. 289–305). Venice, CA: Law and Psychology Press.

CHAPTER 17

Some Needed Research on the Assessment of Hispanics in Clinical Settings

Giselle B. Esquivel

Velásquez and Callahan's review and analysis of research on the assessment of Hispanics in clinical settings in this volume provided a valuable perspective for understanding the development of past studies, the nature of recent ones, and the direction of the research agenda for the future.

The fact that Velásquez and his colleague found an increase in the number of research studies conducted is positive. Past research efforts have concentrated on test bias in intelligence testing with children in educational settings and neglected the study of cultural bias in personality measures and clinical diagnoses. As suggested by Velásquez and Callahan, there is still a critical need to enhance the scope of clinical studies. We need, for example, to include nonclinical populations as a normative reference, and we need to use projective tests. We also need to interpret findings on group-differences constructs of consequence within a meaningful cultural context.

In general, clinical research with Hispanics continues to be scattered and characterized by the same lack of focus alluded to by Olmedo (1981) and Malgady, Rogler, and Costantino (1987). There is a need, therefore, to move beyond psychometric validation to a more comprehensive study of the entire psychodiagnostic process, from initial stages of interview and testing to the development of interventions, emphasizing the relevant cultural variables that impact on each of the phases. Based on Velásquez and Callahan's review, this brief chapter focuses on some of the relevant issues in the psychodiagnostic process and includes suggestions for research.

Clinical interviewing, in general, has received limited attention. Particularly lacking is research on the cultural factors that may affect the interview process. Vasquez-Nuttal and Ivey (1986) cited sources of bias in the interview process. The interviewer variables of social class membership and cultural background, for example, may affect the way in which questions are posed and the nature of the information obtained. In turn, the language skills and acculturation level of the interviewee have an impact on the extent of self-disclosure and the way in which feelings and symptoms are expressed (Marcos & Alpert, 1976). The impact of language and language skills also needs to be explored further, including within- and between-group differences in both nonverbal and verbal communication.[1]

What are some of the issues in the testing process itself? As reflected by Velásquez and Callahan's research review, preferences for a psychometric approach, as opposed to a psychodiagnostic model emphasizing clinical judgment, have led to more research on objective personality testing with Hispanics (mainly the MMPI). Even when objective tests are used, however, their interpretation requires expert clinical judgment in understanding the cultural relevance of the constructs being assessed. Therefore, obtaining culture-specific norms for objective tests and validating the use of projective tests as hypotheses-generating techniques, as well as developing and validating culture-specific projective approaches, will prove valuable. The latter attempt is exemplified by Tell Me a Story (TEMAS), a thematic apperception test for minority children and adolescents (Costantino, Malgady, Rogler, & Tsui, 1988).

The main purpose of clinical testing is to link diagnoses with appropriate interventions. Studies of the most effective types of treatment for Hispanic

---

[1]*Editor's note: Much of this literature has been on industrial psychology rather than clinical psychology and is aimed at employment interviews rather than clinical interviews. (See, e.g., Casio, 1991; McDonald & Hakel, 1985.)*

clients have been scarce. Some of the issues that we need to explore are (a) the effects of cultural consultants as mediators in the treatment process (Acosta & Cristo, 1981), (b) the pretreatment orientations of Hispanic clients prior to therapy, and (c) the use of less traditional forms of therapy, such as folk therapy. Examples of less traditional forms of therapy are Costantino's (1982) folk stories or "cuentos folkloricos" used with Hispanic children and their mothers in a school setting and the use of folk heroes as literary models for adolescents.

Finally, there is a need to validate preventive interventions based on cross-cultural approaches, such as ethnotherapy, and techniques for dealing with stress related to migration and the acculturation process (Esquivel & Keitel, 1990). Relevant, also, is the study of the invulnerable—those individuals who are presumed to have an increased probability of developing a mental disorder, but do not succumb (Garmezy, 1971).

References

Acosta, F. X., & Cristo, M. H. (1981). Development of a bilingual interpreter program: An alternative model for Spanish-speaking services. *Professional Psychology, 12,* 474–482.

Casio, W. F. (1991). *Applied psychology in personnel management* (4th ed.). Englewood Cliffs, NJ: Prentice-Hall

Costantino, G. (1982). Cuentos folkloricos: A new therapy modality. *Research Bulletin, 5,* 7–10.

Costantino, G., Malgady, R. G. , Rogler, L. H., & Tsui, E. C. (1988). Discriminant analysis of clinical outpatients and public school children by TEMAS: A thematic apperception test for Hispanics and Blacks. *Journal of Personality Assessment, 52,* 670–678.

Esquivel, G. B., & Keitel, M. A. (1990). Counseling immigrant children in the schools. *Elementary School Guidance and Counseling, 24,* 213–221.

Garmezy, N. (1971). Vulnerability research and the issue of primary prevention. *American Journal of Orthopsychiatry, 41,* 101–116.

Malgady, R. G., Rogler, L. H., & Costantino, G. (1987). Ethnocultural and linguistic bias in mental health evaluation of hispanics. *American Psychologist, 42,* 228–234.

Marcos, L. R., & Alpert, M. (1976). Strategies and risks in psychotherapy with bilingual patients: The phenomenon of language independence. *American Journal of Psychiatry, 133,* 1275–1276.

McDonald, T., & Hakel, M. D. (1985). Effects of applicant race, sex, suitability, and answers on interviewer's questioning strategy and ratings. *Personnel Psychology, 38,* 321–334.

Olmedo, E. L. (1981). Testing linguistic minorities. *American Psychologist, 36,* 1078–1085.

Vasquez-Nuttal, E., & Ivey, A. E. (1986). The diagnostic interview process. In H. M. Knoff (Ed.), *Child and Adolescent Personality* (pp. 111–113). New York: Guilford Press.

Conclusion

CHAPTER 18

Reflections on Testing: Emerging Trends and New Possibilities

Amado M. Padilla

A book dedicated exclusively to the psychological testing of Hispanics has been long overdue. The uses and misuses of psychological assessment instruments with Hispanics extends back to the earliest days of testing in this country (Padilla, 1988; Valencia & Aburto, 1991). Periodically, there have been calls for a new look at the assessment of Hispanics (e.g., Garcia, 1977), but this is the first volume that actually does so. The contributors to this volume are among the most notable workers in the field of psychological assessment theory and measurement. Many of these individuals have also worked successfully to alter public policy involving the uses of tests. The chapters prepared for this volume represent a marked departure from earlier views of the role of testing summarized in the works by Padilla (1988) and Valencia and Aburto (1991). Furthermore, the work here represents a sensitive awareness of Hispanics that will serve to alleviate some of the fears surrounding psychological assessment instruments found in the Hispanic community. This is the first book of its kind and will serve as the standard for many years to come.

There has been a dramatic increase in the presence of Hispanics in the United States over the past 2 decades. The latest estimate is that there are 20.8 million Hispanics in the United States (U.S. Bureau of the Census, 1990). In addition, demographic projections show that the number of Hispanics in the United States will continue to increase, as well as the proportion of Hispanics to the total population, over the next 3 decades. Hispanics are becoming more important in the work force because of their numbers and youth relative to White Americans who are more heavily distributed among the aging sector of the population (Hays-Bautista, Schink, & Chapa, 1988). These facts attest to the need to consider seriously the problems inherent in the psychological testing of Hispanics in order to ensure their educational and occupational opportunity and success. In so doing, the social well-being of all Americans is fostered. Furthermore, because so many crucial life decisions are in one way or another based on testing, it is important to recognize the heterogeneity within the Hispanic population and the difficulties that this poses for test developers and users alike.

Anyone intent on using tests with Hispanics needs to understand and appreciate the heterogeneity within this ethnic group. The reason for this is simple: The validity and reliability of tests used with Hispanics can only be safely judged when the diversity within the group is recognized. Hispanics encompass people from Mexico, Puerto Rico, Cuba, and all of the other countries of Latin America. Historically, these countries have evolved differently and possess unique national identities, although they also remain linked by some similarities in culture and language. Furthermore, some Hispanics have resided in the United States for many generations and have acculturated into mainstream American culture, whereas others are more recent arrivals from Latin America and maintain their cultural heritage. This heterogeneity needs to be part of any decision-making process that involves the proper use of tests. In some cases, this may simply mean knowing whether the person to be tested is sufficiently proficient in English to be administered a measure (of whatever type) in this language. In other cases, it may mean deciding whether it would be a good practice to administer, for example, a test that has been standardized with Puerto Ricans to later-generation Mexican Americans. Obviously, these dilemmas represent only the very tip of the iceberg in ethical decision making about test use with Hispanics. More important, the necessary dialogue about these issues has begun, as illustrated in various chapters in this book.

Some Historical Concerns

Many recurrent themes have emerged in the nearly 70 years of published literature on the uses of psychological assessment instruments with Hispanics (Padilla, 1988; Padilla & Ruiz, 1975; Valencia & Aburto, 1991). Many of these themes are reflected in the various chapters of this book. For example, the low academic achievement of Hispanic students has been well documented. What has not been successfully explained is the reason for this low achievement. The shortcomings of IQ tests and achievement tests used with Mexican-American students have been well summarized in recent years (e.g., Garcia, 1984). However, questions about the validity of IQ tests were first discussed by a Hispanic psychologist 6 decades ago (Sanchez, 1932a, 1932b), but little attention was given to Sanchez's critique at that time despite his intimate knowledge of the Hispanic culture and the reputation of his publications on the topic. We might ask ourselves why, if questions were raised about the validity of tests by Sanchez and others beginning 60 years ago, and such concerns have continued to the present, has so little attention been given to these problems until this volume? The answer to this rhetorical question probably is that Hispanics have not had the political clout, either in society generally or in the psychological profession specifically, to insist that their concerns be taken seriously. Population demographics, I believe, are beginning to change this unresponsiveness. In the case of Hispanics, their sheer increasing numbers have drawn attention to the group and to their social problems, including the appropriate use of psychological tests to assess Hispanics in school, work, and mental health settings.

The serious underrepresentation of Hispanics in institutions of higher education and also in managerial and professional occupations has become a politically sensitive issue that provokes controversy regarding affirmative action policies. In some cases, the goals of affirmative action run headlong into questions of assessment and test outcomes. We are all too familiar with these dilemmas. For example, in what direction should a promotion board lean when considering promotions to the rank of captain in a metropolitan police department? Should test scores carry more or less weight than experience and ethnicity in setting the equation for promotion? On the one hand, in a meritocracy, test outcomes (such as scores) should be heavily weighted. However, if this meritocracy works for some, but inadvertently discriminates against others because of their race, gender, or social class, then test outcomes might need to be given less weight when trying to establish a more equitable society. Obviously, this is a thorny political and professional issue.

Central to the debate of fairness in testing of Hispanics is the concern for the development and use of assessment instruments and procedures that effectively remove the inappropriate gatekeeping function that many instruments have served and that have kept Hispanics out of higher education and certain managerial positions. The major issues surrounding this debate have been captured in the chapters by Geisinger, O'Brien, Donlon, Pennock-Román, and Ramos in this volume. These authors all tried to show how tests and their outcomes can be made more equitable for Hispanics if the effort is made. These chapters merit careful attention because the information that they convey and the recommendations that they offer are critical to our understanding of the current status of testing of Hispanics.

Explanations for the relative lack of academic success of Hispanics at every level, as well as in the workplace, are common (e.g., Valencia & Aburto, 1991). Not surprisingly, there has been a long history of reliance on assessment theory and measurement techniques to advance genetic or complicated social explanations for the relative underachievement of Hispanics and other minority groups. The most recent example of this is a monograph by Dunn (1987), the developer of the Peabody Picture Vocabulary Test (PPTV), who uses an assortment of findings with Hispanic children to argue that their lower performance on the PPVT may be attributable to a combination of genetic and cultural factors. Explanations of lower levels of achievement that rely on genetic or social interpretations without examining the problems inherent in the tests and in the societal use of the tests are objectionable, as was shown in a special issue of the *Hispanic Journal of Behavioral Sciences*, edited by Fernandez (1988) in response to Dunn's monograph.

It is the historic misuse of tests and the frequent reliance on genetic interpretations, rather than an examination of the deficiencies of the tests or the ethical issues involved in test use, that have created a climate of mistrust of tests in the Hispanic community. The frustration and anger sometimes shown by Hispanics toward tests and the testing industry is juxtaposed with the growing importance of tests in our society. I discuss the increasing reliance on tests in public policy in a later section of this chapter, but before I do so, a few words are in order about cultural and linguistic considerations in test use.

Cultural and Linguistic Concerns

A significant issue concerning Hispanics has to do with acculturation and has been discussed in this volume by Marín. Several researchers are concerned with the cultural and linguistic diversity that exists among Hispanics and appropriately note that acculturation and proficiency in English are important variables when we consider using a test. Olmedo (1979) discussed the psychometric issues involved in developing an acculturation measure. More recently, Rogler and his colleagues (Rogler, Cortes, & Malgady, 1991) reviewed the Hispanic mental health literature in relation to acculturation in order to assess the link between varying levels of acculturation and psychopathology. In their review, they noted the mixed findings with respect to the relationship between acculturation level and scores on various clinical measures used to assess depression and other adjustment-related difficulties. Rogler et al. (1991) attributed the difficulty in understanding the relationship between acculturation and behavioral functioning to the fact that there is no agreed on unitary measure for acculturation. Investigators mostly use their own measures, which suffer from questionable validity and reliability, as attested to by Marín in this volume.

Another issue that merits more discussion than given to it in this volume has to do with arriving at strategies for determining English-language proficiency, especially in school-age populations. There is a profound gap in the availability of tests for assessing English-language proficiency that do more than determine general communicative proficiency. This situation has become a major concern in education today because approximately 10% of all school-age children nationally come from non-English-language homes (Waggoner, 1988). This problem is even more critical in certain states; for example, in California about 33% of all students in kindergarten through 12th grade enter school as limited English proficient (LEP) (California State Department of Education, 1990). A similar situation occurs in other large immigrant-receiving states such as New York, Texas, Illinois, Florida, and Massachusetts. More research needs to reflect a concern for language-assessment measures and how proficiency in English interacts with other variables to predict performance on tests and subsequent performance in school or the workplace. In the chapter by O'Brien, there was an example of an excellent start in this direction. The practical need for a language-proficiency measure by the New York City Board of Education resulted in the very important development of a more serviceable instrument than had existed before. In related work by Pennock-Román in her chapter in this volume and in a separate monograph (Pennock-Román, 1990), it is shown how the Scholastic Aptitude Test (SAT) predicts the college achievement for Hispanic students with different Spanish- and English-language proficiency backgrounds. These are important developments that merit attention because they are improving our thinking about the interface of language and school behaviors for learners who come to school with different language histories.

We also see in this volume attempts by some authors (e.g., Anastasi and Busch) to connect findings from Hispanic assessment studies to cross-cultural efforts to improve general psychological theory. In my opinion, linking testing to cross-cultural psychology poses two significant concerns. The first has to do with the numerous technical problems inherent in tests when used with Hispanics—about which much of this volume is concerned. The second has to do with whether Hispanic Americans constitute a proper comparison group for cross-cultural research.

In regard to the first concern, many researchers have identified technical and interpretative problems with the psychological instruments that currently exist for use with Hispanics. Accordingly, we must then ask ourselves how the psychological assessment of Hispanics can be used to improve on our general knowledge of psychological functioning when the very measuring instruments used for this purpose are imprecise and fraught with problems. The use of suspect assessment instruments does not lead to better psychological science, but only to more error. Gould (1981) made this point very poignantly in his now classic book, *The Mismeasure of Man*.

The second problem has to do with whether Hispanics constitute an appropriate comparison group in cross-cultural research and how this determination is made. I have already discussed the problem of heterogeneity among Hispanics. In addition, I have pointed out the need to understand the dynamics involved in acculturation and how shift in cultural orientation among Hispanics should be determined. However, it is still not clear in what context Hispanic versus non-Hispanic comparisons constitute cross-cultural research and how findings can contribute to psychological theory.

According to Berry (1980), cross-cultural psychology differs from other areas of psychology because in cross-cultural research, the focus is on method rather than content. Thus, cross-cultural researchers are more likely to compare nations or quite different cultural groups, rather than groups from different regions of the same country or ethnic groups within a country. The idea is to maximize the variance between groups in order to determine how culture influences behavioral outcomes. Therefore, comparisons between Hispanics and non-Hispanics contribute more to our understanding of multiculturalism within the United States. Thinking about the comparisons in this way actually allows us to examine processes of psychological adaptation, adjustment, and change rarely given much consideration in mainstream psychology. This view may ultimately prove more productive than simply conducting a study of group A and group B and concluding that resultant differences are due to some retrospectively arrived at interpretation of cultural differences.

An additional point is that improvements in assessment techniques for Hispanics should be made because there is a real need to do so not because Hispanics hold some type of special status as samples for cross-cultural research. The reason for this is simple: A position that maintains that Hispanic research can contribute to cross-cultural psychology can also imply that Hispanics are not part of the mainstream and are only of interest because of their exotic customs. A more productive perspective is that Hispanics are part of the diversity that constitutes U.S. culture, and it is our professional responsibility to ensure that tests that serve as gatekeeping instruments in education and the workplace do not differentially select out Hispanics because of instrument bias or unfair testing practices.

There is one area of assessment that requires greater attention and that may have some use in our understanding of multiculturalism. This is the area of personality assessment. In his chapter, Velásquez summarized all the literature that is currently available regarding the use of the Minnesota Multiphasic Personality Inventory (MMPI) with Mexican Americans. Velásquez's chapter is extremely valuable because it demonstrates the care that is required when personality tests are used with Hispanics. Unfortunately, few other attempts have been made to understand the intricate relationships among culture, ethnic status, and personality functioning. Some recent work is beginning to change this situation. For example, Costantino, Malgady, and Rogler (1988) developed a projective instrument (Tell-Me-A-Story) that has proved useful with urban Hispanic and Black children. Also, Cervantes, Padilla, and Salgado de Snyder (1990, 1991) have developed two versions of a Hispanic stress inventory, one for Latin American immigrants and the other for later-generation Mexican Americans. In short, we need to better understand the advantages and disadvantages of instruments such as the MMPI when used with Hispanics. At the same time, there is considerable room for the development of culturally relevant measures for Hispanics, especially for personality measures, which are widely used for diagnosing and formulating treatment plans in mental health settings. In addition, we also know that personality measures are used extensively as screening devices in industry.

The Growing Importance of Tests

The chapters in this book also reflect several other important considerations in the testing of Hispanics that will draw varying reactions from readers. The first has to do with the assumptions we make on the basis of test outcomes. The second concern is with the increasing, rather than diminishing, importance given to tests in our society. As we know, very important decisions in education, employment, and mental health service delivery are made, at least in part, on the basis of information provided by test results. In education and in the workplace, for instance, there is an assumption that something good happens to those who perform well on tests. Traditionally, this assumption has been a rationale for using tests to select people; however, Hispanics and members of other minority groups are more likely to assume that something bad happens to those who perform poorly on tests. Something bad usually means that individuals get assigned to lower academic tracks, don't get accepted into universities of their choice, or may not be promoted in the workplace. Furthermore, tests are now being given in preschool up through the professional level, with tests of various sorts used to determine competence for licensure or certification in various professional guilds. In every case, there is an implicit message to Hispanics about poor performance and its subsequent negative consequences.

As an example of the growing reliance on tests, we can turn to Darling-Hammond (1990), who very succinctly summarized the new reliance on tests in the context of the growing school reform movement:

> The power of testing is in large part the result of the increasing use of test scores as arbiters of administrative decisions in American schools. To avoid having to struggle with more complex and valid assessments of student, teacher, or school performance, policy makers and administrators have begun to use standardized test

scores to determine student promotion and graduation, to decide class or track placement, to evaluate teachers' competence and school quality, and to allocate rewards and sanctions. (p. 289)

Embedded in the educational reform movement is the question of whether a technologically advanced society such as ours can maintain itself when a significant proportion of the work force is increasingly minority (Black and Hispanic), semiliterate, and lower class (Hays-Bautista et al., 1988). Equally important are findings from cross-national studies that show American students lagging significantly behind students in other countries in mathematics and science. To remedy the problem, which is of increasing concern to industry, attention is being given to school reforms and includes a national assessment program. The intent of a national assessment program is to monitor schools *and* students as the students move toward achieving certain national standards of competency in challenging subject matter—English, mathematics, science, history, and geography.

There have been numerous criticisms of the proposed national assessment program including opposition from national teacher associations. From a Hispanic perspective, there are also problems. The first of these is that by adopting a policy for a national assessment program, many of the recommendations for the use of tests with Hispanics discussed in this volume and elsewhere stand to be lost. For example, concern for English-language proficiency and acculturation level of Hispanic students can be overshadowed in large-scale testing efforts. In addition, the proposed national assessment program, as presented, is strictly an accountability program. However, the use of tests as diagnostic instruments for determining problems in learning and studying strategies for effective teaching are not addressed. This failure to concentrate on tests that can serve diagnostic and instructional purposes as part of the national policy on assessment in school reform makes Durán's chapter especially relevant because he described the design for new ways of using the concepts of assessment to define new approaches to the education of Hispanic students.

The chapters by Geisinger, Donlon, and Durán in this volume specifically address the problems and consequences of testing when the person being tested does poorly. This volume provides many state-of-the-art answers to the proper uses of tests, which will enable us to interpret what it is that tests measure and to assess individual and group performances on such measures. As mentioned earlier, there have long been criticisms of tests when used inappropriately with Hispanics. However, these criticisms have appeared as articles in professional journals or as chapters in books, but never in the integrated form as seen in this volume published by the American Psychological Association. More important, this collection of chapters offers extremely useful recommendations for both test developers and consumers.

Finally, beginning in the early 1960s and lasting through the late 1980s, many psychologists have advocated limiting the use of tests by pointing out the harmful consequences when tests were used with minority students. Some of these efforts have been successful, for example, the Larry P. case in California resulted in the elimination of tests of intelligence for deciding placement of Black, and to a lesser extent Hispanic, students in special education classes. However, despite some small gains in restricting the use of tests with minorities, what we have witnessed recently is a renewed reliance on tests for making decisions of all types, regardless of the consequences (Darling-Hammond, 1990).

Given the increasing importance of tests today, advocacy efforts should be directed at ensuring that policy discussions regarding the development and implementation of national assessment programs include the concerns of Hispanics. There is a real need to worry about what the educational reform movement and other related accountability programs may mean for Hispanics in the future. Furthermore, when tests are used for non-school-related purposes, such as in mental health clinics and industry, advocacy again needs to be extended to guarantee that the highest standards are maintained in the development and use of tests. Clearly, this volume contributes much by focusing on and enlightening any theoretical or applied discussions of psychological assessment with Hispanics.

References

Berry, J. W. (1980). Introduction to methodology. In H. C. Triandis & J. W. Berry (Eds.), *Handbook of cross-cultural psychology* (Vol. 2, pp. 1–28). Boston: Allyn & Bacon.

California State Department of Education. (1990). *Fall language survey results for school year 1990–1991.* Sacramento: Office of Bilingual Education.

Cervantes, R. C., Padilla, A. M., & Salgado de Snyder, N. (1990). Reliability and validity of the Hispanic Stress Inventory. *Hispanic Journal of Behavioral Sciences, 12,* 76–82.

Cervantes, R. C., Padilla, A. M., & Salgado de Snyder, N. (1991). The Hispanic Stress Inventory: A culturally relevant approach toward psychosocial assessment. *Psychological Assessment: A Journal of Consulting and Clinical Psychology, 3,* 438–447.

Costantino, G., Malgady, R. G., & Rogler, L. H. (1988). *TEMAS (Tell-Me-A-Story) manual*. Los Angeles: Western Psychological Services.

Darling-Hammond, L. (1990). Achieving our goals: Superficial or structural reforms? *Phi Delta Kappan, 72*, 286–295.

Dunn, L. M. (1987). *Bilingual Hispanic children on the U.S. mainland: A review of research on their cognitive, linguistic, and scholastic development*. Circle Pines, MN: American Guidance Service.

Fernandez, R. (1988). Special issue. Editor of achievement testing: Science vs. ideology. Introduction. *Hispanic Journal of Behavioral Sciences, 10*, 179–198.

Garcia, J. (1977). Intelligence testing: Quotients, quotas, and quackery. In J. L. Martinez, Jr. (Ed.), *Chicano Psychology* (pp. 197–212). New York: Academic Press.

Garcia, J. (1984). The logic and limits of mental aptitude testing. In J. L. Martinez, Jr. & R. H. Mendoza (Eds.), *Chicano Psychology* (pp. 41–58). New York: Academic Press.

Gould, S. J. (1981). *The mismeasure of man*. New York: W. W. Horton & Co. Hays-Bautista, D., Schink, W. O., & Chapa, J. (1988). *The burden of support: Young Latinos in an aging society*. Stanford, CA: Stanford University Press.

Olmedo, E. L. (1979). Acculturation: A psychometric perspective. *American Psychologist, 34*, 1061–1070.

Padilla, A. M. (1988). Early psychological assessment of Mexican American children. *Journal of the History of the Behavioral Sciences. 24*, 111–116.

Padilla, A. M., & Ruiz, R. A. (1975). Personality assessment and test interpretation of Mexican Americans: A critique. *Journal of Personality Assessment, 39*, 103–109.

Pennock-Román, M. (1990) Test validity and language background. New York: College Entrance Examination Board.

Rogler, L. H., Cortes, D. E., & Malgady, R. (1991). Acculturation and mental health status among Hispanics. *American Psychologist, 46*, 585–597.

Sanchez, G. I. (1932a). Group differences in Spanish-speaking children: A critical review. *Journal of Applied Psychology, 16*, 549–558.

Sanchez, G. I. (1932b). Scores of Spanish-speaking children on repeated tests. *Journal of Genetic Psychology, 40*, 223–231.

U.S. Bureau of the Census. (1990). The Hispanic Population in the U.S.: March 1990. *Current Population Reports* (Series P-20, No. 449). Washington, DC: U.S. Government Printing Office.

Valencia, R. R., & Aburto, S. (1991). The uses and abuses of educational testing: Chicanos as a case in point. In R. R. Valencia (Ed.), *Chicano school failure and success: Research and policy agendas for the 1990s*. London: Falmer Press.

Waggoner, D. (1988). Foreign born children in the United States in the eighties. *NABE: Journal of the National Association for Bilingual Education, 12*, 23–49.

Index

About the Editor

K urt F. Geisinger is Dean of Arts and Sciences and professor of psychology at the State University of New York at Oswego. He earned his PhD from the Pennsylvania State University with a specialization in educational and psychological measurement after earning a master's degree in industrial psychology from the University of Georgia and his undergraduate degree with honors from David son College. From 1977 to 1992, he was a faculty member within the Department of Psychology at Fordham University, where he was also chairperson of the psychology department and director of the psychometrics doctoral program.

He has published in a variety of journals relating to testing and measurement such as *Educational and Psychological Measurement, Educational Measurement: Issues and Practice, Applied Psychological Measurement, Journal of Educational Measurement, Journal of Personality Assessment,* and *Personnel Psychology.* He is currently on the editorial boards of *Psychological Assessment, Educational and Psychological Measurement, Educational Measurement: Issues and Practice,* and *Educational Research Quarterly* and has served on the boards of the *Journal of Educational Research* and *Improving College and University Teaching.*

Geisinger has also contributed generously to professional organizations and is a past president of the Northeastern Educational Research Association and has served on or chaired committees for Divisions 5 and 15 of the American Psychological Association, the National Council on Measurement in Education, and the Joint Committee on Testing Practices. He consults frequently on testing and measurement issues with a variety of industrial, educational, and legal agencies and has served as an expert witness in approximately two dozen legal cases, primarily relating to the topic of test bias.